JACK WEBSTER

WEBSTER'S WORLD

Jack Webster

B&W PUBLISHING

First published 1997
by B&W Publishing Ltd., Edinburgh
ISBN 1 873631 79 0
Articles © The Herald
This compilation © Jack Webster 1997

British Library Cataloguing in Publication Data:
A catalogue record for this book is available
from the British Library.

Cover photograph © B&W Publishing Ltd.
All other photographs courtesy of
The Herald Picture Archive, Jack Webster
except Flora Garry © Gordon Wright Publishing.

Printed by Werner Söderström

To Dad,
   Happy Christmas '97
   love
   Fiona, Alan
      ~ Kathleen.

WEBSTER'S WORLD

Other books by Jack Webster:

THE DONS (1978)
A GRAIN OF TRUTH (1981)
GORDON STRACHAN (1984)
ANOTHER GRAIN OF TRUTH (1988)
'TIS BETTER TO TRAVEL (1989)
ALISTAIR MACLEAN: A LIFE (1991)
FAMOUS SHIPS OF THE CLYDE (1993)
THE FLYING SCOTS (1994)
THE EXPRESS YEARS (1994)
IN THE DRIVING SEAT (1996)
THE HERALD YEARS (1996)
FROM DALI TO BURRELL (1997)

Television Films:

WEBSTER'S ROUP (1985)
AS TIME GOES BY (1987)
NORTHERN LIGHTS (1989)
WEBSTER GOES WEST (1991)
THE GLORY OF GOTHENBURG (1993)
JOHN BROWN: THE MAN WHO DREW A LEGEND (1994)
WALKING BACK TO HAPPINESS (1996)

CONTENTS

CONTENTS

CONTENTS

AN INVITATION TO WEBSTER'S WORLD

FROM the millions of words I have spilled out in the name of journalism over the past 50 years, there is nothing I have enjoyed more than writing a weekly column for *The Herald* in the latter part of my career.

It has been a very personal seam of writing, a point made by the judges when they named me Columnist of the Year in 1996. Week by week I have merely given a reaction to passing events, or raked over memories from the broad spectrum of life, later to learn that I had often spoken for a silent majority whose views are too easily passed over.

In retrospect, the weekly columns have sometimes distilled into the more lasting form of an essay and, come to think of it, that was about the only subject in which I could gain a pass-mark at school.

So the publishers decided to gather them up in the form of a book, which was published in 1996 under the title of *The Herald Years*. That went into paperback edition but left a residue of material which seemed to lay equal claim to inclusion.

Thus a new volume, *Webster's World*, in which those essays range from early days as a journalist in Turriff, through Aberdeen to headier times on the national press.

It tells how I chased Charlie Chaplin, met the richest man in the world and saw Scotland's most notorious murderer, Peter Manuel. It takes you on my travels to the United States, India, the Soviet Union and the Far East, and tells how I covered a royal wedding—and met great war heroes like Alastair Pearson, "Mad Mitch" and Sir Fitzroy MacLean.

Throughout my writing career I have never failed to be fascinated by the day-by-day creation of history, that unfolding of the human story with which the fates will tease and torment us, delight us and devastate us.

Since *The Herald Years* I have had, on a personal level, two of the most joyful occasions of my life—a glittering banquet at which, as one long plagued by a bad stammer, I received the nationwide award as Speaker of the Year; and an invitation to deliver the Founder's Day Oration at Robert Gordon's College, Aberdeen, the school which despatched me at the age of fourteen as an academic reject.

On the broader front we had the dramatic General Election of 1997, bringing Labour's landslide victory. And this volume concludes with my immediate reaction to the biggest emotional upheaval this country has known: the tragic death of Diana, Princess of Wales.

In *Webster's World*, these are some of the events I have tried to portray in a very personal way, as they drift into history.

Jack Webster
Glasgow, September 1997

For the memory of Eden

REMEMBERING THE FAIRM-TOUN

AS I drove across Scotland by the early light of '85, the fields lay glistening in their morning coats, the sky blue and majestic as a backcloth to the wondrous sight of the countryside on a clear day.

Below, the sheep were munching at their winter feed, while less resilient cattle were safely housed in their steadings, pampered as kings and queens in their courts until the first hint of spring tempts them out to graze.

The enduring nature of the land was uppermost in my mind at that time when people are given to moments of philosophising, perhaps as an escape from the horrors of a Hogmanay hangover.

It was only when I came closer to the farmsteads of my youth, in the Buchan corner of Aberdeenshire, that I faced up to the fact that, however much the land itself may have endured, the farming way of life I remembered had not lasted. Gone were the fairmtouns with their cottar houses and whole communities of people who generated the labour of the land; gone even the croft where the solid farm-worker would gain his toehold of ownership and perhaps prosper until he could take on a bigger place.

The farm-worker today would need capital of £200,000 to take over and stock a modest 100 acres—and how could his income even service the borrowing?

So the big machines have come to till the land, and men of greater means have added surrounding farms to their existing units, using grandiose clichés like "more viable operation" where their taciturn forebears would merely have drawn heavily on the bogie roll and spat in contentment.

The Second World War finally ended the way of life I am

1

thinking about, though a relative of mine, who farmed 600 acres of good, arable land in the heart of Buchan, still employed 22 men for that purpose as recently as the late 1950s. Today he would do it with a handful.

Scottish farming has had to accept the inevitable fate of mechanisation and keep itself up-to-date. It is just that, going back to the farmsteads of earlier days, I miss the commotion of the "toun", the bustle of men and horses, the romance of chaumer and peat-stack, cairtshed, and threshing-mill time.

I could still envisage the bailie mucking out individual stalls, and sweeping the greip in a rich pungency of natural smells. There was the stir of the harvest field, the cutting with a binder, the stooking and, best of all, the leading of yellow crop from stubble-field to cornyard, where men of artistry would shape those rucks and tether them against whatever blast the winter might bring.

Then there was the meal-an'-ale for relaxation to celebrate the in-gathering of the hairst, a social whirl of eating, drinking and dancing—and a fine camaraderie which saw decent country folk through good times and bad.

They supped their brose and sowens and had the last laugh on those who scoffed at the monotony of their diet. The fact that heart attacks and high blood pressure were a rarity in the countryside of my youth has more recently been explained by the fact that oatmeal is a merciless destroyer of cholesterol.

But, by and large, the folk have gone from the land, leaving pockets of isolation. Charlie, who looks after my small patch of Aberdeenshire, stands out as an example of that rare species who regarded their job as a way of life and a home, where they produced the sons to follow in their footsteps.

Since youth is seldom regarded in the same category as its begetters, it is a joy to realise that Charlie has three sons who are growing up precisely in the mould of their father. Had they been born in another generation, they would have followed him on to the fields of Honeyneuk as naturally as the dawning of the day.

Instead, they have diverted their skills and enthusiasms to jobs like agricultural engineering, where unsuspecting bosses have found, to their delight, that there is still such a calibre of person around.

So I came away, at that nostalgic time of year, at least with a clearer head about the state of the land and its people in 1985. The life of the countryside has bred into them values and standards which, hopefully, will carry them in their own directions and endure to their personal benefit—even when the life that was lived by their forefathers has passed into the mists of a distant memory.

LET THAT PIANO PLAY

ALL my life I've been a sucker for the performing pianist, those syncopating swingers who give vent to George Gershwin or Cole Porter, Jerome Kern, Richard Rodgers or Irving Berlin. (How strange that America produced so many outstanding composers at the one time.)

As a boy I would drool over Carroll Gibbons and Charlie Kunz or head a queue for the personal appearance of Rawicz and Landauer.

In New York you would find me regularly in the cocktail bar of the Waldorf Astoria Hotel, not through enchantment with the astronomical cost of the beverage but because Cole Porter's own piano, scratched and worn, is still to be seen and heard there, played by a wee man who belongs to Glasgow.

Porter himself spent his latter years as a recluse in the Waldorf Astoria Towers, next door to the hotel which was to inherit his keyboard.

In Los Angeles my favourite haunt used to be the piano bar of the Bob Burns Restaurant, at Santa Monica beach, where I watched an interesting encounter one evening between the resident pianist and an elderly lady who had been enjoying his music.

When the pianist rose for his break, I could hear the lady saying: "Do you mind if I borrow your piano?"

Musicians tend to be wary of such propositions and clearly the man had no idea who she was. I could have told him that his only fear was likely to be unfavourable comparison.

Reluctantly he agreed and she proceeded to play the most magnificent version of George Gershwin's "The Man I Love", the

4

arpeggios rippling with a mellifluous splendour that would have delighted Gershwin's brother Ira, then living just a few blocks away in Beverly Hills.

The lady was Barbara Andrews, whom I had last seen at the Tivoli Theatre in Aberdeen during the war, when she and her tenor-voiced husband Ted were introducing their singing wonder-child, Julie Andrews.

Back home in Scotland—and never having lost the fascination—I soon discovered a pianist who has been my favourite for years. Happily, he plays at my local hotel on the South Side of the city and that is where you will find me any Saturday night in the cocktail bar (always cocktail bars!), soaking up the sweet rhythms of Terry Martin, whose splendid performance is enhanced by his sheer bouncing delight in what he is doing.

Much as I have appreciated his music over the years, I knew very little about Terry himself until the other evening, when I subjected him to the informal interview. How do such people live? Do they have another job?

Terry, I discovered, grew up on the South Side of Glasgow, went to Eastwood School (now Williamwood), and showed such promise as a footballer that he was chosen for the Glasgow Schools team.

But his mother, who died last year, was a pianist for the silent films in the old Crosshill Cinema at Queen's Park and Terry started at the Ommer School of Music in Dixon Avenue at the age of nine. He then moved on to Frank Olsen and also studied the clarinet at the Academy of Music.

Though the background was classical, Terry Martin became fascinated by the playing of Benny Goodman's pianist, Teddy Wilson, and came into his own when he joined the RAF and found himself in Hong Kong.

"Those were the three most wonderful years of my life," he recalls, having seen very little of the RAF, and much more of the plush spots of the Crown colony, where the Terry Martin Trio became a bit of a legend. "People would phone up and plan their functions according to when we could play."

5

He was resident pianist in the early days of Hong Kong Television. Back in Scotland, he was promptly engaged for the Eglinton
Arms at Eaglesham, where he stayed for four years before moving
to the new Macdonald Hotel at Eastwood Toll and becoming a
full-time musician.

He has remained at the Mac, off and on, for more than 20
years, while still fitting in engagements at top hotels like Gleneagles
and Turnberry and spending two seasons in Jersey.

So what is Terry's own taste in music? "I'm basically a dixieland
jazz fan but you can't play that all the time so the choice tends to
be the styles of Berry Goodman, Tommy Dorsey, Glenn Miller
and artists like Sinatra and Nat King Cole.

"As to my style of playing, I try to combine the left hand of
Erroll Garner with the right hand of Oscar Petersen."

Playing for diners who are getting up to dance, he is in no
doubt about the most popular requests. Summoning up visions of
Bogart and Bergman, the public No. 1 is "As Time Goes By",
followed by *The Sting* theme.

Occasionally, another pianist in disguise will try to catch him
out with a bogey tune, one with a difficult middle passage like
"Body and Soul" or "Sophisticated Lady" or "The Way You
Look Tonight".

The way Terry Martin plays tonight and every night—and at
Oceans on a Saturday afternoon—brings immeasurable pleasure
to incurable romantics like myself, whose body and soul are
stirred by those melodic standards which set the fingers a-tapping
and arouse an urge for the freedom of that dance floor.

IT'S JUSTICE FOR J. R. HARTLEY

IMMUNE as I am (or like to think I am) to the seductions of the television commercial, I must confess to a soft spot for the one about the dear old gent who tours one bookshop after another, gingerly inquiring if they have a long-forgotten tome on fishing, written by J. R. Hartley.

Nobody seems to have heard of it and the poor old soul returns to his loving daughter, who seeks to console him by producing the Yellow Pages where he will surely find some more bookshops to try.

He resumes the quest by telephone and, suddenly, joy spreads over his gentle face when a voice at the other end reveals that, yes, they do have a copy of J. R. Hartley's book on fishing. She will put it aside for him.

And the name, please? "My name? It's . . . J. R. Hartley. . . ."

In such circumstances of public indifference, even discounting his natural modesty, I doubt if dear old Mr Hartley would bother to register himself for the possible benefits of Public Lending Right, the modern way of trying to compensate authors for the fact that the vast majority of people who read their books manage to do so from the shelves of public libraries at a cost of absolutely nothing at all.

It was a longstanding and thoroughly justified grouse on the part of the writing fraternity, finally resolved three years ago when the Government provided some funding to pay at least a token sum to the people who provide all that free reading in libraries.

For those of us on the lower slopes of authorship there was a

7

private doubt about applying at all, not that we were disinterested in the money.

But what if we were only making fools of ourselves? The payment was less than 1p per borrowing—and what if the public lending authority responded with a voluminous belly-laugh to say nobody, absolutely nobody, had bothered to borrow our books at all? Or maybe the money due didn't cover the postage! What an embarrassment that would be.

When the first year brought stories of authors receiving only peanuts for their Public Lending Right, I knew I had done the right thing in not applying. The same went for the second year.

But curiosity got the better of me in the third year. Could there possibly be a few people out there in the big, wide world who had lifted my deathless prose from the library shelf, I asked myself. Anyway, it would be fun finding out.

Ever so quietly, I sent for an application form, which asked for details of the books I had written. There were three which qualified under the Public Lending Right Act, one of them "ghosted" for someone else.

Back came the reply, that whatever library borrowings were made in the year to June, 1985, I would receive the appropriate payment at the beginning of 1986. So far so good.

The matter was safely tucked out of my mind till the envelope arrived the other day. The calculations had now been made, at a slightly better rate of just over 1p per borrowing.

Now I can still lose myself in the mystery of computer printouts but this one seemed to have gone a little more haywire than most. According to the electronic brain, a book I wrote eight years ago was still borrowed 9,716 times last year, bringing £123.39. Another was borrowed 3,915 times, producing £49.72 while the most recent publication, "ghosted" and shared with a famous sportsman, had been taken from the library shelves no fewer than 15,055 times, bringing me £76.48. A grand total of £249.59, well worth the application form.

The justice of the Public Lending Right can be gathered from the fact that the first-mentioned book was read, in 1985, by nearly twice as many people as actually bought a copy when it was published. On that basis, the book, which sold around 5,500 copies in 1978, has probably been read by more than 100,000 people.

The money to compensate authors comes from the Government—about £2.75m of it this year—and individual payments are calculated on the basis of sample figures taken from several libraries in the different areas of Britain.

Don't ask me to explain how the final figure is reached but it involves a multiplication factor. In the first two years, the Scottish samples were taken in the libraries of Hillhead and Pollok, both in Glasgow.

This year they were taken at Pollok and Aberdeen, and next year it will be Larbert, Wishaw, and Aberdeen.

But any devious author who may be thinking of engineering his own success at these sampling centres had better think again.

A notice from the Public Lending Right people gives an assurance that "the computer can detect abnormalities in the loan pattern in sample libraries and will reject attempts by borrowers to push the loans of a particular book to artificial levels."

So we had better content ourselves with the natural figures. And what do they amount to?

With a maximum payment of £5,000, that sum has been reached by 63 top authors this year. In the next bracket, 142 have earned between £2,500 and £5,000; 344 earned between £1,000 and £2,500 and another 462 between £500 and £1,000.

I slip in among the 2,433 who reaped between £100 and £500, while a further 6,211 authors received less than £100. Beyond that there were 1,652 who got nothing at all.

Which brings me back to dear old J. R. Hartley. Or does it? On the basis that fishing is said to be the biggest participant sport in this country, the literature attached to it must surely be in demand in public libraries.

Perhaps I should write and tell the old soul. He may be worth a small fortune!

WHEN THE MINISTER TOOK A DRAM

∗ 3 R D   F E B R U A R Y   1 9 8 6 ∗

THE minister man from the North struck a pretty low note of success the other evening when he occupied the dreaded chair of *Mastermind* and faced Magnus Magnussen on the subject of Russian orchestral music.

But, if the performance of the Rev. Michael Chilton was bordering on the off-key-Tchaikovsky, it was nothing to the problem the poor chap is facing back home at Strathdon, where 17 of his 20 elders have excused themselves from duty because the minister refuses to go away.

I would not, of course, presume to judge upon events on Donside because rows involving parish ministers are not only a fairly regular feature of rural life but are invariably a confusion of misunderstanding, intolerance, indiscretion, and not a little hypocrisy.

As with most of life's troubled situations, there are usually two sides to the story.

What intrigues me about the Strathdon stramash, however, is the minister's frank admission that he may have had one drink too many at last year's Lonach Gathering.

At the top table of the Lonach lunch, he says, it was difficult to say no. "As I don't normally drink, it might have had more effect. I may have been in high spirits."

I'm sure he was. And why not? In my recollection of Lonach Gatherings, everyone was in high spirits. From early morning, clansfolk would begin a march around the district, gathering recruits on the march to the big event and downing a dram at every stop.

I'm sure I can recall occasions when the whole jing-bang of them arrived at the gathering both blootered and legless, kilts at the tilt and sporrans awry.

What may have the set the cat among the ecclesiastical pigeons was that the merry Michael, still resplendent in dog-collar, happened to go sprawling in the mud, a matter which may have given rise to some misunderstanding, he says.

I should have thought that, in the context of a summer which failed to arrive, the spectacle of the becollared cleric going thud in the mud would have brightened a grey day on Donside, conjured some delight from depression, hilarity from the humdrum.

Whatever the pros and cons of this right royal rumpus, there is a more fundamental issue at stake—the fact that we have long put our clergy under a pretty intolerable burden of expectation.

We expect them to be Man of God, man of the people, man apart, all at once. The unco guid will sniff haughtily if he shows the slightest trace of human frailty, like succumbing to the occasional modicum of medicine at the Lonach Gathering.

Others will condemn the poor creature for his total abstinence and find him acceptable only when he manages to kick the temperate habit.

How often have we heard it? "A grand chap the minister. Tak's a guid dram, ye ken."

Some will settle only for a sanctimonious sap who will fire them with a holy harangue to be measured by the duration of too many pan-drops.

Others look for contemporary analogy which can become so trite and predictable, offering about as much uplift as an overstretched bra.

The minister's role is presumably to lead his people to God but if he dare succeed too well, the critical tongue will readily turn on any member of the lay flock who is suspected of "going all to hell with religion." It falls into the category of going wrong in the head.

So we tug our minister this way and that and extend our demands to his wife and children, many of whom have been

11

known to kick over the traces in their frustration, incurring other problems of their own.

Many a minister and his family have become social outcasts, held at arm's length as if their well-scrubbed Christianity might conceal a leper's bell.

Through it all, the good Lord himself may never have been consulted on the matter, except by the odd one or two who have offered up a prayer for tolerance and compassion and some practical display of what Christianity is meant to be.

Perhaps somebody will think about that up Strathdon way tonight, on the eve of an important presbytery meeting at which Mr Chilton's case will be taken through hand.

For, if they don't believe in the power of prayer, they can hardly complain about a man who happens to down a mellow malt and put a harmless flush on the face of fellowship. Did the cheerful Mr Chilton really do any more than that?

IN DEFENCE OF LONG JOHNS

* 1 7 T H   F E B R U A R Y   1 9 8 6 *

"WEAR your thermals," said the gent who invited me to dine at the old heckling shed in Irvine, used by Robert Burns 200 years ago.

Restoration of that historic den has not so far included any form of effective heating. So I rummaged in the drawer for my drawers (of the long john variety) and suddenly realised I had quite forgotten the former ritual of wrapping those lily-white legs in wads of wool as a protection against severe winter days which are said, according to legend, to have emasculated brass monkeys.

How strange that I had forgotten, for there was a poignant anniversary to remind me.

On this very day 30 years ago—February 17—I had wakened to what was later declared to be the North-east of Scotland's coldest day of the century and pondered the vital question: Would I or wouldn't I?

In a few hours' time I would be standing in the biggest and barest and draughtiest church in Aberdeen facing up to another question which could have far-reaching effects: "Will you take this woman . . . ?"

It would be no time for chattering teeth. On the other hand, what could I expect in the way of romantic response when I suddenly revealed myself on the wedding night, bereft of boots and breeks and scarcely enhancing a dubious physique with a pair of passion-killing drawers?

Ah well, the lady would have to face reality sooner or later and the johns would at least defrost the libido, which was surely some consolation to a blushing bride on a perplexing night.

13

So caution was thrown to the chill wind and on went the long drawers, which was just as well. For, on this day of all days, a bungling beadle forgot to fire his furnace and that marriage took place in the largest refrigerator in Aberdeen. Icicles hung like stalactites where icicles were never meant to be.

Given that the nuptials are intended for procreation, this particular union must rank in the category of questionable ventures. Oh, it produced children right enough. Three sturdy lads, in fact.

But that wedding day of 1956 (in the run-in to the Suez Crisis but not directly responsible for it) evoked a more immediate response of four or five deaths, as the aged and the infirm, great-aunts and the like, succumbed to a barrage of bronchials and keeled over in the name of pneumonia.

Meanwhile, I survived in reasonable comfort and blessed the tradition which regarded long johns as an obligatory garment in keeping with the good sense of our Scottish rural scene.

Hardy men with weatherbeaten faces and gnarled hands (no shivering softies, them), men who supped brose for breakfast, saw nothing wrong in wrapping up well for the chill air which greeted them as they went striding down the drills of a frosty morning for the ultimate test of pulling turnips.

They wore pink garments of coarse wool, great hairy beasts so formidable that they would stand on their own two feet, overnight in the chaumer corner.

Some saw fit to wear them day and night, summer and winter, peeling them off for no other event but the annual dip in the zinc bath by the fireside.

Temperatures apart, there is little doubt that the power of the long johns lay not only in their effect of generating a cheap form of central heating but in the air of confidence which they instilled in the wearer.

In the barns and haylofts of the farm steading, a man had to be on guard against the peril of rats, which lurked in secluded corners and were known to fancy a frolicsome foray up the leg of a chap's breeks.

Fortified with a pair of long johns, the legs well tucked in at the tops of equally formidable woollen socks, a man could go about his daily business in the sure and certain confidence that, apart from the exclusion of draughts, no roving rodent with mischief on its mind could possibly invade his privacy and threaten his incentive for continued living.

Since these men were part of my heritage, it was hardly surprising I made a firm decision on that wedding day of 30 years ago.

Curiously, the older 1 have grown the less I have felt the need for winter warmth. Perhaps the winters are not as cold as they used to be. Perhaps we become tougher with age.

Perhaps we are prepared to suffer a little for the sake of a thing called vanity.

GOTHENBURG REVISITED

EVER since a memorable night in 1983, the name of Gothenburg has found its way into the standard vocabulary of Aberdonians like myself, coming to mean "A high point of experience; the greatest night of your life—or just magic!"

For that is what it meant to the thousands who followed their football team to the Swedish city that merry month of May, wondering if Aberdeen could put one over on the legendary Real Madrid in the European Cup Winners' Cup final as ultimate proof that fairy-tales really can come true.

As virtual unknowns in the greater arenas of Europe, the men from the North-east had not only broken the monotonous mould of Scottish football, by which I mean the divine right of Rangers and Celtic to win everything, but had demolished all obstacles at the top of European football as well, to stake their claim among the elite.

In 45 plane-loads, hundreds of cars and one ship, 12,000 of us, bedecked in the red of Pittodrie, descended on the neutral soil of Gothenburg, taking over in such a spirit of friendliness that not a single police charge was served in the 48 hours of their stay.

Just as a certain chemistry, brewed up by manager Alex Ferguson, had produced a team for the moment, so had fate decreed that this would be their finest hour.

As we arrived at the Ullevi Stadium, a background of crashing thunder, flashing lightning and torrential rain was conjured up as theatrical effects to a drama which lay, surely, in the skeely hands of nature.

The history books already reveal the cold print of denouement,

16

an Aberdeen victory as famous as any. The emotional details are more carefully hidden in the hearts and minds of those who will always be able to say "I was there!"

When that final whistle blew, we reached for new ways to express delirium, since nothing like this had happened to us before, then stood gazing down on that sodden sward, trying to fix the moment and absorb it into our beings for ever. I shall carry the memory of solid men struck dumb with emotion. Old Joe Mitchell from Rosehearty, hardened from bestriding the furrowed fields of Buchan for a lifetime, allowed the tears to flow freely down his weatherbeaten cheeks. So, too, did Aberdeen's biggest bookmaker, Bobby Morrison, whose ducts might well have been prised open by the fortune he had just lost in loyal Aberdonian bets; but his motives were purer than that.

We had waited a lifetime for this and now that the moment had arrived we were unwilling to let the Ullevi Stadium slip out of our grasp that night. Was there possibly some way to bottle a magic atmosphere and preserve it for ever?

When the stewards finally ushered us out, we embarked on such a night of revelry as most of us had never known, drinking, dancing, and celebrating in a Swedish rhapsody that would reverberate around the city for a long time to come.

Somehow Gothenburg became an untouchable symbol of success for people like me, placed on a pedestal out of reach. Curiously, since the night after my return, I have not even watched the video recording, lest I should wake up in the middle to discover it was all a dream.

The temptation of a nostalgic return to Gothenburg—just as many Celtic supporters have been back to Lisbon—was a prospect for the distant future. But suddenly, it came upon us.

Come tomorrow morning (and whatever the follies of revisiting a scene of triumph) I'll be winging my way across the North Sea, back to the city of Gothenburg, back to the Ullevi Stadium, back to . . . ?

By coincidence, as football followers will know, and having reached the last eight in Europe's premier tournament, Aberdeen

17

were drawn against none other than Gothenburg. The first of two legs took place in Aberdeen 12 days ago, with an outcome which did not augur well for the return.

After a 2-2 draw, the Dons must now go to Sweden with the clear-cut task of recording a win which, in their current mediocre form, seems unlikely.

This time we travel in hundreds instead of thousands and, in all truth, we travel more in hope than expectation. But we shall make our presence felt in the Swedish seaport, exhorting the team to greater feats, against the odds of a powerfully built home side, a vociferous local support, not to mention a diminished challenge from the Granite City itself.

Nature has a fondness for seven-year cycles and it doesn't take a pessimist to sense that the span is running out for Aberdeen, at least for the moment. Great players have gone. The chemistry has become unbalanced. Aberdeen has served Scottish football well by showing the way to other clubs, like Dundee United and now Hearts. Good luck to them. Perhaps it will all come again for Aberdeen.

When I attended my first Scottish Cup final in 1947, I wore a home-made tammy which my mother had fashioned out of her old red jersey. It brought luck. I didn't produce it again until a day in 1980 when they had a chance of winning the Premier Division for the first time. It brought luck. I took it to Gothenburg in 1983 and there again it worked.

Should I risk its reputation in Sweden this Wednesday? I'll think about it. If I do, and it proves once again to be the omen of success, I will take a leap into the Swedish air with such a bounce of joy that you may not see or hear of me in this column again.

Postscript.

The match ended in a 0-0 draw and Aberdeen were out on the away-goals rule.

THE MAGIC OF DRURY LANE

∗ 2 6 T H   M A R C H   1 9 8 6 ∗

UNTIL the other evening, I had almost forgotten the magic of Drury Lane, for long regarded as a theatrical venue without compare.

On second thoughts, a great deal of that magic has been missing this past quarter-century, since rock 'n' roll diverted the musical scene and television upset the habit of a night out at the theatre. But there was a time when no visit to London was complete without a night at Drury Lane, the very heart of the West End, where Nell Gwynn appeared in 1665 and the great names have been gracing its stage ever since.

Even the present building, the fourth to stand on the site, has been there since 1812, when the reopening production of Hamlet was preceded by a prologue from Scotland's own Lord Byron.

Through the twenties it was the setting for shows like *Rose Marie*, *The Desert Song*, *Show Boat*, and *New Moon*, while the thirties belonged to Ivor Novello and four of his romantic operettas, *Glamorous Night*, *Careless Rapture*, *Crest of the Wave*, and *The Dancing Years*.

The Theatre Royal, Drury Lane (to give it its proper name) became the wartime headquarters of ENSA, the organisation providing entertainment for the forces, but it was after the war before I knew anything of that intoxicating atmosphere within the vast auditorium.

The velvet curtains. Opulence dripping out of the boxes. The stir in the orchestra pit. The audience settling down in their seats as the lights dimmed and the overture swelled in anticipation of the spectacle to come.

19

Just as Ivor Novello had dominated in the thirties, the American team of Rodgers and Hammerstein had taken over from 1947 with *Oklahoma!*, running through to 1955 with other hits like *Carousel*, *South Pacific*, and *The King and I*.

I can still re-live the excitement of the boy from the country, keen to write plays and compose music, striding from one London theatre to another, absorbing the splendour of it all, dreaming dreams and generally ending the evening like a real stage-door Johnny, waiting for the autographs of people like Zena Dare, Vanessa Lee, and Ivor Novello.

I had seen the latter in *King's Rhapsody* just before he died in 1951. (Mistakenly, we tend to think of Franz Lehar as belonging to a much earlier generation though he died just three years before Novello, having presented his *Land of Smiles* at Drury Lane before the war.)

Entranced by Rodgers and Hammerstein's *Oklahoma!* and *Carousel*, I returned to the Lane to see their London production of *South Pacific*, in which the part of Nellie Forbush ("I'm Gonna Wash That Man Right Outa My Hair") was played by the ever-popular Mary Martin.

Though we knew nothing of him at the time, I can still turn out a cast-list to show that the minor role of Yeoman Herbert Quale was played by a 20-year-old by the name of Larry Hagman, without any apparent sign of nastiness as I recall, but better known today as J. R. Ewing of *Dallas*. He was also, of course, Miss Martin's real-life son.

Having marvelled at the output of American composers this century, from George Gershwin and Cole Porter to Jerome Kern, Richard Rodgers, and Irving Berlin, I found myself writing to those who were still around.

Finally, there I was, being shown into the Manhattan den where Richard Rodgers worked, fascinated to have arrived at the fount of so much musical creation. The reality was somewhat different from what I expected.

The dapper man behind the office desk could have been any New York businessman. All was so precise and lacking in emotion. Only the grand piano in the corner confirmed that I had not come to the wrong place.

Mr Rodgers seemed to be telling me he did not go around with a headful of melodies in search of a lyricist.

He generally waited for the storyline to arrive and wrote his music according to the moods demanded, no more, no less. It sounded all too much like a tailor and a made-to-measure suit. Yet, through all these assurances, I could hear those melodies in my head, dozens of them, from "Blue Moon", "Lover", "Oklahoma", "The Carousel Waltz", "You'll Never Walk Alone" and "This Nearly Was Mine", through to the later burst of tunes from shows like *The Sound of Music*.

And, just as I could hear them in my head, I knew I could not accept the word of their creator that he was no more than a humble tunesmith, forging melodies as a blacksmith might forge horseshoes. Inspiration came into it, surely. And genius.

These thoughts were with me the other evening as I headed through Leicester Square towards Covent Garden and up the steps of Drury Lane. The show currently packing them in is *42nd Street*, a song-and-dance extravaganza dating back to 1933, when the original dance director was none other than Busby Berkeley.

It is by no means one of the great stage musicals—Harry Warren didn't give it enough wealth of melody for that distinction—but if this is what the London theatre-goers are raving about, I wonder what they would make of some of the truly memorable shows.

Since *My Fair Lady* closed in October, 1963, Drury Lane hasn't exactly bristled with hits. Apart from our own Andrew Lloyd Webber, the stage is not overflowing with that kind of composer either.

But with Frankie Vaughan belting out "Lullaby of Broadway" and Shani Wallis looking even more attractive than she did a generation ago, I just relaxed and enjoyed a lively evening.

Drury Lane had not lost its magic altogether. I hope it never will.

21

WHEN YOU NEVER SAY NEVER

* 20TH MAY 1986 *

THOSE of us who try to string a few words together in a form which will be readable, if not sensible, generally adhere to a code which was probably ingrained in our beings by the time we were 11.

Depending on the primary schooling and our own affinity with the rhythms of language, we may cringe at the sight of advisors and convenors and other bits of modern jargon, like the floppy "disks" of computer-talk, which have been sent to plague the purity of English.

It is not that we are all so steeped in semantics that we can readily recognise our dangling participles when we see them but simply that we still remember some of the basic rules of schooldays which were the better observed if a peaceful life ranked among the priorities.

It was well drummed into you that you never said never unless you really meant never. Since an alternative was a choice between one possibility and another, there was no such thing as a number of alternatives. What was wrong with choices? And so it went on.

But nothing endures for ever, not even the English language. Piece by piece, the words change, new forms of phrasing creep in. In truly American style, we have gotten into the habit of preparing our computer programs without stopping to think about how we are adopting the spellings of another country.

Indeed, it was a member of my own weaving sept, the Connecticut lexicographer, Noah Webster, who began spinning the idea of a different American spelling, which would eventually lead to something quite separate from the English we knew. Whatever may have been felt about Mr Webster and his dictionary, the bare

22

facts do show that the people who speak English as the mother tongue are now heavily outnumbered by those who speak it as a second or foreign language.

The fact that it has become the world's first global language was driven home the other evening when the novelist Robert McCrum came north to Strathclyde University to deliver a lecture on the changes taking place.

Mr McCrum should know what he is talking about. Not only does he write novels but he is the highly-successful editorial director of Faber and Faber, the London publishers.

His was the second in a series of annual lectures sponsored by none other than his rivals at Collins, the company whose long-running bestseller, the Bible, is a clear example of how language will change over the centuries.

Amid the wit of a sparkling address, the 33-year-old Mr McCrum enlightened us on matters like the 1,000 million people who are now using the English language. That is a fifth of the world's population.

There are now more people learning it in China than in the entire population of the United States. It has also become the official language of 34 countries in the Third World.

Of course not all of it is the English we have come to know and love. The Creole as developed in places like the West Indies has been forecast to become the language of hundreds of millions in time to come. In its merging of language, it has been said to be at the Chaucer stage of development.

The Scots played their own major part in taking the language abroad in the first place, and, as McCrum was pointing out, there has been a linguistic version of *The Empire Strikes Back*.

The trappers gave us phrases like working like a beaver. The Aussies have sent back some fairly blunt bullets like as scarce as rocking-horse manure, and as happy as a bastard on Father's Day (which may or may not owe something to Dame Edna Everage!)

McCrum was not slow to lambast the Government for its neglect of matters like grants to foreign students, which has an economic consequence as well as any other.

23

By turning them away towards America and its way of speech, he pointed out, we are ensuring that, once they return to positions in their own countries, they will be more inclined to do business with the United States than Britain.

When the speechifying was over we repaired downstairs to a more informal discussion over a glass of wine and a sandwich. The company was an interesting mixture of Strathclyde academics, bookshop people and publishing bosses like Colin McLean, of Aberdeen University Press, and the chairman of Collins itself, Ian Chapman, as well as an assortment of writers like Lavinia Derwent and broadcasters like Jimmie Macgregor.

Mr Chapman added to the sustenance of the evening by offering us a complimentary copy of the new *Collins Paperback English Dictionary*.

Since we were enjoying what has come to be known as a finger-buffet, I checked the newfangled phrase in the 1,024-page publication but couldn't find it. It was more explicit about pulling one's finger out, though without any reference to vulgar origins.

Presumably with an eye to America, the dictionary gives one of my *bêtes noires*, advisors, as an option. But it goes one further and allows convenors as well. Horror upon horrors!

Not even my *Britannica World Language Dictionary*, published in American in 1956, goes that far. But then, as we said in the beginning, nothing endures for ever. Not even good spelling.

TO PETRA—THE ROSE-RED CITY

* 3 1 S T   M A Y   1 9 8 6 *

FROM high on Mount Nebo I looked out across the Jordan Valley to the Dead Sea and the Judean Hills beyond, with Jericho brooding in the middle distance.

Moses died here, according to the Bible, and this was the view he absorbed in the final moments of his mortal life. The vastness of the landscape, the peace and utter silence and beauty of it all can stir in the human breast a desire to be left up here alone for ever.

That silence is broken only by the call of shepherd to shepherd across the valley, with bouncing echoes accompanied by the tinkle of goat-bells and the lilt of the flute. Yet Mount Nebo was merely an unexpected bonus on the road from Amman to Petra, that "rose-red city half as old as time", according to the poet.

And from Jordan we would fly on across the Middle East to the United Arab Emirate of Dubai in this two-centre package of "Arabian Discovery", which gives you pleasantly hot summer weather from October till May and includes a desert safari.

But first towards Petra, through small communities where little can have changed since Biblical times. Old women sit cross-legged by the roadside, the menfolk laze on mattresses, their wistful faces beaten in bronze. Only the telegraph poles which tether goats are out of context.

As recently as 1955, this journey from Amman could take you 10 days by horse, such was the inaccessibility of Petra. Now the pain has been removed and the pleasure awaits, after an overnight stay at the Petra Forum Hotel.

None of the advance publicity quite prepares you for this mysterious city which is best reached on foot down the narrow

25

gorge, twisting and turning until, suddenly, the full reality is unveiled for disbelieving eyes.

The story of Petra is that of a Semitic tribe called the Nabataeans, who settled there in the centuries before Christ and became "protectors" of the caravans which passed through on the trading routes to Arabia and from there to India and China.

But the main attraction of this vast canyon capital is that they proceeded to create a city, not by building it but by chiselling it out of the canyon walls. And not just tombs but vast cathedrals, public buildings, theatres, and houses that defy the imagination.

The Romans came and added refinements like a colonnaded street but, in time, Petra declined and was virtually lost to the Western world for centuries until it was rediscovered by a German explorer in 1812.

Until last year there were still 500 people living inside the rose-red city, so called for the changing hue of its stone. Even now, when the Government has moved most of them out of the national monument, they return to spend their daylight hours, drawn by the magnetism of the place they call home.

There they laze with their horses and camels as cats materialise from nowhere and miaow for mercy.

Down through the deserted city you turn left into the Roman street, along which there was an inhabited hotel in modern times, frequented by Agatha Christie.

From there you begin a climb through a gorge at the far end of the city, soaring through cliffs upon which they chiselled a stairway to the sky. Once you have reached that rooftop of the world yet another miracle of carving awaits, in the shape of a large monastery no less.

Nearby, a humble lady of noble face, dark and mysterious, lives in a cave with her husband and children, among the few still allowed to remain here, completely cut off from so-called civilisation but civil nevertheless.

There is no way out of here except by that hazardous stairway yet they are compensated with a view from the open door of their cave that stretches down towards the land of Israel and some of

God's most scenic handiwork. (Charles and Diana came here by helicopter on a private visit last year.)

So it was down again, limbs aching, lungs stretching, but spirits soaring. To miss out on Petra, surely one of the real wonders of the world, would guarantee a hereafter of regret.

Then it was on to Jerash, 29 miles north of Amman and widely accepted as the best example of a provincial Roman city to be found anywhere. In this city of a thousand columns, which lay totally buried under sand and rubble until 1806, the main excitement is to be found in the fact that the excavations, begun in 1925, still have a long way to go.

You can stand at one end of a Roman street, with columns totally exposed, and look towards the other end where only the tops are visible. And who knows what lies totally buried beyond that?

There would be so much more to see of Amman and the Wadi Rum, where they filmed the desert scenes for *Lawrence of Arabia*, but it is time to leave Jordan and lift into the night sky en route for the United Arab Emirates, that group of small, independent states which formed themselves into a country in 1971.

The immediate destination is Dubai, a largely modern city from the exploration of oil, which began in 1969 (at the same time as the North Sea), with a rolling hinterland of desert which we would yet discover.

You can flit from the contrasting luxury of the Hyatt Regency to the old part of the city with its alleyways and souks, where gold is a particularly good buy, then sail up the creek which divides the old and new and survey the dhows, which seem incapable of plying those ancient trade routes to the east, as they still do.

This is the land ruled with benevolence by the Al-Maktoum family (they also sustain horse-racing in Britain), where no-one pays income tax and the humblest citizen has the right to approach the ruler on the lines of "Hey Sheik, I have a complaint." The chances are he will put it right.

One evening you may find yourself meeting up at a beach-villa party with expatriates (I met Robin Fyffe, a banker from Ayr, and Ken McKinlay, BP's manager who is a nephew of that well-remembered Scottish golfer and newspaper editor, Sam McKinlay).

The next, you are driving out of town, passing signboards of contractors like Lilley of Glasgow, and heading into the desert on safari, a wiry little English lady called Alison Simms at the wheel of a sturdy Land Cruiser.

Alison lives there and knows the desert and the Bedouin, a reassuring thought as you dip and soar over dunes which deepen into rich pink the further you travel.

We found camp for the night, lit a fire, and ate sausages and chops and drank wine before creeping into our sleeping bags, under the canopy of a million stars. You burrow cavities in the sand for hip bone and shoulder and fade away in the eerie silence of the desert night.

The braying of a stray donkey brought life at 6 a.m., in readiness for an adventure which no-one could guarantee. If you know your desert like Alison Simms, you may be privy to the information that the Bedouin are gathering at an appointed time and place to hold their camel racing.

Off we went in search of the venue and suddenly, there it was, just a stretch of suitable sand with more than 100 camels and their owning families crowding into a makeshift paddock amid dust and noise and excitement.

The jockeys, we discovered, could be as young as six or seven, strapped to the back of the camel by fathers or older brothers, who proceeded to chase alongside in their varied vehicles blaring horns and exhorting their young riders to victory.

The galumphing action of the camel, not one of nature's brighter species, makes for a certain amount of comedy, especially when the dumb creatures zigzag their way down the course—or turn and go in the opposite direction altogether!

That spectacle at dawn in the desert must be over before the sun comes up, bringing temperatures in the 80s by 9 a.m.

So we carried a rich memory back to the encampment where we fried up bacon-and-egg that never tasted better. This was truly the life!

CARNAGE ON A FOREIGN FIELD

* 1 ST JULY 1 9 8 6 *

THE sun came bright into a blue sky over Europe on this same July morning of 70 years ago. The larks went swooping across the picturesque lands of Picardy in Northern France and another heavenly day would have been in prospect. Except that they were holding a battle that day.

It was unlikely to be a lengthy affair because the Germans would be so softened up by the early bombardment of shellfire that the British troops would have little more to do than walk the length of no-man's-land and claim victory at the other end.

The reality was different. The next five miles took close on five months to complete, turning the Battle of the Somme into the bloodiest chapter in the history of mankind, with more than a million dead and wounded on both sides.

As a small boy in the 1930s I can remember hearing tales from lucky survivors, men still in their prime but devastated by the carnage of that foreign field, where poppies bloomed so richly that same morning of July, 1916.

At school we bowed heads on Armistice Day and conjured up pictures of that bizarre battlefield—young men of patriotic fervour rising over the top of the trenches, spurring themselves to battle with oaths on their lips for the German menace which they would silence for ever.

The youngest to die was a 16-year-old; the oldest, a 68-year-old father who had gone to fight alongside his sons. And, just as we were soon to see again in the Second World War, the postman brought the telegrams of dead and wounded, men of the Gordons, Seaforths, Argylls, Royal Scots, Camerons and

Cameronians, HLI, Black Watch, Royal Scots Fusiliers, KOSB and Scots Guards.

In time, they tried to tell it all in our history books, though history is a fickle subject. The First World War had been running for almost two years but the German lines across France had still to be broken.

Back home, they were raising a new army, mainly volunteers, which compassed the higher brackets of physique and education, a loss which later displayed itself, beyond the immediate grief, in a generation of wistful spinsters and a deficiency in genetic reproduction.

They will still argue about the rights and wrongs of the Somme but the first indisputable fact is that the early-morning bombardment had little effect on the resistance of the Germans, who had been well dug into their ridges overlooking the River Somme, established for 18 months and superbly protected in 30 feet of solid chalk.

As our troops moved out of their billets in cottages, barns and byres and headed for the trenches, they lay low to watch the final bombardment, which turned the morning sun into a dull red glow in the dust and smoke. Now it was time for the infantry to emerge from their trenches, over the top and into battle. Time to claim that victory. Time to walk into a solid wall of German attack.

Our men were bewildered and angry, if they were not already dead. On that first day alone, the Germans inflicted 60,000 casualties, of which 20,000 died.

How men gather themselves in the aftermath of such a disaster, comrades left with the parched lips of a last gasp, must be put down to the miracle of the human spirit. When those five miles had finally been gained in five months, the official bulletin hailed it as a great victory. Our revival, with wave upon wave of fresh troops, silently drove a wedge into the German ranks and paved the way for its defeat. But what a price to pay for victory!

In the glaur of that warfare, men had lived like animals, thigh-deep in water and going mad in rat-infested trenches. Great poets like Owen and Sassoon and Graves were trying to capture the

30

scene in words, when they were not escorting each other back to psychiatric hospitals in Edinburgh.

Through it all, the name of one Scotsman became a prime target for criticism. Field Marshal Sir Douglas Haig was said to have commanded from well behind, sending fresh troops to fill the gaps apparently without much idea of the hopelessness of the task.

At the 50th anniversary of the Somme in 1966 I raised such criticism of Haig in a newspaper column of the time, an exercise which taught me to be wary of cool, historical judgments long after the event.

I was subjected to a barrage of abuse from men in their 70s who had actually been there, who held Haig in the highest regard, despite the exposure of their own lives, and wondered if a whipper-snapper like me could have done any better in the heat of a complicated battle.

Most of those men will now be gone, alas, and I can only repeat the defence of their leader, in fairness to their own memory and for the interest of those who might seek to make further judgments.

At least they had survived to live a normal span and could recall how the nightingale still sang through the horror of that July day in 1916.

And the skylark wheeled towards Heaven, perhaps in early warning of souls to follow, those flowers of Picardy who were really too young to fold their petals for ever.

FAIRY-TALE OF FORBES

THE mighty arm of Liberty was raised once more at the weekend, refreshed from a centenary overhaul and still calling upon the world to "Give me your tired, your poor, your huddled masses, yearning to breathe free."

Down the century, countless millions have accepted the invitation, passing under her protective hand with battered belongings in the hope that a better fate might await in this American land of opportunity.

The hypnotic power of her silent, eerie welcome was something I would experience for myself in the 1960s as she emerged from an August dawn and pointed us in the direction of a Manhattan berth.

But I had heard all about her many years before, from a Scotsman who passed that way in 1904 and would return to his native parish in later life to regale us with exciting tales of that brave new world.

I sat open-mouthed at the feet of Bertie Forbes, who had gone away from our own backyard in Aberdeenshire, one of ten poor children from a little country cottage, determined to extract himself from the anonymity of those huddled masses and to "be somebody".

A fascination with newspapers had found an early outlet in Peterhead, Montrose and Dundee, where he learned his reporting craft before heading for South Africa at the end of the Boer War.

But the real goal was New York where he arrived that day in 1904 without contacts, influence, money or a job. That should have meant a bare room in Brooklyn till he found his feet but an instinct for financial writing also told him the value of moving closer to the men of power.

Outrageously for one so limited in funds, he took a room in the old Waldorf Astoria and was soon rubbing shoulders with the famous, men like John D. Rockefeller, Henry Ford, and Frank Woolworth.

The story of Bertie Forbes has now passed into business legend. Not only did the world's most powerful newspaper owner, William Randolph Hearst, give him a blank cheque to write his own salary, but he started his own business magazine, which stands today as the most influential journal of its kind in America.

Appropriately, it is called simply *Forbes*, a fortnightly publication which runs to the length of a novel on most issues.

On his visits back home, I was just as spellbound by the stories as my great-aunt Mary-Jean was horrified by the thought that she had repeatedly turned down the early overtures of a budding multi-millionaire!

In the 1930s, he used to stay at the old Cruden Bay Hotel, a kind of mini-Gleneagles, with his wife and five sons, one of whom, Malcolm, followed him as head of the business after Bertie died in 1954.

Defying that tradition of sons who are never the men their fathers were, Malcolm took the successful base of Bertie's enterprise and expanded it out of all recognition, moving from publishing to real estate and counting among his personal properties a palace in Morocco, a chateau in France, an island in the South Pacific, as well as New York's most fabulous yacht, his own Boeing airliner and more Fabergé eggs than the whole priceless collection within the Kremlin of Moscow.

When he is not flying in that plane or sailing on *The Highlander*, you will find him chalking up records for hot-air ballooning across America or riding his motorbike (he owns the company) to Moscow or Peking.

Malcolm Forbes, in short, is one of America's most fabulous characters as well as one of its wealthiest. His diversion from an early political career (he was a contemporary opponent of

John F. Kennedy) probably deprived the United States of one of its greater Presidents.

While America has been his life, I have sensed that advancing years were turning his thoughts more and more to his father's homeland, appreciating the character and determination it must have taken on that route from a lowly cottage at New Deer to the skyscrapers of New York.

He has been known to slip quietly into Aberdeen Airport in that private airliner or even to pass through the countryside on his motorbike.

But tomorrow night he flies in more publicly. Come Thursday afternoon and the sole owner of the Forbes organisation, publisher, writer, humorist, adventurer, and one of the truly great men of America, will step solemnly into Marischal College for a very special moment in his colourful life.

No doubt he will be remembering that, far away in that land of Liberty, his humble Scots father was recognised by the University of Southern California, who declared him an honorary Doctor of Letters.

Now the situation is being reversed as Aberdeen University confers upon the son the honorary degree of LL.D.

The story will have gone full circle in this week when Malcolm Forbes comes home to the corner of Scotland where his father ran about with patches on his breeks, polishing boots for the gentry to make a precious penny.

Wouldn't Bertie have been proud of the lad?

A ROCKEFELLER AT HAND

THE introductory boom of the organ resounded in the rafters, the filtered light of stained glass fell reverently upon the occasion and soon the academics came stepping in procession, their gowns and hoods of many colours explaining pedigree and discipline.

It took only the dignity of Lord Polwarth, the university chancellor, to set the final seal of importance on a day which would linger in the memory for ever.

Curiously, despite a lifetime of varied experience, I had never before attended a graduation ceremony. Yet here was an event of drama, wave after wave of the nation's young stepping up for that capping ritual which would round off years of effort and set them forth into a bewildering world.

Proud parents gazed from public benches in confirmation of the fact that within the corporate nature of the day there lay as many individual dramas as there were students.

From homes in every corner of the globe they had come to a land where students had been joining a formal learning for 500 years.

They had come with the academic right to be there, built upon that foundation according to their diligence and capacity, and were now offering themselves to the world as a new generation of qualified people.

Whatever personal sacrifice had been made along the way was a private matter to be guessed from the parents who had come to share this culminating day.

For some, the better heeled, it would have meant no sacrifice at all. For others, the hint of hardship was carefully drawn within the contour of a glistened eye.

35

One plain little couple beside me, decked out in their Sunday best, seemed the unlikely progenitors of genius yet this was their day and there was their son, striding forward to receive an Honours degree. I could tell by their buzz of anticipation, the concentration of their attention as the moment approached, and the fumbled touch of unaccustomed hands when it finally arrived.

An exchange of glance between two humble people was a more eloquent account of their own private story than all that words could tell. I must confess, it brought a lump to the thrapple.

And when the pomp and ceremony were over, they spilled out to the quadrangle for handshakes and kisses and the sun came out on cue for family snapshots.

As they headed off to their various celebrations, there were fond farewells among students themselves, vowing that they would write and visit and keep alive the friendships which had matured over four of the most poignant years of their lives. Perhaps they will.

As a mere observer of those graduates stepping up for the climax of their academic careers, my own reflections centred on the high calibre of human being we still manage to produce despite the ravages of modern living.

On the other side, it prompted the daunting thought of what will become of them. Even in normal times, it has always seemed a tall order that the natural wastage of death and retirement will clear enough space for the budding replacements.

The sterner economic times prompted a timely warning from Principal McNicol about the havoc being wreaked by Government cuts. It was reflected in the numbers who might well have been there that day but for whom there was no place.

The efforts of the universities to soldier on in the face of all the adversity were pointed out by one professor who called upon the new graduates to remember them in their prayers—and, better still, in their wills.

If that professor had secret dreams of a Rockefeller on the horizon, he would not have known of the coincidence at hand.

I tell it as a postscript to this column of last week, when I wrote about the honorary degree being conferred by Aberdeen University on New York writer, publisher and adventurer Malcolm Forbes, one of America's richest men, whose father passed in through Ellis Island, a poor immigrant from Scotland.

Over dinner, Malcolm Forbes had introduced me casually to the strapping young man, friend of the family, who was playing a kind of bodyguard role for his Scottish visit.

His name was . . . yes, Rockefeller. Stillman Rockefeller, whose grandfather was a nephew of the legendary John D. and whose grandmother was a member of the Andrew Carnegie family.

Having danced anonymously in Aberdeen discos, he listened intently to those graduation speeches before boarding Malcolm Forbes's private Boeing 727 at Dyce Airport and disappearing in the general direction of America.

FITE STEEN COUNTRY?

IT is one of the sadnesses of our Scottish life that the vernacular speech with which many of us grew up becomes a difficulty when we see it on the printed page. The reason is not hard to find. While we were all taught to read and recognise the English language, our own native tongue was relegated to the level of playground vulgarity, not to be heard in decent places.

It is a flaw of our educational system which, happily, is being put right in several quarters where dialect poets like Charles Murray are in favour at last.

That process should be hastened by David Ogston's recollections of growing up on an Aberdeenshire farm (published as *White Stone Country*), written in the broadest of the Buchan dialect.

Those who write in broad Scots, of course, face a number of difficulties, not least the variations from area to area, as well as the lack of an accepted form of spelling. Writers must set their own phonetic rules and get on with it as consistently as possible. Some, one suspects, write their stuff in English and translate a succession of words into Scots.

Not so David Ogston. His words spring as naturally from his pen as the oats from his father's parks at Kidshill of Auchnagatt, real and authentic and faithful to the idiom which is known best to those who grew up with it.

Like many another North-east writer, David Ogston, who is a minister in Perth, acknowledges his debt to Lewis Grassic Gibbon who opened his eyes to the full meaning of familiar things.

About his discovery of Grassic Gibbon's work, he writes: "The wye that he spak o fowk, trauchled and brave tae, the wye that he held up tae ye the shape o lives lived lang ago (or wis't yistreen), the wye that he brocht ye the atmospheres o parks an sizzens, the muckle furth an the lift, waur that real an direct that faan I laid the beuk doon an put the Howe o the Mearns back in the drawer an gaed ootside intae the sin an aa the sichts an soons an stinks o the close I felt that here, for the first time, in the confines o the stadins o Kidshill, here wis a life foo o the raw materials o poetry an meanin an value, like the life he'd putten intae the nerra mairch-dykes o his pages."

Grassic Gibbon himself bypassed the pure dialect in favour of his ingenious compromise—writing basically in English but with the cadences of the North-east dictating the rhythms to give an impression of total Scottishness.

What encourages me most about David Ogston's book is that he made all these acquaintances with the Buchan dialect in a childhood which was entirely post-Second World War.

I always felt Grassic Gibbon was mistaken in his belief that the old Scots ways and language virtually petered out with the First World War.

I knew that life and tongue in the 1930s so I would have judged it ended with the Second World War. Now David Ogston may have proved us both wrong for here it is, alive and well in the 1950s, and indeed I hear it still in the present day.

He himself left the heart of Buchan at the age of 11, which may account for the occasional word which sounds alien to the local tradition. Thrawn devils that they are, Buchan folk either add to the broadness of standard Scots (as in "stone-stane-steen") or go back the other way.

As a result, their version of "porridge" is not "parritch" but "poarritch". His use of "sterr" comes straight from Stanley Baxter's Glasgow.

But these are minor matters against an overall impression of an evocative piece of prose, distilled from a sensitive childhood, deeply felt and richly expressed.

There might have been no harm in following the Doric to its logical end, calling his book *Fite Steen Country*.

39

IS THERE A BOOK INSIDE YOU?

THERE is a conceit of this profession which says that there is a book inside every journalist, to which the suitable rejoinder might be: and that's exactly where it should stay!

I suppose vanity is the starting point of every decision to write a book—the belief that we have something within us which is sufficiently worth saying to justify the vast expense of a hardback publication.

Yet it would be fatuous to suggest such vanity should be resisted completely, otherwise there would be no artistic creativity at all.

Of course it may all come to nothing. On the other hand, just listen to this story of a lady I met in Glasgow the other day. Hilary Norman was working in an obscure job at the BBC in London, the vivacious daughter of a Jewish couple who fled from Germany to Britain in the 1930s.

At school she was no good at essays nor had she ever been troubled with any ambition to be a writer. But she woke up one morning, several years ago, fresh from a dream which gave her an idea. There and then she decided to write a book. Whatever the gods were up to, her sudden impulse was not as mad as might have appeared.

During spare evenings and weekends she wrote assiduously till the book was finished. Coyly showing the result to a friend, who said it seemed promising, she slipped it into the hands of Hodder and Stoughton of London, who liked what they read.

Without raising her hopes too dramatically, they took it to the Frankfurt Book Fair, where they promptly sold the American rights. Brian Levy of Hodders told me the delightful story of how they came back to tell Hilary of their success.

She would probably be quite pleased with the result. How much had it fetched? A mere 330,000 dollars! They needed to call for the smelling-salts.

The total deal would mean that, even before a single copy of her very first novel was published this summer, the slender Miss Norman would have earned herself around £350,000. She had literally turned a dream into a fortune, something akin to winning the football pools at the first attempt.

Her name will be quite unfamiliar to you at this point. But keep an eye on Hilary Norman's *In Love and Friendship*, which seems to me to have all the ingredients not only of a successful novel but a television series as well.

Against that kind of fairy-tale, I was able to tell her my own funny story, dating back to early manhood when, with all the brashness of immaturity, I thought I had already accumulated a life-story which was worth unleashing on a breathless public.

Once it was written, I gave it the nod of approval, spat on it for luck and sent it off to a London publisher who, for reasons best known to himself, turned it down. Ah well, they all tell stories about the one that got away.

When I then tried an Edinburgh publisher, however, he had strangely similar ideas. At least I had the grace to take the hint and tuck my unwanted masterpiece securely out of sight.

So life wore on and middle-age came knocking, and there I was, one evening, with nothing better to do, rummaging through a drawer when I came upon the old manuscript.

In all honesty, I could now see more clearly why those publishers had not queued up with cheque books. But life had added a few more layers since those lost days of innocence and perhaps it was worthy of a rewrite.

Steeling myself to the task, I wrote a 1980s version of my life-story. And who did I send it to? I sent it to the same London publisher who turned it down the first time. And what did the

London publisher do? With a singular lack of originality, he did exactly the same as he did before.

Once again, I tried the Edinburgh man who, by now, had gained sufficiently in enlightenment to say yes, he would publish it. Celebrations!

To my delight and his profit, the book became something of a Scottish bestseller for a few weeks, running into a second print before being sold out altogether.

Having found a market for that mixture of childhood recollection and more worldly experience, I always intended to write a sequel but time slipped past and nothing happened.

Something of that first book, however, was incorporated into a television programme I wrote last year, a modest film which found itself among the nominations for a top award.

Suddenly, life changed. Instead of me writing to offer publishers manuscripts I had already written, the publishers were writing to ask for manuscripts I *hadn't* yet written. What is more, they were prepared to put their money where their mouths were, much in advance of the event.

Leaning back and drawing heavily on an imaginary cigar, I felt entitled to believe the world wasn't such a bad place after all, capable of the most unlikely turnabouts.

It all came to fruition at the weekend when I signed a contract with Collins to write a book I haven't even thought about yet. As part of the deal, their subsidiary company, Fontana, will bring that earlier book out in paperback next spring.

Therein must lurk a moral. Perhaps there is a book inside every journalist after all—indeed inside every human being, since journalists are nothing special.

So next time you have that urge, don't dismiss it lightly. You might even have a dream like Hilary Norman's, in which case you could be heading round the rainbow.

THE POWER OF COINCIDENCE

EVER since I found myself marooned on a traffic island in Hong Kong, lost and bewildered in a colony of five million people who all looked alike, I have been intrigued by the power of coincidence.

There was only one other person on that traffic island, my only hope of salvation. When I appealed for guidance, the lady turned out to be not only a Scot, not just a Glaswegian, but the daughter of a lady who lived round the corner from my own home on the South Side. Out of those five million people, she was perhaps the one above all who would be best disposed to help me.

You have all had experiences of that sort, some more astonishing than others. Take the case of the London policeman whose phone number at the police station was changed to 40116. Having asked an acquaintance to call him at that number, he went on patrol duty and suddenly remembered he had mistakenly given the number as 40166.

On his way back to the station with a colleague, the policeman saw a light burning in a factory and went to investigate. As he entered the building, the phone rang. He answered and, to his astonishment, it was the friend to whom he had given the wrong number. The number was ex-directory but he discovered that it was, in fact, 40166.

Or what about the express train travelling from Miami to New York on the night of August 24th, 1983? At 7.40 p.m. it struck and killed a woman fishing from a bridge. Sixteen miles farther on, at 9.30, it hit a truck too close to the line.

The shaken crew were replaced but, at 1.10 a.m., the same

43

train hit a tractor-trailer on a crossing, sending 21 people to hospital. Once again the crew were replaced but, at 2.37 a.m., it ran headlong into a car at another crossing.

The authorities had no reason to question the machinery or the skill of the crews but finally declared it a "rogue train" and cancelled the rest of the journey.

Mathematicians and gamblers will work out the odds against such events but, in Scotland this week, I met a scientist who believes there is a dimension beyond mathematical calculation.

Dr Lyall Watson, whose ancestors went from Cupar in Fife to settle in South Africa, takes the view that what we care to call chance really has a pattern of reason of its own. Like Hippocrates, he believes that, in matters of coincidence, sympathetic elements are seeking each other out.

I must confess that most things scientific leave me none the wiser but there seemed a great deal of sense in what Dr Watson was saying. Here was no weirdo trying to promote some cranky ideas but a thoroughly rational and civilised man who has seen and heard enough in his 47 years to convince him that happenings must not be dismissed and ridiculed just because science cannot account for them.

He is impressed, for example, by the fact that we have managed to split the atom and put a man on the moon yet cannot explain, with all our science, how Uri Geller can bend a spoon.

Dr Watson conducted an interesting experiment. He showed a video of Geller to a small girl and implied that anyone could do what he had done. To his amazement, the girl took a solid iron key and bent it in the Geller manner.

"As a scientist, I would have said it was impossible, but the difference between me and the girl was that she did not know it was supposed to be impossible," he explained.

Dr Watson is quite appalled at the hidebound attitudes of many fellow scientists—and more so at the actions of a body which is apparently conducting a witch-hunt against all investigation into anything which smacks of the paranormal.

In his African childhood, Dr Watson was treated and cured by a witch doctor and says: "I was seeing and learning things which predisposed me to accept that there is more than one way to look at the world. I have seen things, like spoon-bending and poltergeists, which my science says are impossible. Reconciling them with my scientific background is not easy."

A quiet, modest man, Dr Watson is clearly not in the persuasion business but he has seen enough evidence of telepathy to convince him there is something in it.

As a guide to how far mankind has yet to travel, Dr Watson instances the vast scope of the human brain compared to the limited use we have made of it so far. He does not believe that nature would have slipped up so badly in over-pitching our capacity.

It is 15 years since Dr Watson produced his remarkable bestseller, *Supernature*, in which he tried to create a kind of demilitarised zone into which both scientists and enthusiasts could venture without abandoning their sense of proportion or their sense of wonder.

Now he has written *Beyond the Supernature*, in which he reckons the evidence of so much that remains unexplained cannot be discounted. Today, he is a British subject living in Ireland and travelling extensively.

He comes up with some remarkable stories. In the state of Nebraska, for example, there is a church choir which meets for practice once a week in the hall. Of the 15 members, you will usually find one or perhaps two who are not there on the dot of 7.30 p.m., as would be the case in any similar situation.

On one particular evening, not one of the 15 arrived on time. For 15 different reasons, they were all at least 10 minutes late. Yet, at the appointed hour of 7.30 p.m., a boiler in the church hall exploded and wrecked the place. All would probably have been killed. Dr Watson does not believe that was a matter of chance. Somehow, unconsciously he reckons, all 15 found a reason for being late. The longer I live the more I would agree that there are fine lines of difference between accident and chance.

OH, THE TALES WE TELL!

THAT glittering Indian Summer, which penetrated bleak October with unaccustomed warmth, simply couldn't last, I consoled myself as the plane lifted off from Glasgow Airport on the southern flight to the Algarve coast of Portugal.

After all, there is nothing more galling than to travel far at great expense in search of that aerial furnace only to find that you would have done just as well by staying at home.

By the time we were high in the sky—and higher still on a floating cloud of mellow malt—I was magnanimously conceding that the folks back home were perfectly entitled to their modicum of warmth. Good luck to them.

It was no skin off my nose (metaphorically at least) since I would be basking on the golden beaches of Alvor, lapping up the luxury of Penina and toning up the tissues for the long dark winter ahead.

Such generosity of spirit was well maintained in the clear blue heavens over Biscay and survived the first tremors of shock when visibility deteriorated over Portugal and we went dipping through dark, ugly clouds to land at Faro Airport.

Ah well, even the glorious Algarve must have its odd day of cloud, we agreed, as the taxi driver sped us westward along that Atlantic fringe.

As regular members of the time-share fraternity, we knew our Algarve weather pretty well. Years of experience told us that tomorrow would burst forth with all that unbroken blue which follows the odd intrusion of cloud.

But tomorrow turned out to be as dull and miserable as today

46

and, by late evening, the rains had arrived in such an aquatic convention as to perform a night-long deluge, vying for airspace with the lightning and all accompanied by the orchestral drums and cymbals of thunder. Tam o' Shanter never had it so bad.

But if those first three days were disappointing, the fourth was merely the prelude to the bleakest day of all. Thursday lashed us without respite till cars were reported to have floated away in the floods of nearby Portimao.

Meanwhile, having scunnered of scrabble and re-read Edwin Muir's *Scottish Journey* with a new-found level of nostalgia, what else was there to do but read the papers from back home?

And what joys did I find there but the news that that confounded Indian Summer was blazing away as before, bathing Glasgow in sizzling sunshine and reaching an enviable 72 degrees one day in Aberdeen.

"Come home to Sunny Scotland!" was the invitation during a phone-call back home, in response to our postcard, which had said: "Having a torrential time—glad you're not here!"

To cut short a catalogue of misery, let me just tell you that we reached the ninth day of our holiday before we saw the kind of day we had come to expect in that idyllic corner of Europe.

And when those grey skies did finally clear and the fury of thunder, lightning, flood and tempest receded like a fading nightmare, we awoke one morning to a rattling of windows and inexplicable rocking of beds. Yes, believe it or not, we were in the midst of an earthquake!

Yet, peculiarly, out of all that mayhem, we ended up with an overall impression of a thoroughly enjoyable holiday. People were thrown together in the spirit of emergency and, when the hot days finally came, they were appreciated as never before.

We bared our bodies and tanned the torsos, strolled on balmy evenings and dined to soft lights and music, ready for a new day on those magnificent beaches of the Algarve, broad and clean. In the sand dunes behind, Steve's café was ready with the lunchtime sardines and the bottle of wine; then it was back to the sun-cream, spinning like a chicken on a spit to cover every exposable corner

47

of the anatomy and convince ourselves that the journey really had been worthwhile after all.

And when the sun had soothed away the worst of that earlier nightmare, we joined the plane at Faro and landed back in Scotland—in time to catch the tail-end of that Indian Summer.

So what do you tell the folks at work? The whole truth or just parts of it?

I was no sooner home than I found myself in a company where holiday experiences were being exchanged. In response to tales of astronomical temperatures elsewhere, one lady was holding forth about her recent holiday . . . in the Algarve of Portugal.

She was just back, she said. Glorious, just glorious, it was. Oh, there were a couple of days that weren't just as glorious as the others but she could hardly remember a thing about them.

Had I been away? she asked. Yes yes. I'd been to the Algarve, too.

"Oh, when was that?" she queried with the first hint of concern.

"The same two weeks as you," I replied, with the rise of knowing eyebrow.

I was far too much of a gentleman to say more. Her secret was safe with me. Yet I could swear that, for a few moments at least, her suntan deepened and a bead of sweat came trickling down her brow. Perhaps it was no more than a delayed reaction from that glorious fortnight on the sunny Algarve.

THE POWER OF LOVE

UNDER the soft lights of an Italian restaurant in the heart of Glasgow the other evening, you would hardly have noticed the unusual composition of a small party quietly celebrating a rather special event.

There were two priests, an assortment of journalists and a guest-of-honour, whose name of John Fagan might give hint of the occasion.

For it was just 10 years ago that this modest little man, a former Glasgow dock worker, was plucked from obscurity and thrust into the limelight as "the miracle man", whose cure from stomach cancer was credited by the Vatican to the intervention of the blessed John Ogilvie.

A Banffshire man, Ogilvie was the priest and martyr who was hanged at Glasgow Cross in 1615 for refusing to accept the supremacy of King James in spiritual matters. Only one Roman Catholic parish in the world bore Ogilvie's name but it was there by chance, in the Easterhouse district of Glasgow, that John and Mary Fagan happened to live.

The stomach cancer had reduced John Fagan to a ramshackle five stones as friends gathered round his bedside and prayed through John Ogilvie for some kind of recovery. Dr Archibald Macdonald, the local GP, was not a religious man and faced the harsher medical reality that Fagan was already without pulse and in the very last stages of his life. The last rites had been delivered.

But, instead of signing a death certificate, Dr Macdonald suddenly found himself faced with a man who had come back from the dead, complaining only of hunger. He was dumbfounded.

49

From that moment on, John Fagan rejoined the human race and, when they took him back to hospital, that massive tumour had vanished completely, from an area where natural regression is little known.

That all took place in 1967 but it was nine years later before the Vatican finally accepted the opinion of a panel of experts that there was no explanation for John Fagan's cure except a miracle.

Since Roman Catholics often reach their God through a third party, that miracle was credited to the intercession of John Ogilvie. It was all that was needed to hoist him from a state of blessedness to one of sainthood—Scotland's first saint for over 700 years.

Come that autumn day of 1976 and 20 plane-loads of Scots lifted off for Rome, 4,000 people altogether, including John Fagan and Mary, the latter never having been farther from home than Blackpool.

Amid the glitter of St Peter's, looking rather like a Hollywood set, the Pope declared that John Ogilvie from Banffshire was a saint in Heaven and, in the uninhibited way of Catholic worship, the congregation burst into spontaneous applause.

Especially for a non-Catholic like myself, it was a truly astonishing spectacle, lending itself to the colourful journalism of the national paper for which I worked at the time.

For much of the time in Rome, by coincidence, I was in the company of that talented journalist, the late Colm Brogan, my predecessor in this Tuesday column, who was covering the event for the *Glasgow Herald*. As a Catholic, Colm was a helpful colleague, acting as interpreter of events and making good the shortcomings of sinners like myself.

There was just one event which he failed to interpret in time, an incident which lived with him for the rest of his days and about which he was magnanimous enough to relate as a story against himself.

It happened on the day after the canonisation, when Pope Paul presided over a gathering of the 4,000 Scots. When that ended, Colm and I sauntered down from the press gallery, to be confronted by a pin-striped gent who ushered us along a private corridor and into an ante-room.

A few people were already poised on the edge of their seats, the whole atmosphere exuding a sense of occasion as, two by two, they were ushered into the room beyond.

In the stiff silence of the moment, Colm and I were unable to communicate satisfactorily. But gradually, as we moved towards the big door, the bewilderment of our situation began to come clear. By some extraordinary misunderstanding, we had been included in the small group being granted a private audience with the Pope.

A fairly honest chap by nature, I was prepared, on this occasion, to ride along with the misunderstanding and present myself for the newspaper scoop of a lifetime. Simultaneously, however, the cool of young Mr Brogan was visibly cracking. As those pin-striped Papal attendants motioned us to rise for those last few steps towards his Holiness, he called out "Stampa! Stampa!" which told them we were from the press and shouldn't be there.

As we had been ushered in with dignity, we were just as swiftly ejected with a lack of ceremony which bordered on the indecent. In the Vatican courtyard, my reproof of poor Colm would not bear reprinting. He threw up his hands in apology, confessing that he had lost his nerve, and, in the circumstances, couldn't have faced the Holy Father. On reflection, that made him a better man than me.

Until his premature death this year we kept up our standing joke about the scoop that got away. Alas, we missed him the other evening but he was well remembered.

John Fagan has now moved to Livingston, where he lives alone but near his daughters. At 72, he counts every day a bonus. As we dined, the leader of the musical group announced the presence of John Fagan, then played "The Power of Love". Strangers came across to shake his hand.

"The Power of Love" was appropriate indeed. Somewhere along the way, it must have played its own special part in the amazing story of the modest little man from Easterhouse.

A GOLDEN VOYAGE

WITHIN the span of an average lifetime there may be no more than a handful of events which stand out for special remembrance, highlights of experience which linger like a poignant perfume and will still be there at the last of our quieter moments.

One such event in my own lifetime was crossing the Atlantic on the great *Queen Mary* for my very first sight of America, an experience which distilled emotion from many different levels. There was the arrival at Southampton Docks to stand in awe beneath the bows of that majestic ship—and a patriotic pride in the Scottish craftsmanship which shaped her beauty.

There was the glitter of a five-star hotel in motion, reaching out to the lonely acres of the Atlantic, and the day-by-day approach to the New World, a mounting adventure of socialising which, for all its sense of anticipation, did not quite prepare us for the wondrous denouement of the Manhattan skyline. I re-live it often and shall do so again tomorrow night, when the BBC give us the latest in Desmond Wilcox's series, *The Visit*, which takes us through from the early story of the great Cunarder at John Brown's Shipyard in Clydebank.

It was a troubled start in 1930, with a shortage of money which led to all work being stopped just in time for Christmas of 1931.

When work did restart on the distinguished hull, No. 534, the men of John Brown's were led back to the yard by the Dalmuir Pipe Band and the great lady of the sea was finally launched in September 1934 before an audience of 200,000. She was fitted out in time for her maiden voyage in the spring of 1936.

The fiftieth anniversary was marked earlier this year when the survivors of the first voyage were among those to sail the same route, from Southampton to America, on board the *Queen Mary's* successor, that other Clydebank creation, the *QE2*. The film cameras pick up the stories of those who sailed both times, alternating shots from 1936 and 1986, and presenting people like the former Thelma Viner, then a young girl being treated by her parents but now better known on the South Side of Glasgow as the wife of Dr Sam Lazarus of Milverton Road, Giffnock.

Among Thelma's shipmates was the young Larry Adler, who paid his own fare but joined in as an additional entertainer with Henry Hall and his orchestra giving the inimitable rendering of George Gershwin's "Rhapsody in Blue".

Not everyone on board knew that the fellow-passengers included people like Frances Day and Jack Buchanan but Larry Adler's biggest discovery was none other than Joseph Kennedy, father of the future President, who was evidently returning to tell President Roosevelt that Europe's future lay not with Britain but with a certain Adolf Hitler!

The stories abound but one of my favourites from the build-up to the maiden voyage concerns the adventurous Joe Hepworth, of the well-known clothing empire, who was then a young clerk on the London Stock Exchange. Having booked his passage he rushed back to tell his colleagues. But pride quickly turned to consternation when his superior called him in and said: "Don't you know, Hepworth, that you never sail on a British ship?"

"But why sir? I don't understand."

"You must always sail on a French ship."

"But I still don't understand sir. . . ."

"On a French ship, Hepworth, there is none of this damned nonsense about women and children first!"

Such precautions were hardly necessary, though on the Golden Voyage of 1986, there was enough ice flowing south to put the *QE2* well off course and bring about a rather dramatic announcement from the captain.

Because they were now behind time, the old engines could not hasten them to New York in time to disembark and pick up passengers at Baltimore for a cruise to the Caribbean. So they would just head straight for Baltimore!

Needless to say, elimination of the Manhattan arrival, the real climax to many a voyager, did not extract a round of applause for the skipper. Not even the alleged persuasive powers of Desmond Wilcox, with all the presence of tell-tale cameras, would change his mind.

So there was anticlimax, which rather gave me second thoughts about an ambition to repeat my earlier voyage to America. Since then, however, I have been reassured by the fact that the *QE2* has been in dock for a total refit and will now have the power to make good any lost miles in future.

One of these days I may be heading down the M6 for Southampton and treading the boards of the *QE2* for the first time since the day she sailed downriver from John Brown's to dock at Greenock. At that time she was still a tangle of loose wires and unfinished decor, with mechanical troubles to come on her trials.

Once the teething troubles were over, however, she took her place on the high seas of the world in the proud tradition of the Cunard liners. For me that tradition is epitomised by the majesty of *Mary* as she sailed under the Verrazano Bridge, acknowledged the curtsey of Liberty to the left and headed proudly for the Hudson River.

That last gala night, on which I had won the week's accumulated jackpot of 160 dollars and celebrated accordingly, had left many of us in poor shape to absorb the Manhattan skyline. But there we were, wrapped up against the rigours of hangover, standing in silent wonder at the sheer hypnotic power of it.

New York, New York. It was H. G. Wells who said the distant view was not so much that of a city but of a collection of boxes from which a city might be unwrapped.

Soon they were unwrapping it before my disbelieving eyes. And I have been a sucker for the Big Apple ever since.

TURRIFF—
MY START IN JOURNALISM

* 1 6 T H   D E C E M B E R   1 9 8 6 *

FOR a variety of reasons, upon which I need not dwell, the newspaper business has broken no records in its progress towards the technologies of the twentieth century.

When you consider the veritable wonderland of communications tricks which can now be performed on little green screens, it is surprising that there are publications in Britain today which are still being produced by the age-old system of hot metal.

Even that old, traditional method was a bit of a mystery to me that day in 1948 when I picked my way through a joiner's yard and mounted the ricketty staircase of the *Turriff Advertiser*.

I had come to be interviewed for the junior's job, which would either admit me to journalism in a post-war period of few opportunities or consign me forever to a banker's booth.

With the bree of his pipe running down his chin, old Willie Peters eyed me up and down, asked if I could do shorthand, then called for a second opinion from his delicate son, Bob.

"Fit d'ye think?" asked old Willie.

"Oh, I suppose he'll dae a' richt," said Bob, in frank assessment of a doubtful prospect.

Happily, nature protects her young from the full brunt of insult and self-confidence was riding high when they promptly gave me the job and Bob conveyed me on a conducted tour of their Dickensian premises.

Intrigued by the world of print, I was nevertheless surprised to find that headlines and advertisements were still set by the hand-picking of letters from little boxes, in exactly the same way as we had done with our children's printing sets.

The main body of the newspaper was set from a Linotype machine, that old workhorse of the iron age which stamped letters on molten lead and spilled out hot slugs of metal at a laborious pace.

Line by line they fitted together until a column of the size you are reading now would form such a solid chunk of heavy metal that you might imagine it was built to last for ever.

Instead, as soon as that page was printed for the next edition of the paper, an apprentice boy would melt it all down in a large black pot, skim the scum from the surface and remould the metal bars of lead so that the whole process could begin all over again.

Even in my total ignorance of things mechanical, I was left with a clear impression that here was a cumbersome process of unjustifiable effort which lingered from a bygone age.

Surely there must be a smarter way to set the columns of a modern newspaper than this.

At the mid-point of the twentieth century, however, there were few such thoughts on the *Turriff Advertiser* or anywhere else. Bob Peters continued to sit stolidly at his Linotype, a kind of symbol of a longstanding tradition of newspaper production, which persisted as far south as Fleet Street until modern times.

By the same token, along with the boy who skimmed the hot lead, I used to tramp the streets of Turriff in the early hours of Friday morning, delivering bundles of newspapers to shop doors, much as they had done in the darker days of last century.

But changes had to come and the recent events in Fleet Street are only one part of the revolution which has come to spread itself through the entire fabric of the newspaper industry.

Bob Peters lived to see the new technology applied to his beloved *Turriff Advertiser*, now under the direction of his son, Duncan. Indeed, the local papers showed a clean pair of heels to Fleet Street when it came to progress.

But it was his death the other day which rather symbolised for me the end of the old newspaper era. Gone is the hot metal and the solid slabs of lead which reeked in your nostrils as they melted and re-formed from one day's print to the next.

56

Here at the *Herald*, where there have already been strides of progress, we are poised for yet another generation of technology, by which the writing fraternity will type in their stories by means of "direct input", even from locations far removed from the office.

Miraculous happenings on those little green screens will transfer it all to the desk of the sub-editors, who will perform their various feats of trim and titivation by computerised methods to baffle the innocent.

Further refinements are in store for the years to come, all of which is a far cry from the days of Bob Peters up that ricketty stair in Turriff.

Mind you, the best laid schemes . . .

Just the other day, on one of Holland's leading newspapers, the very latest technology went hopelessly on the blink—and there wasn't even an old-fashioned typewriter on which the journalists could produce their stories. Mercifully, they had not forgotten that other outmoded practice of handwriting and the paper came out on time.

That, in turn, reminded me of a famous editor of the *Aberdeen Journal*, a certain William Forsyth, who was reputed to have the worst handwriting in the whole of journalism. Compositors dreaded having to set his "copy" and on one occasion, when it was returned for deciphering, Forsyth had to confess he could not make head or tail of it himself. He had to bestir his memory to find what he was writing about.

The same William Forsyth was the subject of another amusing tale. One typesetter, completely baffled by his calligraphy, declared he was damned if he could read it but, if somebody would fetch his fiddle, he might well be able to play it!

MY COLLEAGUE KEVIN

* 1 3 T H J A N U A R Y 1 9 8 7 *

I ONCE had a colleague called Kevin Fitzgerald, one of those delightfully Irish characters with all the charm and some of the failings of that extraordinary race, around whom a well-justified legend has grown and grown.

As one of a distinguished family which gave society an inordinate number of doctors and nurses, Kevin felt obliged to balance matters by becoming a journalist. After all, every family must have its black sheep.

But Kevin's brain was as keen as any of his brothers or sisters and, apart from the charm of his personality, he possessed a very special talent for the selection of fleet-footed horses.

So he settled himself in Glasgow after the war, from which point he became one of Britain's most successful racing tipsters, under the name of Scotia, carrying off the nationwide trophy on one occasion when he lay horizontal and motionless in the annexe of the Victoria Infirmary, able to make his selections only when a willing nurse would hold the race-list at a suitable angle.

Kevin, as you will have gathered, simply lived for the race-course, travelling day by day from Glasgow to Ayr, Kelso, York, Redcar, Thirsk, Beverley, or wherever the fraternity were due to assemble that day.

After 25 years of making a name for himself, Kevin, who lived in the Simshill district of Glasgow, went home for a holiday to the Emerald Isle, back to the community whence he came, and there he was fêted by the locals who gathered round to hear great tales of life on mainland Britain.

"Sure," said one dear lady, "it must be a wonderful thing to be living in Glasgow, so near to the bonnie, bonnie banks of Loch Lomond." Then she sat back, bless her romantic heart, to await a first-hand account of the legendary loch and its scenic attractions.

For once in his life Kevin, whose brogue was intelligible only to a fellow Irishman, was lost for words. In rather embarrassed tones, he had to admit that, in all his 25 years in Scotland, he had never even seen the bonnie, bonnie banks of Loch Lomond!

"You mean to say you've never been to Loch Lomond?" the lady persisted in disbelief. "But why not? There used to be a tramcar going all the way from Glasgow, was there not?"

"Well, it's like this," Kevin said, searching for something more than a lame excuse. "It's not on the road to any racecourse."

After a recent experience, I can now appreciate how Kevin felt. Having passed my own quarter-century in Glasgow, I was revisiting the native heath when I was asked a similar question about the splendours of the Burrell Collection.

Yes yes, it was true, I lived within 10 minutes' drive of Scotland's greatest public attraction. But no, I had to admit I had not yet been to the Burrell.

Come to think of it, there are many more things I have not done in my 27 years in Glasgow. I have never been to the People's Palace or Provand's Lordship.

I have been inside Barlinnie but I have never been to the Barras on a Sunday. Worse still, I have never set foot on the picturesque island of Arran nor sampled the pleasures which every other citizen of Glasgow will tell you exist in that other island resort of Millport.

Lest this should begin to sound like a boast, I had better say I am making it a New Year resolution to put right some of these shortcomings. So, when most people were heading back to work after the festive holiday, I took myself to the pastoral peace of Pollok Park for a quiet look at this mammoth collection of the fabulously wealthy Sir William Burrell, former Glasgow shipowner and hoarder of artistic objects.

And there I strode respectfully through room after room,

59

peering knowledgeably at Chinese ceramics, precious tapestries, paintings and stained glass windows.

Then I came upon Sandy Kinnaird—not among the fossils, I should add, but acting as a guide to visitors. I used to know Sandy as a man who ran fruit shops around Maryhill, though I did always feel he was more suited to culture than cucumbers.

Anyway, he sold out in good time and took the highly civilised course of gaining an honours degree in French and marketing from Strathclyde University at the age of 64.

The transition from bananas to Burrell might seem like what they now call a quantum leap but a jolly good job he makes of it, unveiling the secrets behind this impressive collection and heightening the interest for that vast majority of us who don't know our art from our elbow.

Hereabouts, I suppose, I must confess I have a fairly limited energy for traipsing round galleries and museums and, in the case of the Burrell Collection, the most interesting feature I found was the reconstruction of three rooms from Sir William's home at Hutton Castle, near Berwick.

To see the exact setting in which a man of all that wealth actually lived brought him more alive for me than anything else.

I feel I should have been interviewing him; instead, I must confess I knew nothing about him at all in his lifetime. Being the football philistine that I am, I would have known a lot more about Willie Bauld than Willie Burrell in the 1950s.

Now, had I been smarter, I could have substituted that football excuse for Kevin Fitzgerald's horse-racing one when I was asked about the Burrell Collection in my native village.

"You see, it's not on the road to any football ground," I could have said, half-joking. But the half that wasn't joking would have had to admit that the Burrell was very much on my route to Ibrox, Firhill, Love Street, Cappielow, Boghead . . .

Dear old Kevin wouldn't have given me an outsider's odds on getting away with that one!

RICHEST MAN IN THE WORLD

WHEN someone you regarded as a good friend describes you, after death, as "a lecher, a miser, a womaniser, whose private life was often beyond belief; he was totally unlovable", it doesn't leave too much scope for your enemies.

Such was the fate of a figure who has intrigued me for a long time, the late Jean Paul Getty, the oil tycoon who was once the richest man in the world.

The catalogue of tragedy which that wealth seemed to attract, typified by the kidnapping of his grandson who had his ear cut off before the ransom was paid, is now legendary.

The task of bringing the whole story together was undertaken by the English writer, Russell Miller, who, in Glasgow the other day, was giving me some idea of the hurdles he had to overcome.

His two years of research began in Los Angeles, where he was so little connected with the story that he couldn't even discover exactly where the Gettys lived. After five weeks of getting nowhere, his first break arrived when he found that a lawyer friend in San Francisco happened to know Judge William Newson, a close contact of the family.

He introduced him to one of the sons, Gordon, an enthusiastic composer and singer, and that in turn opened a few doors, though he did not reach people like the present Paul Getty, who lives in London and gives away a fortune every other week.

But he did meet some of the women who figured in Jean Paul Getty's "harem" at the Sutton Place mansion in Surrey and, piece by piece, the story fitted together.

And what a story it is. Having married five times and failed in

61

every one of them, Getty was reduced to statements like "A lasting relationship with a woman is only possible if you are a business failure. Women can be divided into two types—those you pay to stay with you and those you pay to stay away."

At the age of 60, he was boasting of sleeping with five women in one day, which seems to me like an awful lot of sleeping.

From the general picture, of course, there emerges a man of such meanness that you wonder if it can all be true. At the Crufts dog show, Getty apparently walked round the block for 30 minutes until the cheap entrance rate applied. When it came to paying the ransom for the grandson with the cut-off ear, he lent his son the money—at an interest of 4%.

In the oil business, of course, Jean Paul Getty was quite brilliant. With an uncanny instinct for detecting the stuff, he also gave geologists their proper place.

The first-born son, George, was groomed to keep a Getty at the helm, but George went and committed suicide in 1973. The last-born son, Timmy, died in 1958, aged 12, his last wish being to see his father, who was too busy to come to him.

In between there were Ronald, a failed film producer; Gordon, who gets slated by the critics for his compositions; and Paul, the ex-heroin addict who lives as a recluse in Chelsea, still mourning the wife who died of a heroin overdose.

He blames himself for the tragedy and believes he could have saved her if he himself had not been so stupefied with drugs at the time. Perhaps it is a comment on their condition in the late sixties that they gave their son the impossible name of Tara Gabriel Galaxy Gramaphone Getty (they couldn't even spell "gramophone" correctly).

As if all that were not enough, there was Paul's son by a previous marriage, the boy who had his ear cut off. After that incident, his wild instincts took him deeply into drink and drugs and, at 24, he suffered a massive stroke, which has left him blind, dumb, and quadriplegic. He is now 30, with no hope of recovery.

Of course, we are talking about a total tragedy yet, when I read all these dreadful things about Paul Getty and his family, I found myself thinking about Max Garvie, the Laurencekirk farmer whose murder in the sixties led to a particularly sordid trial, which ended with his wife and her lover going to prison.

As the sexual permutations unfolded, revealing what Max himself had been up to in that swinging decade, his neighbours, solid farming folk of the Mearns, felt sufficiently moved to issue a statement saying that, whatever had been said in court about Max, they had always found him a fine, decent, hard-working man. There had clearly been two sides to his character.

Now my one advantage over Russell Miller in the Getty saga was that I had actually met the great lecher himself. Paul Getty once invited me to Sutton Place and there, after passing through the electronic gates and past vicious guard-dogs in the driveway and human minders who were hardly more desirable, I had 90 minutes of his time all to myself.

The richest man in the world, by the way, was sitting in a plain little room with his shoe and sock off and his foot up on a stool, suffering agonies from a goutish ailment in his big toe which not all the money in the world could put right.

When I told Russell Miller that I had found him a man of high intellect and great depth of culture, charming, kindly and a little pathetic, he acknowledged that the women closest to him had given a similar account.

While Miller had started out not particularly liking the Getty family, he had to concede there were qualities in the old man not readily observable.

The public image of the richest man in the world was hard to fit to the man I found in solitary confinement at Sutton Place. But then, as my granny would have said, "there's naething queerer than folk."

ABOUT MAKING LOVE

THE volume of verbiage which has been spilled around in the name of love and its attendant pleasures, over the years, is beyond all means of measurement, much of it dull, boring, and banal. Perhaps the best of it keeps a sense of humour, giving it the saving grace of a hearty laugh.

The Marx Brothers produced their fair share. Attempting to keep up with the wit of Groucho (who said he knew Doris Day before she was a virgin!) brother Chico tried this one on his wife when she caught him kissing a chorus girl: "I wasn't kissing her; I was whispering in her mouth." Then again, I liked the one which said the best present a woman can give a man is a sleepless night. And Mae West could always be depended upon for such bawdy quips as "Is that a pistol in your pocket—or are you happy to see me?"

I don't know whether love makes the world go round but I do know it makes Lailan Young go round the world (14 times so far) in search of its statistics. Some of them are positively bed-rocking. For example, did you know (or do you care?) that at any given moment, according to Ms Young, there are 7,666,667 people making love?

If you still remember your division tables and wonder about the uneven figure, she will surprise you further with the news that about 57,000 of these people are engaged in some form of multiple activity which we had better not explore too specifically in the columns of a family newspaper.

Leaving head counts aside, however, Ms Young comes up with a fair old ragbag of romantic facts and figures which tend to raise more questions than they answer.

The Chinese, she tells us (and Ms Young herself is of Chinese origin), have a unique way of making love: back to back. Over a cup of steaming hot coffee (which came steamier by the minute), she tried to assure me that all things are possible for the acrobatically agile. I must leave that one to the individual imagination. No stamp-addressed envelopes, please.

The Japanese, on the other hand, have an obsession with something called the J-Spot, which evidently puts an entirely new complexion on love. Hereabouts I could perhaps offer a limited amount of practical guidance. The first difficulty with the J-Spot is in finding it. Having found it, the second is in knowing what to do with it.

Ms Young's instructions put me in a quandary straight away. Her book says: "Raise your index finger and run it along the hairline." There was I, trying to remember where my hairline used to be, when I spotted a diagram and realised she was talking about the hairline at the back of the neck.

Once you find the centre of that line, measure one inch immediately below it and—hey presto!—you have found the J-Spot. Thereafter, you need a partner to kiss it, nibble it or some other such nonsense.

Other pieces of intelligence in Ms Young's book include the fact that the most married man in history was King Mongut of Siam (the monarch in *The King and I*), who proved himself a real glutton for punishment with 9,000 wives, before dying of fatigue (what else?) and exposure (of course) while watching an eclipse of the moon in 1868.

There is also a health warning for men over 50 with a mistress: you are more likely to have a heart attack. Making love to your wife at that stage in life is to be compared to climbing three floors or taking a three-and-a-half mile walk. With a girlfriend, it is like racing up the stairs of a skyscraper or sprinting for five miles. In defence of the over-50s, I do think she is laying it on a bit.

The attractive Ms Young grew up in Australia, of Chinese parents, and was educated at the Presbyterian Ladies' College in Melbourne, under the stern eye of Principal Mary F. B. Neilson from Glasgow. It is not easy to ask a lady of that background how she comes to have such an intimate knowledge of love's kaleidoscope. But I tried. Yes, some of it was from personal experience but, spoilsport that she was, she wouldn't tell me which bits.

As a writer and anthropologist, she did tell me, however, that she had moved to live in Paris, where she married a Frenchman.

That seemed to be the kind of accident which encouraged her to say: "Don't marry a Frenchman. They may think they are the cat's whiskers but they are certainly not the greatest lovers in the world."

Needless to say, she is no longer married to the Frenchman. Ms Young then moved to London and married an Englishman, and seems to have no regrets about that one after 17 years.

She was apparently so appalled by the low level of books on the subject of love that she set out to raise the standard. Well, we are given such mind-boggling information as the fact that a Burusho bride in the Himalayas shares the bridal bed with her mother-in-law till the marriage is consummated.

And we hear from Sir Robert Helpmann about the problems of nude dancing. "It is simply that not everything stops when the music stops," he explained. And that was the cue for Ms Young to hope that her book will go with a swing.

MAKING LIGHT
OF LIFE IN 'DARKNESS'

∗ 1 4 T H   A P R I L   1 9 8 7 ∗

PULLING a collar high against the bite of an April morning—much colder than it had been in February—I could hear the moan of the wind that matched the moan of those who suffered its winter sting.

Yet all things are relative and I knew there was very little to moan about as I headed for the concourse of Queen Street Station, Glasgow, to await the arrival of the train from Aberdeen.

Aboard the train was a man who would soon dispel the meteorological gloom of the morning and put to shame those of us who have so much for which to be thankful and who take it for granted in most ungrateful fashion.

As the diesel ground to a halt and the hordes spilled out, there was Duncan Simpson striding purposefully down the platform with Beth by his side.

Beth is the Golden Labrador who guides her master through his daily routine. For Duncan is stone blind. From birth he has suffered from retinitis pigmentosa, usually a hereditary condition which can lead to total blindness.

Duncan's father was a farm servant on the scene of my childhood more than 40 years ago and it was there, as a four-year-old, that he first realised his handicap.

Gazing over the Buchan landscape, his three-year-old brother exclaimed at the sight of the White Horse of Mormond Hill, a famous landmark in Aberdeenshire. Hard as he peered, Duncan couldn't see it. His sight then was good enough only to distinguish one colour from another but never good enough for reading. Year by year it deteriorated till the fading light was gone for ever.

67

By then Duncan had been to the Royal Blind School in Edinburgh, where he met a young lass from Dundee. "She thocht I wis a bit o' a nuisance," Duncan recalls with a hearty laugh.

But she changed that opinion in later life and married the lad from Aberdeenshire.

"So, if you'll pardon the pun," says Duncan, who invariably sees the funny side, "it wisna love at first sight!"

In fact Jean lost her sight at the age of three and has virtually no recollection of vision. Colours mean nothing at all. Both are agreed that it is better to have seen and lost than never to have seen at all. Duncan just appreciates the fact that he can remember the difference between blue and red. Jean wears a lot of blue because everybody says she suits it and within his world of darkness, Duncan can picture exactly how she looks. Not only does he remember blue but he remembers what his Jean actually looks like from his days of partial sight.

She, on the other hand, has never seen her husband, a matter about which the irrespressible Duncan can produce more humour.

They live in joyous union in their Aberdeen home, like many another blind couple, able to attend to most of their needs but helped by their 20-year-old son Kenneth, who has mercifully been spared what could have been a hereditary condition.

Duncan used to turn a useful hand at mat-making in the workshop for the blind in Dundee but pined for his native Aberdeenshire, its music and poetry and the wild outdoors and the sough of the wind in the trees. For sound has replaced his vision as a compensation of the senses.

Returning to Aberdeen to work as a skilled craftsman, making furniture, he devoted all his spare time to a tape-recording service for the blind. What ran for years as a labour of love eventually became his full-time occupation, but still a labour of love, involving the production of a weekly tape with news, interviews and various publications to keep the blind up to date.

A whole range of books can be found on Duncan's Grampian Tape Service, bringing pleasure and independence to those who want to "read" at their leisure.

He had come to Glasgow to turn the tables on me, acting as the interviewer in a discussion conducted in the broad dialect of my native Buchan. When our session was over, I drove him out to the Knightswood district of the city to visit his sister.

She took a little time to answer the bell, but, when she did, I realised once more that nature can deal some cruel blows.

Apart from a crippling arthritis, sister Sheila (Mrs McCready) is stone blind like her brother. In that special world of their own, those two who had gone together to the school for the blind now hugged each other with loving tenderness.

Sheila works as a telephonist for the DHSS at Clydebank, managing to get by but grateful for the kindness of friends.

I left the two of them alone for a while, feeling that, despite all its depressing viciousness, the world can still produce its saints and minor miracles.

I am trying to think of ways of raising some money for Duncan's work for the blind.

As he and his beloved Labrador Beth went striding off in that uncanny harmony, I felt the better for being reminded once more that we live in a wonderful world—and should pause from time to time to count our blessings.

THE FACE OF COURAGE

* 2 1 S T   A P R I L   1 9 8 7 *

I MET a quite extraordinary woman last week, waif-like on the outside but strong and courageous where it matters most.

I must confess at the outset that mountaineering is not my favourite subject nor reading about it my favourite pastime. Equally, I must admit the story which Cherie Bremer-Kamp had to tell was riveting—an experience to put all of us to the ultimate test of endurance, physically, mentally and emotionally.

In the Himalayas just over two years ago, Cherie and her doctor husband, Chris Chandler, were poised to become the first people. ever to make the winter ascent of the north side of Kanchenjunga, the third highest mountain in the world.

They were already at 26,000 feet, dug into a snow-cave for the night, and in the morning they would make the final push for the summit. Chris Chandler had already conquered Everest but this time he was with his wife in a special union of spirits which lent an exhilaration to their adventure.

At that height in winter the wind roars eerily, like the thunder of the Niagara Falls or the rush of an express train coming at you through a tunnel. The brain may be starved of oxygen and the fingers numbed to lumps of lead but Cherie stretched herself that morning and gazed up at the summit of "Kanche" in anticipation of their final triumph. Then she turned towards Chris, still lying in the snow-cave, and suddenly realised he was in some distress. Soon he was gagging and gurgling in what he, as a doctor, well knew was the onset of pneumonia.

"The only possible treatment at that height was a rapid descent," Cherie told me in the comfort of a Glasgow hotel.

70

With the help of their only porter, who was largely intent upon self-preservation, she tried to mastermind a quick return to safer levels, but they staggered down like drunks on a Hogmanay night, frozen and exhausted till darkness came quickly.

Digging out a platform, she tried to warm and comfort Chris. They tried to move again but her husband just staggered and fell. "Will somebody help me?" he cried in desperation.

But there could be no more help. Chris Chandler, handsome, brilliant doctor and mountaineer was, to all intents and purposes, dead. On the heights of the Himalayas, sheer and frightening, what on earth do you do?

His slender wife knelt beside him. She said: "We turned him over to look at his face. His finely sculptured features, gaunt from weeks of gruelling work, had relaxed into an expression of bliss. All the tensions and cares of mortal beings had dissolved; there was only peace and beauty shining forth."

In the account which she has since written, she adds: "As death and love met, my whole being was filled with terror. I felt him letting go of the past and all we had shared, yet the future had not yet arrived. I couldn't let him go easily. 'I need you, Chris, don't leave me!' I screamed in silence."

As she embraced his body the sounds which came from within were empty and hollow. Apparently when someone dies on a mountain the traditional burial is to put them in a crevasse or push them over a cliff. Cherie could face neither.

She propped him up and said goodbye, photos of his children tucked next to his heart, before concentrating on her own means of returning to the land of the living. Indeed, the first half of the story, which I have not yet mentioned, ensured there would be some fairly discordant music to face.

For Cherie Bremer-Kamp, who grew up in Australia and trained as a nurse there, met her first husband, Terry, in those same Himalayas. He was an American musicologist by whom she had two children.

It was when she and Terry joined the 1978 American Expedition to the K2 Mountain, second highest in the world, that she

71

met and fell in love with Chris Chandler. On that K2 climb, she and Terry were roped together in a kind of symbolism that was about to take the strain. They continued for the sake of their children but Cherie later married Chris Chandler.

Now that he was dead, she had to return to Seattle to face his parents who reacted with some anger at first though they have now accepted the situation. At first Chris's ex-wife prevented her from seeing his three children but that, too, has now been re-solved, with the children wishing to have a first-hand account of their father's end.

Doesn't she regret the entire heartbreaking involvement with Chris and his tragedy? Even in the devastation of her life, Cherie Bremer-Kamp views it all as part of an inevitable pattern of life.

Now she plans to help the kindly village people who so helped the pair of them on their way up the mountain. She has even been tempted to return to the scene but, instead, asked a Yugoslavian expedition, who were following the same route, to look out for Chris. They reported nothing but she wonders if they were sparing her feelings.

At that altitude, there would be no decomposition, only shrink-age. For the moment she gets on with life.

As I bade her goodbye, I realised the hand I shook had no fingers. "No, I lost them all in the frostbite of the occasion," she explained. "They had to be removed in the surgery." Similarly she lost all her toes.

With all her handicaps, the slender little lady walked away, a brave spirit driven on by some compulsion that lies beyond the understanding of most of us.

That urge to conquer mountains grips them like a drug. But what a price to pay for the pleasure.

GLASGOW'S MILES CLEANER

MY turbulent love affair with Glasgow has been running now for the best part of half a century. To be precise, it began in the summer of 1938 when I was brought south on the longest journey of my tender life, to visit the Empire Exhibition at Bellahouston Park, the biggest event ever staged in Scotland.

As a sign of the changing times, incidentally, it was also the longest journey for my 64-year-old grandfather, an authority on Robert Burns who insisted we carry on that little bit further to pay homage at the birthplace of the Bard.

To complete the grand tour, we took in the building of the *Queen Elizabeth* at Clydebank and headed north with enough wonders to mesmerise us indefinitely.

Within a year, however, Glasgow was paying us a return visit, 200 children and parents invading our rural peace in their flight from the bombs which would surely come with the Second World War.

As the two cultures mixed, I fed madly in love with a girl called Margaret and suffered a broken heart when she went off back to her bronchial backstreets in time for the real bombing to start.

The letters of a love-lorn swain, all of nine years old, were addressed—I remember it well—to No. 13 Vine Street, Partick.

When that war was over, I became a regular visitor to the industrial capital. I was here on the day of Benny Lynch's funeral in 1946, the same year as my first visit to Hampden Park (for the Victory International in which Scotland beat England by that last-minute goal from Jimmy Delaney).

Finally I came here to work as a journalist on Leap Year Night

73

of 1960, and, on such a night of romantic connotation, who should be sitting in the same office, as an editorial secretary, but my beloved Margaret from 13 Vine Street!

In preparation for the culture shock of coming to Glasgow, I read *No Mean City* and Cliff Hanley's evocative *Dancing in the Street* and found myself absorbing the true essence of the city in all its grotty warmth.

To clear our heads after a smoke-filled night of producing tomorrow's newspaper, we would walk home through the Gorbals in the early hours of the morning, keeping an eye on close-mouths as if some Johnny Stark might be lurking there with well-honed razor.

To my surprise, the streets of the Gorbals were wide and handsome and the rich character of the place could surely have been retained with some sensible planning instead of the hideous rebuilding which passed for architecture in the 1960s.

But all that is in the past. In modern times, as the world now knows, Glasgow has washed its face, brushed itself down, put on some finery and begun to step out of its complex. With a chest-beating defiance, which comes generally from the downtrodden, it has declared rather immodestly that "Glasgow's Miles Better", though better than what, is as unclear as it is grammatically incomplete. Than it used to be? Than Edinburgh?

The official seal of having come up in the world will finally arrive when Glasgow becomes European City of Culture in 1990, having already upgraded its cultural image with attractions like the Burrell.

At one time I thought it had the makings of an artistic festival which could creep quietly up on Edinburgh but the nature of Mayfest seems to have become such a socialist indulgence as to alienate one half of the people from what was supposed to be a people's festival.

So Glasgow has made mistakes but then who hasn't? Once it gains real confidence in its own ability, there will be less need to brag about being miles better; less need to boast of being the friendliest city in the world which, for all its warmth, it most certainly is not.

74

It confuses friendliness with matiness, that back-slapping bonhomie which seeks to impose its generosity with such aggressiveness that the slightest hint of rejection is liable to produce that most unfriendly phenomenon of "pittin' the heid oan ye".

True friendliness, I have found, comes more naturally and genuinely from people like the Borderers.

But Glasgow will learn. Glasgow will mature. In reaching for its fur coat it will not be allowed to neglect its knickers.

As an appropriate way to mark the fiftieth anniversary of that memorable Empire Exhibition next year, Glasgow will throw wide the gates of a horticultural paradise and invite the nation to step inside its Garden Festival.

And there they will find a fragrance which is somewhat different from that of the dear green place in days gone by.

SUPER-EIGHT MEMORIES

• 7 T H   J U L Y   1 9 8 7 •

AS one still recovering from the miracle of the telephone and not remotely prepared for the technicalities of how to work a video recorder, I have just been exposed to yet another example of scientific magic. It's too too much.

And it all dates back to the cine-film craze of the affluent sixties when more and more ordinary mortals were able to make their own home movies and Super-Eight was all the rage.

I duly trotted along to a leading photography shop in Glasgow to buy a well-known brand of cine camera—and foolishly allowed myself to be talked into a lesser-known Japanese model which the assistant was no doubt pushing on account of a better commission.

The confounded thing, dogged by a faulty light-meter, went back to the shop time and time again in an attempt to have it put right but without success.

I should have given the shop a piece of practical advice on what to do with the Japanese camera and demanded a replacement with the model I had sought in the first place. But, in those less claim-conscious days, I didn't. And after a few years of trial and error, I finally gave up in disgust and shot no more cine.

The pathetic little reels, of three-minute duration, lay in their canary-yellow containers, tucked away in a cupboard for nearly 20 years till I unearthed them recently and wondered if there would be anything worth salvaging from the mediocre mixture. And, if so, could they possibly be transferred to video?

I found a chap who would do his best with my miscellaneous celluloid and just the other day he brought back the results of his labours.

76

To my delight, he had not only transferred the entire footage to video but had also extracted some of the more personal shots, woven them into a pattern, added appropriate music and presented me with a splendid little keepsake of the sixties.

And there was my father, at his vigorous best, striding about the farmyard in typical posture, while my mother wandered down her garden picking flowers and turning coyly to face the camera. Thank heavens for such a precious remembrance.

Those three little nippers following at their grandfather's heels are now grown men in their twenties. Familiar faces and long-forgotten incidents sprang out to jog the memory and call for a reassessment of time.

Having taken that camera further afield, I found myself walking the decks of the old *Queen Mary* in mid-Atlantic, sauntering in the gardens of Versailles, and through the Expo Exhibition in Montreal in 1967; posing outside the White House in Washington and alongside the thundering waters of the Niagara Falls.

There was a poignant visit to that branch of the family which emigrated to Canada, still living on the same small farm which greeted them after a horrendous crossing from Greenock around 1910.

Back home, who was that walking across George Square, Glasgow, with Lord Provost John Johnston? None other than the Russian leader of the day, Mr Kosygin, on his way to the City Chambers.

In my own back garden, another historic shot featured the former flyweight boxing champion of the world, the great Peter Kane, who fought Benny Lynch and Jacky Paterson. Having come to lunch one day, he was now engaged in a three round bout with my five-year-old son.

So it went on; the innocent faces of childhood, the hairstyles and short skirts of the sixties, the candy floss of the fairground, the flotsam of life itself.

Sudden recognition brought cries of delight and peels of laughter before the living spirit of departed faces would just as quickly have you down to tears.

I'm glad to have that cinematographic record of an age gone by. As I watch it now, I can hear the echoes of Herb Alpert and the Beatles and Martin Luther King and so much else that constituted the essence of the sixties.

I can also envisage a square little man in a grey suit, fair hair and rimless glasses, standing behind a counter and persuading me to buy a camera which would soon put me off the idea of cine film altogether. Ultimately, that was bad business for him as well as years of lost opportunity for me.

When I think of the years between, when I could have continued that record of the children growing up and so much else that was happening in my life, I could happily throttle the little blighter.

If I were to resume my amateur filming career, it would now be with a video camera. If that day comes, I'll make a decision about the model I want. And no whipper-snapper behind a counter is going to change my mind!

AN UNUSUAL PILOT
AIRS HIS VIEW

MOST boys of my generation were hooked on aeroplanes by the exploits of Biggles. Biplanes soaring into the air from Croydon Aerodrome (whoever heard of an airport?) came to be one of the symbols of glamour in a land which was soon to need all the flying machines it could muster.

Having spotted Spitfires and Hurricanes, Lancasters and Liberators throughout the war, I myself did not venture into the air until 1952, when a journey to London in an old Pionair convinced me that, in the interests of comfort and peace of mind, not to mention speed, it would be better to go by train.

Those doubts were gradually overcome, however, and 20 years later I was soaring 11 miles into the sky over the Arctic Circle, completing a historic flight in the very first prototype of Concorde, having left Prestwick at midnight, gained sunrise within half an hour, watched a premature sunset a few minutes later and returned to Prestwick in time for a second sunrise!

It was Charles Lindbergh, the first man to fly the Atlantic on his own who said: "Science, freedom, beauty, adventure—what more could you ask of life? Aviation combined all the elements I loved."

Well, aviation takes in that other element of fear as well, the one which lurks at the back of our minds every time we surge into take-off and wonder, amid vague prayers, if it is a natural thing for great lumps of metal to be lifting large human cargoes into the celestial stratosphere.

Much as we entertain such fears, of course, we will still sit transfixed watching a nail-biting horror movie of the skies, just as

79

we'll watch a gory murder mystery which would appal us if it happened in real life. Such is the perverse nature of the species, sometimes explained away by psychologists as a safety-valve for phobia.

Such matters came together in my mind during a lunchtime meeting last week with Tom Block, a man whose dual role in life makes him something of a rarity.

For Tom is a regular airline pilot on the one hand, flying passengers from the American east coast to California, an occupation which alternates with a lucrative career as a thriller writer. Needless to say, his thrillers are culled from first-hand knowledge of planes, fired into action by an imagination which never goes beyond the bounds of what is technically feasible.

After three novels which put him sky-high in the best-selling lists, Tom Block has come along with *Skyfall*, a pretty alarming business about terrorism in the air, with a bomb on board, shots being fired, leaving the hijacker and co-pilot dead and the pilot badly injured.

What do his employers at US Air think about all this, I wondered. Evidently the president is so delighted that he has given him an award and loves to receive autographed copies.

And he is not the only one who likes autographs. Whenever that intercom hums into action with the announcement that "This is Captain Block speaking", you can be sure there will be a few double-takes from passengers who have just bought the captain's latest sizzler at the airport. Convinced that this is really the same Captain Block, they then send their copies forward to the flight deck for autograph.

It could only happen in America, we say. (Maybe the airline president wasn't so daft giving him an award.)

On last week's visit to Britain, Tom was travelling for the first time on Concorde when, as a fellow-pilot, he sent forward his identification. Once again there was instant recognition and in no time he was being invited up to the flight deck.

Over a gin-and-tonic on the terra firma of a Glasgow bar, Tom agreed that, in his role as a thriller writer, he capitalises on the sense of horrific tragedy. It has something to do with the approach-avoidance syndrome.

In reality, the shock-horror-dramas like mid-air collisions or hijacking don't perturb Tom Block. Even with all the apprehension about defects in air traffic control, he makes the point that it still takes a combination of mistakes and a large slice of bad luck to bring two planes together. Having been struck by lightning 20 times, he takes that kind of thing in his stride.

But there is one danger in the air which Tom Block respects above all others—the violent storm. At the extreme end, for example, no aeroplane can survive a tornado.

But storms are fairly localised events and it is here that we are in the hands of the human skill factor, aided by technology, in threading a way through a storm, diverting this way and that to remain on paths of safety.

From that Concorde trip, incidentally, he came away with two main impressions. One was the speed with which he felt at ease on the flight deck of this fastest-ever passenger plane.

The other was the fact that, 15 years on, our prized possession is falling behind the American Boeings in computer technology. Of course we cannot be smug about our invention which may have been so far ahead of its time those 15 years ago.

On the other hand, the Americans were never very happy about the way we stole the limelight with our supersonic star.

THE LEGEND OF
BUFF, STEVE AND GEORGE

∗ 1 7 T H   N O V E M B E R   1 9 8 7 ∗

CLOSE on 28 years of living in Glasgow has done practically nothing at all to blunt my North-east accent nor, I suspect, would another 28 affect the situation in any noticeable manner.

Broad as the bannock which used to spread across my granny's girdle, thick of speech as the brose of the old-time fairm-touns, I am well beyond redemption in the eyes of those who would hear us sink our native speech in a sea of uniformity.

There is nothing consciously fostered. It is just the way I am. The problems would start if I let loose that accent on the actual dialect with which I grew up.

While Glaswegian friends joke about my North-east "twang" (I always thought it was Glaswegians who had a twang) and have their bit of fun over the "loonies and quinies" who lie within their understanding, they might be less tolerant if I started complaining that my queets were fair connacht but I was aye knypin' on for a' that.

That distinctive North-east dialect needs some dilution when you step beyond the Grampian drawbridge. Like German red wine, it doesn't travel too well.

Yet its flavour is retained to fine effect by that satirical trio of entertainers who glory in the title of Scotland The What? Regularly they travel to theatres well away from the glaur of Sharnydubs, as far as Edinburgh and Glasgow, even London, where they are gradually educating the natives towards an appreciation of a richly expressive form of speech.

So successful have they been that all three men, in their middle years, have given up lucrative professional posts to become full-time members of show business.

82

Buff Hardie, brilliant graduate of Aberdeen and Cambridge, was secretary of Grampian Health Board. Steve Robertson was a local solicitor (and they don't come more lucrative than that) and George Donald was assistant rector of Perth Academy.

Their cult following is just about as well versed in the various sketches and songs as the trio themselves, demanding repeat performances of material to which they already know the punch-line.

That alone makes Scotland The What? a rather unusual act. Their records and tapes sell abroad in large volumes to exiled Scots who have never had the chance to see them.

Now they have gone one step further and put large swatches of their material into book form, so that the faithful can re-live the humour, sing the songs, while sitting at their own firesides.

It is a brave step, maybe even a shrewd one, by a bunch of canny Aberdonians. Putting your material into print is a simple way of putting a copyright on your words!

To me, those very funny men are a modern extension of the mood portrayed by the great Harry Gordon of a previous generation. They are addressing themselves to the descendants of those same "Fittie folk, Kitty folk an' folk fae Rubislaw Den".

Satire is never far from the core of their humour. The way they take off acts like the Alexander Brothers can reduce a solemn man to tears of laughter. No need to say who they have in mind when they give us "The Scottish Plumber". (*There was a plumber, a Scottish plumber, no finer man than he, to mend your W.C.*)

Alien ears soon pick up the rhythm of speech as Buff Hardie appears as The Baillie (Councillor Alexander Swick), taking his place on the bench of the local court where justice has not only to be done—it has to be seen to be believed. Example:

Baillie: Right. 2.30, time for the first race—the first case. Right, Mr Physical, bring in the first criminal. Eh. fit's that? Innocent till proved guilty? Fa's side are you on? A' right, a' right. Bring in the hooligan onywye. Right, stand up there, Jim. An' tak that smile aff yer face fan I'm spikkin tae ye. An fit wye are ye nae handcuffed? Oh, you're the solicitor!

83

The Oldmeldrum Sports is an old favourite from 1975 which endures through all repetition. Sandy Thomson, the sports convener, calls up a famous London number to ask if Her Majesty would care to perform the opening ceremony.

When they come to discussing a possible royal contribution to the bring-and-buy stall, Sandy asks the Queen: "Tell me now, can ye dae a bilin o jam? Fit could ye dae? Rhubarb? Oh ye could. An' dinna forget tae write on yer ticketie—yer sticky label—ER 1975. No no, yer Majesty, nae Elizabeth Regina. Early Rhubarb."

Predictably, the *Beechgrove Garden* gets a humorous airing. And Sandy Thomson turns up again on *Desert Island Discs*, from 1979, to be interviewed by the late Roy Plomley.

Sandy is the Bowling Champion of Auchnagatt, not just once but four times. "An achievement worthy to rank alongside that of Bjorn Borg," ventures Mr Plomley.

"Oh it's better than Bjorn Borg," says an indignant Sandy. "He's never won the Bowling Championship o' Auchnagatt."

So it goes on. When you link into the rhythms of their imaginary village of Auchterturra, with its Glaiket Stirk hostelry and guest house called Middenview, even the southern English can begin to get the drift of it.

If the trio's title baffles, all comes clear when they sing their song called "Reputations", which ends:

> Pope John Paul the Second
> Is a Rangers fan.
> Sylvester Stallone is gay
> And Dolly Parton is a man.
> But the strangest reputation
> Is the one that Scotland's got:
> When folk sing Scotland the Brave
> We say Scotland The What?

PITY ABOUT THE SNOWBOOTS

THERE is nothing quite like sending your wife away on a long weekend for starting to unravel the mysteries of the microwave or the video recorder, both of which continue to baffle my singularly unscientific mind.

Yes yes, I would manage fine. Pay the milk, water the plants, feed the birds, walk the dog (who would water the lamp-posts)—and if I forget to record *Fortunes of War* I'll suffer the fate of Prince Yakimov. I know, I know.

Just off you go. You've had a bad year. That special offer of a long weekend in New York is just what you need. By the way, I've been in New York in November and it can be bitterly cold at this time of year. So wrap up well, take the woollies.

As we drove to Prestwick Airport, the news confirmed my warnings. Snow was falling to the depth of a foot in Washington and that is well to the south of New York.

So off she went, soaring into the western sky by Arran on a route which would lead to Newark Airport, under the Hudson River tunnel and into what is perhaps the most exciting city in the world.

Singing like an idiot, as I tend to do when alone in the car, I drove back up the Ayrshire road to Glasgow, turning over in my mind the long list of instructions.

At least the cookery part had been taken care of. That was pinned up on the kitchen wall on a day-to-day basis and in a form of Simple Simon language which assumed a backward mentality.

The pre-cooked dishes would come straight from the freezer and the instructions would go like this:

85

Day One: Meat roll + beans + pot. Put unwrapped pot. on plate, open microwave door, insert plate, close door and press for High at 4 mins. Sponge pudding—High 1 min.

Day Two: Chicken dish. Put water in veg., cover dish with another dish. High for 8 mins. Take tarts out of foil. . . .

And so it went on, all very scientific.

Come to think of it, why do you take the tarts out of the foil? Ah, something to do with the rules of microwave. Whether they would explode, melt or vanish I never did find out. Perhaps that old adenoidal chap, Mr Kipling, could have told me but I couldn't be bothered phoning him up.

I followed the ritual day after day, through the steak and mince, flan and scrambled egg. More water in the confounded vegetables. But, as one who had hitherto struggled to boil an egg successfully, I did make some spectacular progress.

For example, did you know it is possible to make a cup of coffee in a microwave? You did? Ah well, I was only trying to extend the bounds of knowledge.

As the mounting pile of unwashed dishes threatened to obliterate all light from the kitchen window, I retreated to the lounge and thought I had better undertake a dress rehearsal for recording *Fortunes of War*.

Those newfangled systems of remote control really do hover on the fringes of magic. Can anyone explain to me how, by the pressing of a variety of buttons on a slim panel, the television set will jump through hoops while, by the operation of a second little handset, the video recorder will start, stop, reverse, do three-point turns and dance a jig for good measure?

Giving up all hope of enlightenment, I turned to the more familiar feel of the newspapers to see how the snowstorms were building up in America. Right enough, the given temperatures were in line with all that was forecast. In the forties one day, the thirties the next.

Just as well my wife went prepared with warm, heavy clothing. Perhaps she would be sledging in Central Park by now. As I cast an eye over several papers I found, as frequently happens, some disagreement about what the temperatures in New York really were.

There are some English papers, so far behind with the news anyway, which put an asterisk to indicate they are talking about the day before yesterday. Others give themselves a let-out with a midday tag, leaving room for vast differences on either side.

As a defender of the accuracy of quality newspapers in this country, I would concede nevertheless that this is one area of coverage which needs improvement. Inconsequential as it may seem, temperatures abroad are a much-read feature of the morning papers. How many of us, lying at some holiday poolside reading day-old British papers, have contested the accuracy of local levels?

Anyway, the weekend passed with a minimum of catastrophe. The cooker cooked, the video recorded, and the stereophonic gramophone spilled out orchestral volumes to which I gave the accompaniment of the poor man's Pavarotti.

And soon the Jumbo was lumbering in from New York, New York, which had indeed turned out to be a wonderful town, and I was hearing all about soaring to the top of the Empire State Building, crossing to the Statue of Liberty, window-gazing on Fifth Avenue and listening to Cole Porter's piano being played in the Peacock Alley of the Waldorf Astoria.

"Just a pity about the weather," I ventured.

"A pity about the warm woollies and snowboots, you mean. Why, didn't you read it in the papers? It was sweltering in New York. Upper sixties it was. We lunched out in Central Park and cast all the clothing we could."

"Really?"

"Yes. And by the way, what's happened to Harriet and Guy?"

HOW I TELEVISED MY CHILDHOOD

•15TH DECEMBER 1987•

AS evenings go (if you'll pardon the indulgence) this is a fairly significant one in my own personal trail through life.

For the past year or so, much of the spare time has gone towards creating a television film about my childhood. It all grew out of a previous adventure into television, my first, which ended up with a nomination for an award.

Now the BBC were encouraging me to try something more ambitious and that was how I came to casting an eye over a book I once wrote, mainly to do with that fleeting introduction to our lives which we call childhood.

First there was the synopsis to be prepared, taking its chance with scores of others, all vying for the final nod of acceptance from the hierarchy of television.

Only when that was achieved did the real work begin: a more detailed structure, linking up sequences which would follow logically and with interest.

Into the fabric of documentary I would write some drama scenes, my first venture into dialogue, depicting various aspects of the early years. So there were meetings with director Dick Colthurst, who had shaped my previous film, and with the man who would direct the drama sequences, David Blair. Ideas were bounced between us before we set out for the childhood setting in Aberdeenshire to map out possible locations. But there you run into technical problems.

I wanted to write a scene about the day before war started, when the evacuated children of Glasgow arrived at our village station. Thanks to the sixties vandalism of Dr Beeching, however, there no longer was such a thing as a local railway station. So we had to find a real steam engine and create a bit of make-believe.

You read about film crews flying off on location to exotic spots but, for this particular adventure, there was nothing more exotic than the village of Maud, where I was born. But that was good enough for me. In fact, it ended up as one of the special events of my life.

The village turned out and stood at a respectful distance to watch the activity which recreated the scenes of the Second World War, when 1,000 soldiers came thundering down the brae to enliven our rural backwater. What excitement!

The directors had managed to unearth authentic military vehicles from the period (there is a restoration society for that purpose) and to obliterate such tell-tale evidence of 1987 as television aerials and modern bank signs.

Perhaps the most poignant moment of all arrived when I noticed the entire school population being led over the hill by the headmistress, Gina Walker, who was at Maud School in my own day. As a project, it seemed, they had come to witness the work of a former pupil and that, I must admit, choked me up a little.

For me, one of the intriguing aspects of making a film was the casting. For a couple of cameo parts, I made a special request to have those splendid Scottish performers, Bill Riddoch and Eileen McCallum, playing respectively my father and Lizzie Allan, a woman without legs who ran the village sweetie shop.

But the biggest acting role of all goes to an 11-year-old boy, who plays my own tender self as a child. The drama director interviewed a dozen North-east boys for the part and I sat in on the final selection from four.

It was a difficult decision but we settled for young Neil Elphinstone from Techmuiry, near Fraserburgh, a farmer's son who lives about eight miles from where I grew up.

Though he had never acted in his life, Neil turned out to be a real "pro", patiently coping with all the tedious rigmarole of filming and responding magnificently to his co-performers.

So we filmed through parts of June, July and August and ended with the drama episodes in September, basing ourselves at hotels from Peterhead to the rural hinterland I know so well.

I am left, I suppose, with the lingering impression of how much sweat has to be shed over the making of a one-hour film. The costume and make-up departments must strike the right note for the period. The design and props people have the daunting task of scouring various centres in England to come up with the effects of a pre-war sweetie shop, for example, and to recreate the decor of those bygone days.

And the weather plays its part. For the final scene, which needed more than a blink of sunshine, we waited a full ten weeks! So human temperament is put to the test.

Finally it is all in the can, as they say, and you await the result with trepidation. So tonight I shall sit down at the television set, service myself with a glass of whisky, and wonder if the *Nine O'Clock News* will ever end. Because, once that is over, my future as a television writer is on trial. There will be no hiding place.

I'm narrating as well as writing, which is an adventure in itself when you have my kind of speech imperfections. Anyway, the die is cast. Cross your fingers for me—and if there is a blank space here next Tuesday, I may have fled for ever.

DIARY OF GOOD INTENTIONS

AS another year recedes into history, the diary for 1988 presents itself on the desk and brings its own reminder of all those good intentions so firmly declared exactly twelve months ago.

In 1987 I would not only keep a regular diary but summarise each week in that space at the bottom right-hand corner.

It started out with promise, if not inspiration: "The year arrived quietly. Guinness rumpus still raging."

By January 12 the storms of winter had well and truly broken and I was recording: "A week of Arctic weather—the worst that Glasgow can remember. Country folk have it much worse but it is a novelty in the city. All public transport off. Not at work Tuesday."

Then the most extraordinary weather pattern developed. Ten days after that storm of January 12, I recorded that we were "sitting out in the sun. Also installed as Honorary Member of Irvine Burns Club, along with the Poet Laureate, Ted Hughes."

On Sunday, January 25, as well as being Burns Night, "I sat up till the sma' 'oors watching the Superbowl of American football on television: New York Giants 39—Denver Broncos 20."

Monday, February 2: "Writing an obituary notice on novelist Alistair MacLean, who died today."

Saturday, February 14 (St Valentine's Day): "My football match for today called off because of frost—yet I sat out sunbathing." (In retrospect, that was the summer that was.)

Thursday, April 9: "Given final go-ahead from the BBC to make a television film. Met producer and drama director."

Saturday, April 25: "Another burst of glorious weekend weather.

91

Aberdeen had a record 75 degrees. Farmers running into deep financial trouble. Heard today of a fifth suicide in my native corner."

Saturday, May 16: "At Hampden Park to see St Mirren beating Dundee United in the Scottish Cup Final. (Bet my fellow-columnist Willie Hunter is turning somersaults tonight.)"

Wednesday, May 27: In America for 70th birthday celebration of *Forbes* magazine. (Liz Taylor there—some night!)"

Thursday, June 11: "Back home—General Election."

By midsummer, the weekly summary was faltering badly, though I managed to record for July 29: "Became a paperback writer today. Strange experience to see your book on racks at airport and railway stations, rubbing shoulders with Agatha Christie and Alistair MacLean!"

Wednesday, July 29: "Off to sunny Cyprus."

All that Mediterranean sunshine may have baked the brain-cells a little because the whole diary system was threatening to collapse. I had to wait till November for the next full summary, which said: "Saw Eden [my wife] off to New York and sat down to write the script for that television film. A chance to have the house to myself—to stride about and speak to myself without any threat from men in white coats!"

Tuesday, December 15: "This is the night. My film on BBC1. As the last credit rolled off the screen, phone began ringing. How did all these people get my phone number?"

The postscript to that final entry, dear reader, is that your letters have been flooding in by the fistful, to the point that I have never seen such an avalanche in all my years of writing. I'm ploughing through the replies as quickly as possible.

Happily the tone of reaction has been one of undiminished pleasure, a sentiment which spread even to most newspaper critics, who might not have been expected to rush compliments on a writer from a rival journal.

Of course, you cannot please everybody. There was one fellow who became so disgruntled that he called the film a crashing bore. That was before he started on the really insulting parts. But then,

as my old granny used to say, there's naethin' half as queer as
folk.

Your own letters had their idiosyncrasies as well. One chap was
close to ecstasy about the film. He was so often moved to laughter
and tears that he seemed to be having a good old emotional rave-
up (or was it booze-up?).

He wanted to compliment me all the more since I had achieved
all this "with a face like yours!"

I'm afraid it is the face I'll have to settle for and, with the luck
of survival, it will be there at the top of this column in the new
year which is about to break upon us. (Memo to picture desk: can
you improve the mugshot?)

By then I shall have embarked on a whole new set of resolu-
tions, which may include the keeping of an orderly diary.

In the meantime, have a good Hogmanay—and an even better
New Year.

IN SEARCH OF SCOTLAND

* 1 6 T H   F E B R U A R Y   1 9 8 8 *

THE winter which looked as if it would never come was mild enough to tempt me out of suburban shelter last week and into the wide open spaces of Scotland.

After all, some of my most memorable drives around this glorious country of ours have taken place in the so-called dead of winter, when the tourists were safely out of sight and the roadways had reverted to local usage.

So I headed up through Perth and across to the east coast, where a warming sun shone out of a clear sky and inspired in me an alarming burst of fractured Pavarotti.

Oh what a beautiful morning! What a privilege to be alive on a day like this, surging up through Angus to the red-clay soil of Grassic Gibbon country in the Mearns and onwards to Aberdeen, with its grey granite spires.

A plate of mince and skirlie and I was on my way northward again, into that cold shoulder of Scotland where first I saw the light of day. By now, that daylight was drawing in, under threat of ominous cloud, so I pulled into the Saplinbrae House Hotel at Old Deer for the night and found solace in some antifreeze of an amber hue, enjoyed all the more since its glow was matched by the flicker and warmth of a real log fire.

Out-by, the storm clouds looked as if they had brought winter at last, with showers of sleet displaying a ghost-like image on window panes. And so to bed (a four-poster at that, complete with canopy).

Whatever would the morning bring? Blocked roads and snowploughs? Well, the morning brought its own surprise—a crisp, invigorating frost and more of those same blue skies of yesterday.

Onwards by New Pitsligo, once known as Cyaak and as famous for its lace as it was notorious for its tinkers and illicit distillers, and through the Moss of Cowbog, where I used to accompany my grandfather with horse and cart to cut the peat of winter's fuel.

A thin shroud of snow had dressed the dead fields of winter as sheep went in search of anything that hinted of grass. Straw rolled up from a disastrous harvest wormed its way along dykesides and some crops had not been cut at all, a grim reminder of the current plight of farmers.

Along that Moray Firth coast, which can boast the best climate in Scotland, the little whitewashed villages sat smug on their shelves, from Pennan to Crovie, before the road dipped down to Gardenstown, a place renowned for holiness.

Last time I passed this way, a few years ago, I came suddenly into the tiny village square, where an evangelist was holding forth about the sins of the flesh. When two men in a speedboat came roaring along the shore, he turned his threatening fist to condemn this desecration of the Lord's Day.

Three days later, I opened my morning paper to read that two men had died off Gardenstown when their speedboat . . .

I put the chilling memory behind me and drove on over the Longmanhill to find Macduff and Banff in mellow mood, bathed in the sunshine which drew a sparkle from the still waters of the Moray Firth.

From a vantage point overlooking Macduff harbour, I lunched on haggis, neeps and tatties, as the television set crackled on about George Bush having a tough time in the American caucus.

I was absorbing a landscape which would endure for ever, peopled by some hardy individuals who seemed as if they might follow suit. A call on an elderly relative was a heart-warming reminder of the calibre of folk we produce in this great old country of ours.

Jean Ann Webster has been infant-mistress to generations on that Banffshire coast and there she was, in her 90th year, still

95

putting the world to rights, defying all disabilities to dirl her piano and scrape her fiddle and recite for me the rich, immortal verse of Charles Murray.

By nightfall I had skirted those coastal towns of Whitehills and Portsoy, dipped through that dramatic viaduct at Cullen, which gives the illusion of driving into the sea, and pulled in for another night at Elgin.

In the town hall that evening, I joined the audience at a concert, which brought the delights of Bill McCue, Anne Lorne Gillies, Tam Reid (of bothy ballad fame), and the Elgin Strathspey and Reel Society.

But the surprise of the night was an up-and-coming pianist I had never heard of—Derek Barron from Huntly, now based in Glasgow. Give that young man a break and a few strings of backing and he will knock your Richard Claydermans clean off the piano stool.

Come the morning and the sun was shining once again. Now I would drive on by Grantown-on-Spey and Aviemore and reach Glasgow by sunset. Well, that was the plan.

But a safety check with the AA revealed that Drumochter Pass was already blocked with snow and there was worse to come.

So there was nothing for it but to retrace my steps down the east coast, stopping off at Stracathro for a plate of stovies and skirlie. (Trencherman would pale at my culinary habits but I offer no apology!)

Nothing much came of the dire forecasts and still we waited for a real winter. But we would suffer yet, folk said, in the traditional tones of Scottish foreboding.

Well, the consolation must be that we won't suffer for too long. March is just two weeks away and spring will beckon thereafter. The buds will sprout and lambs will gambol and new life will come to the land.

Of course I am an incurable romantic. So don't blame me for tempting Providence if you awaken to a blizzard tomorrow morning.

96

Speaker of the Year banquet: acceptance speech at Central Hotel, Glasgow

Author receives award as UK Speaker of the Year
from national president Ken Sharpe

Left: Author with Charlie Chaplin outside the old Tivoli Theatre, Aberdeen

Below: The favourite Hotel—Beverly Hills on Sunset Boulevard

Above: Native village of Maud, with Webster farm of Honeyneuk top right

Below: Author (right) leads parade of 1000 pupils from Robert Gordon's College, Aberdeen, to give Founder's Day Oration

Above:
Peter Manuel,
double hand-
cuffed, arrives
at court for
his appeal

Above right:
Mass murderer
Peter Manuel

Right:
Col. Colin
Mitchell—
"Mad Mitch"
of the Argylls

*Opposite top
right*:
Flora Garry,
authentic poet
of the North-east

Opposite top left:
Jim Clark, from
Chirnside,
Scotland's World
Champion
racing driver,
at the Monaco
Grand Prix 1964

Opposite below:
Jim Clark
at the wheel
of his Lotus

Ol' Blue Eyes himself, Frank Sinatra on stage in Glasgow

Mary Garden, Aberdeen's world-famous
opera singer

Hugh McIllvaney—charted lives
of Shankly, Stein and Busby

Above left:
The legendary
Jim Rodger
with his OBE

Above right:
Author (left) with
Tommy Gemmell
of Celtic, Drew
Rennie of the
Express and the
Rev Stanley Mair
of Netherlee

Right:
On the conductor's
rostrum at Glasgow
Royal Concert Hall

Diana, Princess of Wales 1961–1997

THE MAN WHO MADE MAJORCA

• 7 T H   J U N E   1 9 8 8 •

A GOLDEN glow of Mediterranean sunshine radiates from the warm personality of Lloyd Davies, a tanned, wiry little figure who must surely rank as a living legend of the travel trade.

From within the business founded in Glasgow by his father, Llewelyn Davies, in the early part of the century, young Lloyd virtually discovered the Balearic island of Majorca in the 1920s and, as far back as 1934, was initiating what became the annual trek of the Scots to their favourite resort in the sun.

In particular, the old Roman town of Pollensa more or less owes its existence as a summer attraction to the jovial Scot who guided its progress from a small town with no more than two hotels (and an appalling sewage problem!) to the classy resort it is today.

Appropriately, therefore, the ex-Mayor of Pollensa, Miguel Pericas, and his wife were in Glasgow the other evening for one of those rather special occasions which become overlaid with a fine sense of history.

They had come, like myself and many more of his friends, to pay tribute to Lloyd Davies at his 80th birthday party in a South Side hotel. And what a night of reminiscence it turned out to be.

For Lloyd Davies belongs to that era of travel which knew variety well beyond the reach of the package tour. In those pre-war days, as well as pioneering Pollensa, you would find him involved in such an unconventional tangent of the travel trade as despatching Clydesdale horses to Australia.

When that war arrived, it was Lloyd Davies who was asked to

arrange speedy transport for Jewish refugees as they fled from Hitler's Germany.

And of course there was Mrs Stewart. She was the Glasgow lady who emigrated to America and ended up as housekeeper to the notorious Al Capone in Chicago. But she always came back to her native city and invariably her travel arrangements were handled by the Llewelyn Davies office in Queen Street.

Any reference to her gangster boss would bring the loyal response that "Al may have been a rascal but he was always very good to me."

At that birthday dinner, Lloyd was recalling a gent of his pre-war acquaintance who came in to arrange transport for 20 of his compatriots who were returning to the Indian subcontinent.

In those days, that involved a truly hazardous journey over land and sea, with intolerable stretches cooped up in a steamy bus. Some time later, Lloyd ran into the gent in Argyle Street.

"Hello, Bashir. Tell me, how did the trip go?" he inquired.

"Ah, no good, Mr Davies, no good," was the reply. "Four deid and the rest no' weel!"

It was during a world cruise as a young purser with the Anchor Line that Lloyd Davies landed at Majorca, which was then only a winter resort for the truly well-heeled.

Rejoining his father at 21 Queen Street, he took on the travel side of the family business—his late brother Llewelyn ran the currency side—and pursued the hunch that Majorca could extend its winter attractions to become a summer resort for sun-starved people like the Scots.

He had also noticed that Paddy Henderson's shipping service from Liverpool to Rangoon had lots of empty berths between the Mediterranean and Merseyside, mainly because homecoming passengers from the Far East tended to leave the ships at Marseilles and speed home to Britain by train to gain an extra few days.

So Lloyd Davies did a deal with Paddy Henderson, sending his customers from Glasgow to Liverpool by train before shipping them to the sunshine.

In those early days, he came to know a certain hotelier called Herr Strohmeyer, who seemed to employ an unusual number of young German waiters. At a much later date, he discovered they had been trainees at a secret U-Boat base and that there was more to Herr Strohmeyer's activities than running a hotel.

Lloyd Davies was in Majorca just days before the outbreak of the Spanish Civil War, which was so closely followed by the Second World War that his full plans for the Mediterranean island had to be shelved until 1950. Even in those post-war times the trip involved a tiring marathon which needed plane changes between Prestwick, Paris, Barcelona and Palma.

But it all came right in the end and the pioneer himself was hailed as a local hero on the island, co-opted to the tourist board and decorated by the Spanish authorities.

He and his charming wife Jean took a particular liking to the hotel bellboy on one of their earlier visits and never lost touch with the lad. How splendid that that bellboy progressed in his career to the point of becoming the owner of the Pollentia Hotel—the same Miguel Pericas, former Mayor of the town, who came to Glasgow for the birthday party!

So the vibrations of the night were full of friendship and good-will. That incomparable Glasgow pianist, Terry Martin, set the musical scene with ripplings of Cole Porter and George Gershwin, while Lloyd and Jean Davies went dancing the night away.

He has been the complete denial of a popular notion that you need to be ruthless and unscrupulous to succeed in business. For here is one of nature's gentlemen, enjoying his eventide all the more because he knows that he set a new pattern of relaxation for generations of people in the West of Scotland.

'MY COUSIN DATES LIZ TAYLOR'

LIFE is full of rich moments. So let me tell you about the brothers Andy, Chic and Arthur, friends of mine who grew up in a tenement in White Street, Partick.

When you get them together, the sparks of waggish wit begin to fly. They really are a bunch of jokers. Andy is the best-preserved 72-year-old I have ever seen, a lean, fit man who still runs for Victoria Park. Down at the club the other week he was giving them the biggest laugh they had had in ages.

"See that Malcolm Forbes who is dating Elizabeth Taylor?" said Andy. "Well, he's my first cousin."

"Ay, that'll be right," they chorused. "Him that's among the richest men in the world? Pull the other one, Andy."

Brother Chic from Irvine, another stylish runner in his day, told a similar tale at the Partick printers where he works, without cutting much ice. Talented athletes though they are, incidentally, both concede that third brother Arthur, from East Kilbride, is one man they can never beat. He is a tax inspector at Centre One.

Leaving behind all disbelief, however, the three brothers bundled into a modest car last weekend and headed for Aberdeenshire, where the same Malcolm Forbes happened to be flying in on his private Boeing 727 to buy up a historic castle, fly one of his spectacular hot-air balloons, entertain the parish to a memorable picnic—and re-bury his Scots father who died in New York in 1954.

When the Happy Billionaire stepped on to Scots soil, there were plenty of willing hands of welcome. But the readiest

100

recognition and warmest reunion were reserved for . . . yes, you've guessed it—Andy, Chic, and Arthur from Glasgow.

"Great to see you, fellas," said America's most flamboyant citizen, whose wealth you begin to count around the £500m mark. And Malcolm Forbes's brother Wallace joined in the general embrace.

At a family lunch, the five of them were like kids once again, recalling happy times together in the 1930s. Was it really 50 years since they played in a world still innocent of Hitler's war? Yes, they were first cousins all right. Down at the club, Andy wasn't kidding.

So how did it all come about, this close link with the man who owns a palace in Morocco, a chateau in France, an island in the South Pacific (as well as the largest collection of the priceless Fabergé eggs)—and can sail or fly to his various homes in a luxurious yacht or private Boeing?

It sprang from a little country cottage at Whitehill of New Deer, Aberdeenshire, where Bertie and Duncan Forbes were two of the ten children of a poor country tailor. While Bertie made his way to America in 1904, founding the prestigious *Forbes* magazine and making his fortune, brother Duncan gravitated to Glasgow, where he became a box-maker with Tomlinson's of Partick, a humble citizen of White Street, whose pleasures seldom stretched beyond a welcome dram.

Though poles apart on the social scale, Bertie and Duncan were brothers still when the millionaire came home every two years, sailing into Southampton with his wife and five sons. Established in a suite at Glasgow's Central Hotel, he would take the local relatives on a tour of the Rob Roy country and treat them to a slap-up meal. Andy remembers the ritual before family Forbes departed for the opulence of Manhattan. The American boys were ordered to divest themselves of their best clothes and hand them over to their Glasgow cousins!

The war put an end to the visits and when Bertie resumed his pilgrimage, it was without the sons, who were now leading their own lives in America.

Malcolm Forbes entered politics and was a hot tip to become a Republican President, a contemporary of John F. Kennedy.

Back in Glasgow, the war had cut across a promising athletic career for Andy Forbes. By the time it was over, he was already past 30 but his potential as a long-distance winner could not be ignored.

An injury kept him out of the 1948 Olympics but he was chosen for the 1950 Commonwealth Games in New Zealand. That meant a lengthy sea voyage so Andy along with that other legend of Scottish sport, high-jumper Alan Paterson, withdrew because of the absence from work.

When word reached Sir Alexander King, the cinema magnate, he ordered that the two Scots be flown to New Zealand at his expense. So off went Forbes, at the age of 35—to win the silver medal on the very first day of the Games!

It didn't bring material wealth but another Forbes had proved himself among the greatest in his field.

Today, aged 72 but looking in his 50s, he still runs eight miles a day and ten on Saturdays, a shining example of how to look after yourself.

So much had happened since the Forbes brothers last met their American cousins. Without knowing it, while Andy was landing at Arromanches after D-Day, cousin Malcolm was storming ashore further along the Normandy coast, showing such bravery as to gain the two top American war honours.

There was so much to talk about at the Forbes reunion last week. Malcolm had brought back Uncle Bertie to be re-buried in his native parish so Andy, Chic and Arthur had cords at the lowering of the coffin.

But this was no occasion for sadness. On the contrary, there was much laughter in their recollection of times gone by. And when it was all over, the Forbes brothers set out for Glasgow, with a few more tales about their famous cousin from America.

This time, I suspect, the boys in the club will pay more attention.

THE BALLROOM DAYS OF
JACK CHAPMAN

∗ 2 6 T H   J U L Y   1 9 8 8 ∗

THE name of Jack Chapman will conjure up romantic memories for countless thousands of Glasgow folk whose courting days were sometimes measured by the strict tempos of his mellow dance orchestra.

Who, in their heyday, did not sow the seeds of a romance at the old Albert dance hall in Bath Street or later in the Plaza at Eglinton Toll?

For Jack Chapman was not only the most popular dance band leader in Glasgow but widely accepted as the Victor Sylvester of Scotland. A superb musician, playing violin or saxophone, he led his 10-piece orchestra with tail-coated style, creating an appropriate atmosphere for those generations who, face to face, used to mould their bodies into a single unit of rhythmic movement.

Yet I wonder how many of those people, scanning our classified advertisements, had recognised a man who died recently at Grantown-on-Spey as their very own Jack Chapman. Aged 84, he had spent his latter years by the mellow climes of that gentle valley, not far from his son Ian, who lives in Elgin.

But it was in his native Glasgow that Chapman was known and loved. Here was the lad, brought up in Springburn and brimful of music, who managed to study violin at the Royal Scottish Academy in time for the Roaring Twenties and all that that meant in terms of ballroom dancing.

The age of the palais-de-danse had arrived, all the way from Hammersmith to Dennistoun. Alec Warren, whose family owned the Albert, remembers how he first became aware of Chapman.

Himself a professional dancer and now aged 85, Alec returned from an engagement at the Winter Garden in Blackpool to help reshape the family dance hall of the 1920s. It was time to get away from the old image of the Quadrilles and give a lead in the new fashion.

"We had a scratch orchestra at first. Then the leader brought in this fellow called Chapman," he recalls. "I soon realised the others were not up to much but that here was a real find. So I got rid of the rest and put him in charge. He went on to form his own 10-piece orchestra."

For the next 25 years, the Albert was synonymous with the name of Jack Chapman. Through the 1930s into a stormy war-time, with its constant flow of uniformed personnel, including vast numbers of Americans, he was there on the bandstand, remembered by all as a kind and thoroughly gentle man whose exquisite tones were balm to a troubled world.

Alas, his departure from the Albert was prompted by a note of discord which would have seemed alien to a man who lived for harmony. Alec Warren still winces at the thought of it.

With the changing musical mood of the 1950s, he had received some complaints that Jack Chapman was not keeping up to date with the music. He merely mentioned the fact to the bandleader. But the effect was devastating. He took it very badly, handed in his notice—and Alec Warren, with whom he had had a splendid relationship, never saw him again. It is still a lingering regret.

Chapman moved over to the Plaza on the South Side, and enjoyed another decade of strict tempo before retiring to teach music in Renfrewshire. Meanwhile he had moved from Giffnock to Pollokshields and Paisley before his final destination on Speyside.

After the death of his first wife, he married his brother's widow, Cissie. His stepson, Malcolm, is an accountant in London.

As if to trace the ghost of a legend, I ventured along to the Plaza the other evening and discovered a scene I thought had all but vanished. The magnificent ballroom, with its central fountain, still vibrates to the tempo of quickstep, foxtrot, modern waltz, or tango, largely unchanged in appearance from its opening day in 1922.

Where Glasgow was once the dancing capital of the world, boasting no fewer than 11 great halls, the Plaza stands today as sole survivor, recalling an age when people danced with decorum and were spared the devastation of their eardrums.

There I watched a tall, handsome man guide his partner round the floor with grace and style. He turned out to be Farquhar MacRae, former manager of Glasgow's Berkeley Ballroom and still tripping the light fantastic at the age of 83!

Farquhar went dewy-eyed at the mention of Jack Chapman. Yes, he remembered him as well as anyone, having first danced to his music in the Dixon Halls as far back as 1924. At that time Chapman was playing the Japanese violin.

Jack and Nancy Haran from Kelvindale were another couple cutting a fine figure on that ballroom floor, to the music of Manny Ferri, moving with the ease of 20-year-olds, as if blessed with the elixir of life. In fact, Jack Haran will not see 73 again. Once more, they glowed at the mention of Chapman's name.

This last oasis of ballroom dancing in Scotland owes almost everything to one man—Plaza manager Adam Sharp, a Banff loon who came to Glasgow in 1952 and has given his life to maintaining this particular art form. He can hardly find the words to do justice to his old bandleader's memory.

But, as we sit in his office, the best memorial is to be found out there on the floor, where more than 300 people are gliding into the night—perhaps the last, slightly sad, remnants of the ballroom generation, proving to the bitter end that they don't come dancing any better than in the city where Jack Chapman reigned supreme.

FRAGRANCE OF
THE GARDEN FESTIVAL

THEY lowered the final curtain on the great Glasgow Garden Festival last night.

It was farewell to Scotland's biggest spectacle for 50 years, an event which took time to imprint itself yet, finally, so caught the public imagination as to break the wildest estimate of attendance.

This was the great festival of the people, fortuitously caught in the upswing of Glasgow as the flavour of the decade among British cities. This, in turn, has further boosted the confidence and morale of Glaswegians and broadened the horizons for the future.

So what do we do this morning as they begin to dismantle the rollercoaster and Clydesdale Bank Tower, dig up the gardens and fold away the tent, with that flat sense of anticlimax that comes with the circus leaving town?

Do we just allow the new-found confidence and enthusiasm, not to mention a vast reservoir of expertise and know-how, to melt away like the snow off a dyke? To do so, I suggest, would be nothing short of lunacy.

Fifty years ago, with the Empire Exhibition at Bellahouston Park, Glasgow, we Scots proved we were capable of putting on one of the greatest shows on earth. On a more modest scale we have shown, with the Garden Festival, that the enterprise and talents have not deserted us.

So what are we waiting for? As soon as they draw breath, I suggest the various agencies reconvene and begin to plan for the Big One. On the world platform the most obvious event is probably Expo, the regular international exhibition which takes in major cities around the globe.

I have seen it at work—and have yet to witness anything more spectacular than our own Bellahouston of 1938.

To join that Expo queue, it needs someone to make the move, to spark off the enthusiasm. If no-one has thought of it, then THINK!

Meanwhile, a whole generation of Scottish children resume school today, having distilled in their young minds a treasure of memories from the Glasgow Garden Festival which will stir conversation for the rest of their lives.

Who will forget the Tower, which now returns to the care of its owners in Switzerland? Or the tramcars they had heard so much about from their elders, those monuments to a bygone age which attracted 1.25 million passengers and will now return to the stillness of the museum?

Who, most of all perhaps, can ever forget the terrifying drama of the rollercoaster, which turned the world upside-down for 700,000 people at £1 a ride (it cost more than £1m to hire) and was surely the most imaginative loss leader of all time.

In quieter moments we'll remember the landscaping and the gardens, the beauty of which encouraged a retired antique dealer from Leicestershire to pay £215,000 for the transfer of the National Trust enclosure to his home in England.

We'll remember the bustle of the restaurants, the beat of the jazz bands, the speedboats on the Clyde and the gentle ride around the festival on the little blue trains.

Of course we all have our own minor reservations. Personally, I would like to have seen a night-life, with lights and music, and a site which would have allowed for tumbling waterfalls, an indispensable part of any major spectacle.

But, as the chief executive, Air Vice-Marshal George Chesworth will return to his home on the Moray coast in the knowledge that he masterminded the Garden Festival with the precision of the Falklands War, in which he was deeply involved; knowing, too, that he generated interest among five times as many foreign visitors as are present in Seoul for the Olympic Games.

Marketing director Bill Simpson will know that he made the

right decision to stick with a historic event at home, in preference to a post in the warmer climes of California.

At a cost of £42m, a large share of which has been recouped, I reckon we had a bargain, as well as a festival to remember.

Now comes the redevelopment of the riverbank site. But, when nostalgia hits us in years to come, it will still be possible to cross Bell's Bridge and turn right or left along the riverside, meandering through acres of landscaping which are to be retained, or round by the marina, which will be further developed.

Screams from the rollercoaster will still echo in our ears, no doubt, as the memories flood back. But most of all, I suspect, we shall catch the fragrance of a garden which grew where once they built the mighty ships—and left us with a balm to enrich the rest of our lives.

WHAT A CENTURY!

EVEN with 12 years still to run, it goes without saying that we have already lived through the most remarkable century in all human history.

Anybody's granny who saw the 1880s and lived till the 1960s was a witness to the entire development of transport from the horse-and-cart to the supersonic aeroplane. (My own granny was born before the Tay Bridge disaster of 1879 and was still here to marvel at a man on the Moon.)

We have endured the two world wars, made a dramatic advance in all branches of science but, in the end, created perhaps as many problems as we have solved.

I was taking it all through hand last week with Robert Carvel, the distinguished parliamentary correspondent, whose father worked as a journalist in this Albion Street building until 1936, when he moved to London.

Young Robert entered the Press Gallery in 1939 and was in the privileged position of catching the final whiff of that decade which would lead us to the Second World War.

Looking over this bewildering century, Robert Carvel was recalling how he had always been able to claim that he had covered 12 of the 24 General Elections since 1900. Now, to his delight, he can claim to have written first-person reports on all 24.

To clarify, he has just been working on a gigantic tome which seeks to chronicle the month-by-month history of the twentieth century.

The result is a book of well over one million words, much heavier to lift than it is to read. An array of capable journalists, marshalled by the former editor of *Channel Four News*, Derrik Mercer, have put themselves into the position of writing about the events of the century as if they had been doing so at the time.

Thus Robert Carvel, who heard Lloyd-George speaking in the Commons, found himself reporting what the colourful Welshman was doing in 1909 as well. In the same way, he was writing about those 12 General Elections which preceded his time as a practising journalist.

He turned out 57,000 words and, along with Peter Lewis, acted as a kind of copy taster at the weekly meetings. It was all very scientific and computerised, with researchers providing the choice of stories from the files of the *Daily Telegraph*, which they claim to have been the best all-round newspaper of the century. (We are talking about London-based newspapers, of course!)

So, in newspaper format, they have charted how people's lives have changed through the century, from fashions and rations to pop tunes and package holidays.

At the first dawn of 1900, Nigeria became British, the Boer War was raging and Lillie Langtry was packing them in at a Washington theatre. Lord Mountbatten was being born as Oscar Wilde died in poverty at the age of 45.

In 1910, reports of Mark Twain's death were not nearly so exaggerated as he had once claimed them to be. This time, the man christened Samuel Langhorne Clemens really was gone for good.

So we squelch our way through the First World War to Charlie Chaplin's first full-length film in 1921 (*The Kid*, with Jackie Coogan).

In 1925, when Mrs Thatcher was born, everybody was doing the Charleston, that energetic dance which took its name from the town in South Carolina where it all started.

In 1927, Garbo was eclipsing the beloved Mary Pickford and Clara Bow, just as Hitler was plotting to eclipse the freedom of Europe. Back in Britain, we were heading for a decade in which we would be obsessed with the abdication of Edward VIII, an event which so mixed politics with royalty and sex as to be totally irresistible.

The Second World War brought the second great divide of the century while, on this corresponding day of 1952, the former General Eisenhower was about to sweep triumphantly towards the White House after his victory over Adlai Stevenson. (George Bush will be looking for a repeat performance.)

The Coronation year of 1953 also brought the conquest of Everest, Gordon Richards' only Derby win and, at long last, an FA Cup medal for the greatest footballer who ever lived, Stanley Matthews, by then 38.

So to rock 'n' roll, Elvis, Bill Haley and the Beatles, *Coronation Street* and the scandals of the Profumo affair, a certain candidate for Story of the Year, we all said, until it was quickly put into perspective by the Kennedy assassination which, excluding the world wars, would make a strong bid for Story of the Century.

This mammoth undertaking of a book was, surprisingly, completed in eight months and is expected to sell 275,000 copies in three months, making it the biggest-selling production of its price in publishing history.

An item from 1957, incidentally, drives home how quickly the world around us changes. It is a report of a hotel being built at a Spanish village which is trying to make itself into a holiday resort. The village in question? Benidorm!

ESCAPE TO THE ORIENT

* 3RD JANUARY 1989 *

RE-BOARDING the jumbo jet at Abu Dhabi, on the way home from the Far East, I was commenting to a fellow passenger on the monstrous nature of those flying machines and expressing the usual layman's bewilderment about lifting 312 tons of aeroplane into the sky.

Several hours later, having worked out the time adjustments, I realised that, at that precise moment, a similar machine had been exploding into the night sky to give us the ultimate in human horrors, which will forever be remembered with the label of Lockerbie.

It was my first renewal of contact with the wider world after three weeks of almost total separation from the on-goings of this crazy globe. It does journalists no harm, from time to time, to fall out from the daily columns of news and comment and take themselves away to the balm of distant tranquillity.

I could hardly have gone farther than my trail from the paddy fields of Thailand and the garish excitements of Bangkok, through the bustle of Hong Kong and along the island chain of Indonesia to the idyllic peace of Bali. (A mere two-hour hop and I would have been in Australia). It had been 15 years since last I sampled the magic of the Orient.

On the verge of the Balinese winter, with temperatures still in the 90s, I wandered through the lush countryside, so green and picturesque, with its terraced valleys of palm trees and profusion of foliage, yielding everything from rice, bananas and tapioca to vanilla, cloves and coffee, as well as a colourful burst of bougainvillaea.

112

Through village after village on the road to Mount Batur, the women balanced baskets on their heads and bore themselves with dignity, while their menfolk scraped and tilled the fields with oxen, and well-dressed children made their way home from school.

All around there was an air of industry, arising perhaps from the absence of unemployment benefit and the knowledge that you work to survive. Of course it is not a condition that would commend itself to the so-called sophistication of our western standards, yet the outward signs were of serene contentment and a touching family protectiveness for less fortunate members.

I have always harboured the thought that I could put up with poverty as long as it was hot poverty—and Bali could be just my scene. There you could always pull a crust from a nearby tree and curl up under canvas in the steaming heat of the night. Air-conditioning might be the problem.

High on the volcanic Mount Batur, the black grime of lava from the 1963 eruption still leaves its tidemark as a grim reminder that the slumbering giant could growl into action at any hour.

Back down by the golden sands, the year-round climatic expectations are made clear from the fact that the foyer and public areas of the Bali Hyatt Hotel consist only of a roof and stilt supports. In other words, it is never cold enough to warrant walls.

So I listened to the quiet melody of the south sea ripple as it broke gently upon the beach, a soothing sound interrupted only by the raucous rasp of a Scottish voice in foul-mouthed flight and the public address of a yapping yuppie from London, holding court about property deals in the City. (Was this Bali or Benidorm?)

Mercifully, those embarrassing ambassadors of western culture were soon on their way, leaving the Balinese to their more simple but civilised ways. At least that heightened my appreciation of the temporary respite from a different world.

When the sun had bedded himself down and the moon came soaring in the night sky, you would find me in the piano bar, with its open-air terrace, listening to the call of the jungle bird as it provided weird accompaniment to "Blue Moon" or "Strangers in the Night".

As tall palms swayed sensuously in the balmy breeze, with all the grace of Balinese dancers, it occurred to me that this might be as close to Heaven as I could ever aspire. So I made the most of it, trying to fix it all in the consciousness as a source of future consolation.

But now, from the distance, came the first rumblings of the monsoon. The rains would come any moment now to fill the reservoirs of a lush land and ensure another year of nature's bounty.

Tomorrow, it would be time to leave this island paradise and resume contact with a troubled world; to learn the full extent of Armenia and to hear of Clapham Junction; to know that Edwina Currie had gained egg all over her face and that lowly Hearts had beaten Rangers.

That journey back home would be undertaken in a jumbo jet which would, in itself, become a chilling symbol of the reality which dictates our daily lives. It is an appealing thought that you can escape from it all. But, in the end, it is no more than an idle dream.

HOW I CHASED CHARLIE CHAPLIN

* 2ND MAY 1989 *

THE lecture tour has never been my forte but I must confess to a certain pleasure in the recent round of public engagements which brought some of the most delightful audiences I have ever encountered.

It is a consequence of writing paperbacks that publishers encourage this sort of thing, on the basis that it inflicts no injury at all on their sales figures. That novelty of meeting the public is in sharp contrast to the loneliness of the long-suffering writer, who labours over a typewriter, unaware of what the reaction might be.

My recent face-to-face with live audiences, ranging from the Scottish National Trust to Bothwell Rotary Club and the Buchan Heritage Society, produced some chastening moments, not least when I was confronted by such diverse questioners as my mother's first boyfriend (early 1920s) and my own qualifying-class teacher of 1943.

Once you have delivered similar addresses to different groups, the most intriguing point of all is the utter predictability of what will interest and amuse. Among subjects which go down well, I have found the story of Charlie Chaplin a matter of fascination for all ages. Appropriately, I was speaking about him on the recent centenary of his birth and telling of the sweat I shed in trying to interview him.

Chaplin had no liking for journalists and vowed he would give no more interviews after the McCarthy witch-hunt of the 1950s. My eternally optimistic pursuit of the legendary clown went on for more than five years, particularly in the Swiss retreat of Vevey, where he lived in later years. Ever so politely but firmly, I was fobbed off by a protective secretary.

Chaplin, however, had a fondness for Scotland and sometimes came here on touring holidays, particularly along the Moray Firth coast. In 1970, I received a tip that he would book in at the Tor-Na-Coille Hotel in Banchory. The precise date was uncertain and the reception desk was sworn to secrecy but, determined to confront the man, I booked in and bided my time.

I was reading a book in the foyer, with one eye on the main entrance, beginning to question the quality of my information, when suddenly a limousine drew up and out stepped the unmistakable figure of Chaplin, accompanied by his wife, Oona.

I let them settle in, but before they withdrew for the night I approached Oona, hoping that she might explain my innocent purpose to the great man. She reminded me of his no-interview policy but promised an answer at breakfast. My heart sank when she came down to say she was sorry; he refused to break his rule. So near and yet so far.

In desperation, I approached the man himself and asked if he would at least sign my copy of his marvellous autobiography. He agreed. I sat him down on a couch and asked if he would add some autographs for my children. How many did I have? Three. I wished I had said 10!

He began to draw caricatures of himself—bowler hat, moustache, baggy trousers and cane—for each one. All the while I was asking questions and finding to my delight that he was giving answers, which I desperately sought to memorise.

Finally I reminded him that, around 1906, he had appeared at the Tivoli Theatre in Aberdeen, as one of Fred Karno's knockabout lads. On his way south, how would he like to call at the old place, now a bingo hall, to remind himself of bygone days?

"Yes, I'd rather like that," he said—and I arranged that his chauffeur would follow my car to Aberdeen. Meanwhile a photographer was alerted so that a historic moment would not be missed.

Chaplin stepped out of his limousine and surveyed the old Tivoli, still displaying the signs of parterre stalls and fauteuils, recalling his days with Fred Karno. Word spread like wildfire that the great Charlie Chaplin was here. As if by magic, a crowd materialised from nowhere.

Could this really be the great clown of Hollywood? He signed autographs, patted young heads and spread a hand of thanks to an adoring crowd. The congestion began to alarm Oona so we ushered him back into his limousine and waved him goodbye for ever.

I made my way to the telephone with the story they said I would never get—and recorded one of those rare experiences which come to brighten our lives.

THE GLAMOUR OF MARY GARDEN

• 9TH MAY 1989 •

IT was a radio play by Frederic Mohr which sent me scampering for the family photo album. And there she was—opening the school fête in our rural village in the 1950s, with my father-in-law in attendance.

Yes, I had met her briefly but, more often, had merely observed her at a distance, sweeping down Union Street in Aberdeen with all that aura of mystery to be expected of a prima donna.

Mohr's dramatic version of her life had reminded me once again of how we neglected Mary Garden, Scotland's greatest female singer and perhaps the finest lyric soprano of all time.

How shameful that I had grown up with a knowledge of Melba and Patti but knew very little about the operatic singer on my own doorstep.

In fairness, though she spent the last 30 years of her life in her native Aberdeen, the family had emigrated to America and the bulk of her career was spent in Chicago and Paris. And what a remarkable career it was. While the traditional opera singer was liable to resemble a battleship in full blast, Mary Garden was the born actress who learned to use her devastating appearance as well as her voice, lending a wickedly sensual touch to her performance.

She scandalised society with her "Dance of the Seven Veils" in Richard Strauss's *Salome*, so much so that the police chief of Chicago declared her act indecent. She told him in no uncertain manner to go devote himself to the exploits of Al Capone and other hoodlums of the day.

Recalling her procession down Union Street, I can well imagine her walking from her home on the Champs Elysée to Montmartre to meet her varied circle of friends.

Paris crowds adored her, showering flowers on stage. Long after the casting couch, impresarios tended to want her not only for her voice but for her body.

The great Debussy was obsessed and one piece of local gossip I do remember from my youth was that she was mistress to the famous composer. Mary Garden herself denied it. She certainly created the role of his famous Melisande and prompted him to marvel, in reference to her Aberdonian background, that she had come from the cold far north to do so.

She revelled in her power over an audience, concluding that, once you have experienced that, there is nothing more to do but go home to a glass of milk and 10 drops of iodine!

She enjoyed her power over men too, accepting their favours and attentions but treating them with a measure of scorn. When people called her an insatiable man-eater, she responded that "I can take it or leave it." Indeed, there were hints of a lesbian interest.

Instead of marrying, she steeped herself in her art and achieved much for women in the theatre. From prima donna, she made the unique switch to general manager of the Chicago Grand Opera company, with total control.

Mary Garden was courted by European royalty and was not unknown at Windsor. Melba was there on one occasion and behaved very badly, according to the Scot.

In fact, she had reservations about the great Melba, paying her the left-handed compliment of saying she was a wonderful singer as long as you kept your eyes shut!

No man kept his eyes shut when Mary was around. Born in 1874, the same year as Winston Churchill, she must have been pretty outrageous for Victorian times, exposing herself from thigh to toe with splendid relish.

Already 65 at the start of the Second World War, she caught the last plane out of Paris before the Germans arrived. Back home in Aberdeen, she settled into a long retirement, broken with

119

lecture tours of America, where she was greeted with standing ovations.

After all, this was the woman once coupled with President Theodore Roosevelt in a public vote as one of the two best-known personalities in the United States.

Yet we knew so little about her at home. There she was, a ladylike figure with a veil, gliding down the main thoroughfare of Aberdeen with her sister, the remnants of a star in old age.

She kept up appearances in Union Street coffee houses, tipping much more than the price of the coffee. Yet word was that she far outlived and outspent her means.

People would whisper that that was the great Mary Garden though, in all truth, she was less familiar to the Scottish public than her distant cousin, my good friend Neville Garden, who presents *Good Morning Scotland*.

Mary ended her days in the psycho-geriatric setting of House of Daviot, near Aberdeen, and died in 1967. According to Frederic Mohr's drama, there were only 14 people at her funeral and nobody to claim the ashes.

Happily, I hear of Aberdeen schoolchildren planning to portray her life and there is word of some recognition at the Edinburgh Festival. It is not before time that we paid some fitting tribute to a quite remarkable lady. My thanks to Mr Mohr for reminding us.

THE SCOTS CONNECTION
OF EDVARD GRIEG

6TH JUNE 1989

IN the still of a late spring evening, the music of Edvard Grieg came filtering from the concert room of Hutchesons' Hall, right in the heart of Glasgow.

On the 175th anniversary of Norway's statehood, the audience I found, when I wandered into that historic building, was predominantly Scottish—and that was surely as appropriate as the evening itself was truly civilised.

For, without too much presumption, we can lay fair claim to some part of the man who became the national composer of Norway but whose origins were to be found near Fraserburgh, where his forefathers used to farm at Mosstown of Cairnbulg. It was from there, just three generations earlier, that Alexander Greig set out for a new life across the sea, having been engaged to work for the British Consul in Bergen, a Mr Wallace from Banff, who happened to be a friend of the Greig family.

In time, Alexander himself became the British Consul and was followed in the post by his son and grandson, by which time they had conformed to the continental way of spelling and changed the Greig to Grieg. Year after year, however, they continued to cross in a little boat to take Communion in the kirk back home. We might have been perfectly happy to let our emigrant family disappear into the folds of Scandinavian obscurity except that, in 1843, it happened to produce a musical genius.

Edvard Grieg became one of the great composers, friend of Ibsen, Liszt and Hans Christian Andersen, Dvořák, Delius, Paderewski and Tchaikovsky (What a coincidence of living talent!)

From his music for *Peer Gynt* to his Piano Concerto in A Minor, he sent the world a-spinning with his tumbling fjords of melodic delight, guaranteeing himself a niche of immortality in musical history.

My interest in Edvard Grieg was aroused at my grandmother's knee, when she told me about the day her own father set out from their schoolhouse home in Aberdeenshire to attend a recital by the great composer. She was unclear about where he was going but she thought it was to Edinburgh. For certain, he was going somewhere—and he went with the special family interest of being a Greig himself, from the same Rathen-Cairnbulg district near Fraserburgh.

Having long known of the distant cousinship, Gavin Greig nevertheless went to hear the recital and came home without having gone backstage to introduce himself. Can you imagine such reticence? Nowadays, there would have been a televised reunion, no doubt a personal appearance on *Wogan*—and certainly a Tuesday column in the *Glasgow Herald*.

There is, incidentally, a distinct lack of evidence about Grieg's presence in Scotland. So we are all the more indebted to a well-documented account of a visit by a Morayshire minister, the Rev. W. A. Gray, to a Norwegian hotel:

"Scarcely had I taken my place in the hotel porch after supper, for a smoke in the cool night air, when Grieg stood beside me alone and lit his cigar," he wrote. "His figure was even shorter and slighter than I first imagined it to be."

Introducing himself as a Scot from the North-east, he became engaged in an animated conversation with the composer who spoke, in fluent English, about Fraserburgh and his Scottish friends and connections, his godmother (a Mrs Stirling from Stirling), his fondness for Carlyle and his appreciation of Edinburgh's beauty.

"Edinburgh people are very kind," he said. "They have asked me repeatedly to visit them and to play and I would do so willingly if it were not for the sea. I am the very worst of sailors. Once, some years ago, I crossed from Bergen to Aberdeen. I shall never forget that night of horrors, never!"

So Edvard Grieg came to Scotland for sure. And here we were, on that evening in Glasgow, listening not only to his music but to his life-story, as revealed in his own essays and letters. That was put together, quite delightfully, by John and Margaret Hearne, who came down, rather appropriately, from Aberdeenshire as a last-minute replacement for Agnes Walker, who was to have provided her own programme on Grieg.

John Hearne, well-known member of the John Currie Singers, is a lecturer and composer, while his wife (formerly Margaret Jarvie from Glasgow) is a teacher of speech and drama, who directs the Children's Theatre in Aberdeen. Together they have toured with the SNO Chorus in America.

With the piano accompaniment of Robert Howie, a music lecturer in Aberdeen, they transported us to the world of Edvard Grieg, a man strongly influenced by the tradition of folk song.

As testimony to the power of heredity, isn't it strange that his distant cousin in Scotland, Gavin Greig, was himself a composer and brilliant organist, a poet, playwright and a folk-song expert whose collection is counted among the greatest in the world?

How much they would have had to talk about—if only my great-grandfather had plucked up the courage to go backstage at that piano recital!

ALASTAIR PEARSON—
MAN OF COURAGE

◆ 3 R D   J U L Y   1 9 8 9 ◆

BY yon bonnie banks of Loch Lomond, he wanders across his rolling acres with a sheepdog at heel, his gruff, asthmatic voice belying the kindly nature which radiates from a rare and rugged character.

Farmer Alastair Pearson has battled long with ill-health but then battles have been the speciality of this extraordinary figure who collected a Military Cross and no fewer than four DSOs in the Second World War, marking him out as one of the most decorated and heroic soldiers in the history of warfare.

From his job in a Glasgow bakehouse, Pearson became a legend of the Parachute Regiment, a battalion commander at 27 who led his men by example through the campaigns of North Africa and Normandy.

With a special talent for woodland fighting, he stood poised like a defiant stag, daring the Germans to invade his territory and gaining for himself a distinctive by-name—Monarch of the Woods.

Today, at Tullochan Farm, by Gartocharn, he is cajoled into recollection by an adoring grandson, 13-year-old Miles Stuart, who is so fascinated by the exploits that the pair have already been to visit the D-Day landing area—and to identify the exact spot where Grandpa's bum hit the ground!

Alastair Pearson has also been persuaded to relate his story to Julian James, a young officer of the present-day Paras.

The exercise started in 1983 when Pearson was seriously ill with a stomach complaint. James was advised that an obituary of the legendary Para should be prepared. But the old Red Devil recovered and what should have been a death-notice will

124

soon be out as a book, *A Fierce Quality*, to be read in his own lifetime.

And what a story it promises to be, all the more appropriate since it coincides with the 50th anniversary of the Parachute Regiment. The foreword has been written by the Prince of Wales no less, and never was the royal nod more richly deserved.

Life began in Wilton Street, Glasgow, during the First World War, but moved to Cleveden Drive, where Alastair Pearson grew up. His father was a grain merchant who did well on the Stock Exchange and was able to send the boy to Kelvinside Academy and then to Sedbergh School, Cumbria, in 1930.

But he left without academic qualification and returned to Glasgow in the midst of the Depression, gaining an apprenticeship in his uncle's bakery at Port Dundas.

The starting wage was 18 shillings a week (90p), rising to £3.17.6d, but it was possible to buy an old Ford car for £6 and to enjoy life as a member of the Territorials in Glasgow's own Highland Light Infantry.

Off to war in 1939, Alastair Pearson volunteered for special service and found himself in the 1st Parachute Battalion. In 1942 he arrived back in Glasgow, en route to the North African campaign.

In the very first battle, Colonel S. J. L. Hill was shot in the neck and lung and Pearson became the youngest C.O. in the British Army.

His men were inflicting such damage on the German troops, raiding outposts, ambushing convoys, blowing up supply dumps, that he was soon collecting his Military Cross. It was just the beginning.

In the midst of bloody warfare, however, there was always time for light relief. Pearson recalls his padre visiting Beja on Christmas Eve, joining a queue of soldiers for what seemed like some bargain shopping—and finding himself next in line at a house of ill fame!

At one stage the War Office thought the C.O. too young and a chap with the impossible name of Lt. Col. Gofton-Salmond turned up to replace him, saying: "Terribly sorry, old man. Nothing personal, you know. Fortunes of war and all that."

"This is my battalion and it is going to stay my battalion," growled Pearson.

The doctor came to the rescue by discovering that Gofton-Salmond had piles—and declared him unfit for service!

Pearson collected his first DSO after a bloody battle at the hill of Mansour. It is hard for lay people to understand that opposing forces were sometimes so close as to call to each other.

"Good morning, Tommy, what regiment are you?" the Germans would ask.

"Come a little closer, Hermann. We're just having a brew-up," the paratroopers would shout back, before slinging their remaining grenades at them.

"We would go in search of our wounded and so did the Germans," Alastair Pearson explained to me. "So there was quite a close personal contact in which we would swop wounded."

He himself developed an uncanny sense of when and where the Germans would strike next. He could do without sleep and live for days on a can of sardines. But the tough commander had great generosity of spirit.

A distraught soldier came up to him one day, laid down his rifle and said: "I'll have to pack it in, sir. I can't fight any more."

The soldier had to be put under arrest but action broke out and he was sent to help establish a first-aid post in a cave. A shell hit the cave and all were killed. When Pearson came to the arrested man's papers, he stamped them "Killed in action."

"We don't want to shame his people," he said. "He wasn't a coward. It took a brave man to come up to me and lay down his rifle."

No such consideration was given a sergeant-major who stole the rum ration. He was court-martialled and sent home in disgrace.

"I can understand an honest doubt of conscience," said Pearson. "But I cannot stomach a man who will use his position to take advantage of soldiers fighting in a war."

126

It was actually the Germans, recognising the ability of the paratroopers, who christened them the Red Devils.

Though the aim of war is to destroy the enemy, Pearson's Paras developed a sensitive awareness of life, to the point of venturing into no-man's-land to rescue any wounded man.

One of their own officers, brought back dying one day, reported that another man lay out there in distress. Sergeant Jock Rainnie from Aberdeen and another soldier went out to find him.

He turned out to be a young German. Pearson bent over him and said: "The war's over for you, my lad; we'll look after you."

The German smiled: "You are Scottish? I studied at Glasgow University. The Scots are wonderful people. I admire your poets. Do you know: My heart's in the Highlands; My heart is not here; My heart's in the Highlands, a-chasing the deer. . . ."

The Scots were silent. Tears streamed down the German's face. "I wish to thank you for saving my life," he said.

The big advance in North Africa began on March 27, 1943, the Allies bulldozing their way across hot plains, guns booming, tanks grinding and ruddy-faced men sweating over a front which stretched for 100 miles.

Pearson was essentially a night fighter: "I made only one attack in daylight—and I swore I would never do another one!" he tells you. "Once your troops gained confidence in fighting by night, you got on much better and had fewer casualties."

Pearson agrees he was a born survivor but thought his last moment had come in the valley of Tamera, when he was leading 300 men against 600 Germans.

"I found myself face to face with a German in a tree just a few yards away. We were in the process of being overrun and I thought I had had it," he now confesses.

The situation had been spotted from behind the lines by a certain Sergeant Clements, who gathered a motley collection of cooks and so on and came charging through with a war-cry to save the day. Pearson did not hesitate to recommend Clements for a Military Medal! He himself had added to the DSOs.

127

The crossing to Sicily threw up the bizarre situation of the American Navy managing to shoot down 32 of our own planes—and the British Navy coming close to emulating them.

Pearson was reading a book on the Dakota crossing, ready for the big jump, when he saw Mount Etna on the wrong side. The American pilot had mistaken burning haystacks for burning Dakotas and was turning back in fear.

The commander squeezed into the cockpit, where the co-pilot sat weeping.

"I'm not prepared to go in," said the pilot.

"And I," bellowed Pearson, "am not prepared to go back."

In the knowledge that he had a trained pilot among his Paras on board, he took out his revolver and threatened to shoot them. The pilot obeyed orders but went in on a dive, which meant that Pearson had to jump at a mere 200 feet.

"My batman jumped after me but the others who came after us were either injured or killed," he recalls. "My own knees have not been the same since."

Alastair Pearson had also suffered his first bout of malaria but was back home in time for the D-Day preparations.

He went to a cocktail party at Devizes and met Joan, a young war widow, to whom he proposed. She fixed their big day for June 8, 1944, and the dashing Scot was not allowed to tell her that he wouldn't be at his own wedding!

On the morning of June 6 the bride-to-be heard it from an old chap pumping water at the well. He had heard it on the wireless. The greatest invasion in all history had started. Early that morning, Pearson, now commander of the 8th Parachute Battalion, had dropped 10 miles behind German lines, with the task of blowing three bridges.

Joan managed to put out new invitations for a September wedding and this time there were no hitches.

By now Alastair Pearson was realising his war was over. The superhuman effort had caught up with him. Soon it was back to the bakehouse in central Glasgow, but asthmatic attacks made that an unsuitable career. He borrowed enough to buy the 240 acres of Tullochan Farm, on Loch Lomondside, for £12,000, and there he farms to this day.

The couple's only daughter, now Fiona Stuart, became Scotland's finest horsewoman, the first to be nominated for the Olympics, though her horse had to withdraw. She is married to Ian Stuart, a deputy chief executive of Strathclyde Region.

Despite his own ill-health, Alastair Pearson continues to look after the men who suffered in war, as vice-chairman of Erskine Hospital. He attends reunions every year and, at the age of 74, undertakes the arduous duties of Lord Lieutenant of Dunbartonshire as well.

Gazing out from his big, white farmhouse, he expresses no romantic notions about war.

"It was a job to be done," he says simply. "If you didn't kill them, they would kill you. You were fighting for survival. I met only one chap who was fighting for honour."

Of his own part in it, he will say only: "It gave me confidence. But I maintain that wars are won by private soldiers."

Those private soldiers will pay the highest possible compliment to the leadership qualities of Brigadier Alastair Pearson by telling you that they would gladly have followed this extraordinary man to the very ends of the earth.

A WARTIME DIARY—
THE FINAL DAYS

A WEEKEND of wartime memories was all the more poignant since the current calendar coincides with that of 1939. Then and now, September 3 was a Sunday, the day we gathered round the wireless and heard Chamberlain announce our fate.

On the Saturday, I stood at our village station with mixed emotions—excitement over the fresh faces of Glasgow evacuees, sadness over village lads departing for destinations unknown.

Each would gather a story of individual experience, perhaps to be told one day, perhaps to perish on some foreign field.

I have chanced upon the wartime diary of just another Scottish soldier, whose scribblings may give a new generation some hint of what was endured by so-called ordinary men and women.

Gordon Munro from Troon was off to war in the 51st Highland Division, soon to be captured at St Valery and transported to prison in Poland.

There he worked on a farm for five years until the Russians came close from the east. Now it was time for the German guards to set their wretched prisoners on a 1,000-kilometre march towards Germany in the dead of winter.

Despite hunger, exhaustion and frostbite, Gordon Munro struggled to record the forced march. Let us just linger with snatches from the frozen hand of a courageous Scot as he pencilled secretly into a pathetic little notebook.

His journey began on Burns Day, 1945:

The Russians very close. We could see German tanks firing. Started marching on roads thick with refugees and snow. Spent the most miserable night of our lives.

130

Nothing to eat or drink; temperatures down to 25 below. Practically everyone suffered from frostbite. Saw a chap with one side of his face frozen—and he was unaware of it.

Terrible amount of dead horses lying at roadside. This is a procession of cripples but we see worse than ourselves. The Russian PoWs in a bad way. Should one be unable to keep up with the column he is shot and left lying.

Things going from bad to worse—but the war news is good. German civilians admit the end is not far off and they will be pleased. The Big Chief means nothing to them now.

We are all in a weak condition and with lice to feed besides. Though we march miles with no conversation, when we pass through a town, it starts up and jokes are cracked. It takes an effort but shows the spirit is not dead.

Many refugees have lost touch with their wives and children. As they go along, they stick notes on trees. I've seen a complete trunk covered with notes. Signposts are also used. They sign their names on the finger-posts which they are following.

Guards refused us a drink of water. What a reception they got! Should this lot be with us when the war finishes, I guarantee one or two won't live five minutes. . . .

I arrived here bad-tempered. Shortly after, the church bells started ringing. It's Palm Sunday and they have composed me. There must be a bit of belief in me yet.

Now 50 kilometres north of Hanover . . . the Germans are in an awful muddle. . . . I think April is now the month. The guards broke into a store and got well oiled. Under the influence, they became sentimental and were saying before long we would be the guards and them the prisoners and not to be too hard on them. That depends!

Yanks are getting pretty close. Last night I had the opportunity and have taken a walk. . . .

That "walk" meant escape for Gordon Munro and some friends. They hid in a wood, cold and miserable but helped with food by some Poles. Then the great moment arrived:

The Poles came rushing madly down, shouting that the Yanks were there. They started us on a mad gallop too. The Yanks must have

131

thought we were mad. We were laughing, shouting and clapping each other on the back. The Yanks received us well. Then to bed but not to sleep. Too excited.

First full day of freedom after five years. What a breakfast! After 5¹/₂ years we are going home. No seats on the plane. We just sit on the floor. Most of the lads have never flown and are a bit apprehensive. Landed at Amersham, to be greeted by the WRI.

At Euston, I caught the Glasgow train which was crowded and stood all the way. But great to be back in Scotland for the first time since October 1939.

Gordon Munro came home to marry his girlfriend, Margaret Bulloch from Larbert. They had two children and he became a sales manager with Appleyard in Ayrshire.

Margaret died and Gordon later married Myrtle Shields from Netherlee, Glasgow. They took over the Dunvegan House Hotel in Banff and then the Croft Inn at Glenlivet.

They retired to Garvald in East Lothian in 1983. Gordon died of a heart attack last year, aged 71, and Myrtle lives with her memories—and his.

No medals. Just another story . . . well, maybe. But doesn't it tell us something about the courage, endurance and heroic nature of the human spirit?

WHY ALY BAIN WAS PLAYING
THAT NIGHT

∗ 3 1 S T   O C T O B E R   1 9 8 9 ∗

SAUNTERING past the home of Robert Louis Stevenson in
Edinburgh's New Town last week, I was reminded that our
famous writer once said he did not expect the dialects of Scotland
to survive his own lifetime. It was one of his less accurate forecasts.

Certainly the poor man died when only 44 but, even if he had
lived a normal span, he would still have been well out.

If proof of that fact had been needed, I found it just a few
nights earlier at a most extraordinary night of celebration, hon-
ouring the work of Gavin Greig, Scottish poet, playwright and
novelist, whose main task in life was to rescue and preserve a
vanishing tradition of Scots folk song.

Gavin Greig, distant cousin of Edvard Grieg, had been writing
operettas, like *Prince Charlie*, which were much in vogue in the
latter part of the nineteenth century.

But in the year of Stevenson's death, which was 1894, he
fostered a tradition of Scots drama which grew straight out of the
lives of local communities—a kind of kitchen-sink drama of its
day but mostly to do with the rich humour of the rural areas.

With characters written around the local scene, it meant that
amateurs could more or less play themselves, whether they were
the shepherd, the gamekeeper or the prosperous farmer, Mains,
who had his eye on a future wife.

That first play of 1894 was *Mains's Wooin'*, to be followed by
Mains Again, and it was from the sequel that a local drama group
performed a hilarious excerpt in the village hall at New Deer the
other night.

It was pure, undiluted Aberdeenshire dialect, from the fairm-touns and bothies of 100 years ago. And if we needed confirmation that there were still people who spoke and understood their native tongue, this was surely it.

The reaction of a packed audience revealed complete familiarity with the words and instant recognition of the sentiments. Robert Louis Stevenson should have been there.

Ill-fitted for the task, Mains was in the travails of composing a love letter, aided by his younger servant, Peter, who was more acquainted with the wily ways which lead to a woman's heart. Human nature changes very little.

Appropriately, that concert took place in the same village hall where Gavin Greig held his premieres in the 1890s. For in that parish he conducted a centre of learning which spread his reputation far and wide. Scholars would journey from as far as Edinburgh to enjoy his conversation and company.

Drama was just one side of his well-rounded life. As well as being writer, composer and brilliant organist, he collaborated with his close friend, J. Scott Skinner, the king of strathspey, and arranged much of his music. Scott Skinner would come to the house with his fiddle and play on the front lawn while Greig's children beat time with sticks on pans!

I heard it from my grandmother, who was the eldest of Greig's nine children. They didn't understand the genius of the man they were accompanying.

But Scott Skinner was creating another musical tradition, which found its place in that memorable evening at New Deer. And, if we believe that that style has also vanished from our midst then we are making the same mistake as Stevenson made about the dialects.

For there, before our very eyes, was surely one of the greatest traditional fiddlers of this or any other day, the inimitable Aly Bain from Shetland, wielding that instrument as if it might have been an appendage to his chin from birth.

By coincidence, Aly Bain's early projection to public attention was largely due to a BBC producer, the late Arthur Argo who, like myself, happened to be a great-grandson of Gavin Greig.

134

Bain is now an international star, performing far beyond village halls, but it was as a tribute to Arthur Argo, who died tragically young, that he travelled north to give the musical treat of a lifetime to country folk who came in from farm and croft, as they might have done a century ago. Arthur's parents were there to appreciate the gesture.

But Aly Bain was not alone in carrying on a fine tradition of Scots fiddle playing. There was the splendid bowing of Bill Brian from Elgin and a host of youngsters whose generation might seem to have forsaken their heritage. But it is not so.

Remembering, from my own childhood, that great accordionist, Jean Stewart from Fetterangus, it was a special delight to hear her daughter, Elizabeth, intoning the tradition of the travelling folk, along with that other fine performer, Joe Aitken from Kirriemuir.

There was a joy and a warmth about that evening which showed that, for all the superficial changes, there is a basic Scottishness about us which endures. At the end of the night, we stood and sang one of Gavin Greig's musical finales, conjuring up those "red skies far ayont Benachie".

In his own time, we would then have filed out to pony-and-trap. Instead, we boarded motor-cars and roared off into the night. But the spirit of his "Hame and Guid-nicht" was much the same.

CLASSROOM HOWLERS

• 7TH NOVEMBER 1989 •

ONE of the joys of making last week's television film, *Northern Lights*, was the chance to meet up again with two schoolteachers from pre-war days. At my age, you don't expect to have your infant mistress still around to keep an eye on you.

But I have Miss Catto, a welcome survivor in her 90th year, who was not only there to receive me on that first school day of April, 1936, but was teaching in the same classroom 10 years earlier, during the General Strike.

Along with her younger colleague, Miss Morrison, who took me into the war years, she represents continuity and stability and a sense of cushioning against the limits of this earthly trip.

And when the cameras had stopped their whirring, the three of us were lost in reminiscence, Miss Catto remembering that I had stated an early ambition to be "jist like Robbie Burns". Retelling it in the staffroom, she had expressed the hope that I would not become too much like the Bard!

We all remembered a droll arrival in the infant class, fresh from the farm, who sat studying a ventilation grille in the ceiling, not unlike what he had seen in the barn. Then in serious adult tones he inquired: "Are ye ill wi' rottens?" (Are you bothered with rats?)

Most teachers have a repertoire of school howlers and I was no sooner back at my desk than I found such a collection, gathered together in book form by John G. Muir, who is primary schools adviser in Caithness and Sutherland.

In fact Mr Muir has struck such a rich seam that he has been encouraged to produce *Even More Classroom Clangers*, as a follow-up to two earlier volumes which have totalled sales of 75,000.

136

Not all classroom humour transfers to cold print with success but Mr Muir manages a good percentage. He tells, for example, of the infant teacher who kept spare clothes for "accidents". Discreetly, she changed a little girl who had wet herself and sent the soiled pants home in a carrier bag.

Next day, travelling on the bus with her father, the little girl noticed her teacher in a seat in front. In a loud voice, she announced: "Mrs MacFarlane, my daddy's got yer knickers in his pocket!"

Ann, a hard nut of the upper secondary, arrived in class having obviously been involved in a fight. When the teacher inquired, Ann admitted that she had started it and was finally persuaded to say why.

In a broad accent, she explained: "She called me a bad name, sur. I cannae tell ye whit it wis, but it starts wi' an H."

Parental response is always good for a laugh, as witness this one: "My husband and I feel that William should drop history as we both feel there is no future in it."

"When Lorna came home she had bad pains in her stomach so we kept her at home to see what would come out of it."

Or how about this for the ambiguous? "Susan did not come back to school after lunch because her dad turned into a big tree on his way home from work."

That kind of humour is grist to the mill of George Glass, a head teacher from Inverness, who has illustrated John Muir's book to full effect.

Another parent wrote: "Robert came home today and told us that a teacher had said he was illiterate. I have to tell you that this is not the case as we were married five years before we had him and have his birth certificate to prove it."

Writing wrongs can range from "A gargoyle is a liquid used for a throatwash" and "When you sneeze you should use atishoo paper" to "The subject I lick best is speling."

One child wrote that "People who are immortal can have the time of their lives" while another thought that Robert Redford was the Archbishop of Canterbury!

One bright spark thought Galileo was "the first man to make the earth go round the sun" and another thought Samuel Pepys kept a dairy.

Teachers themselves have contributed to the more conscious humour, like the one who gave this report: "Writes imaginatively—particularly good at absence notes." And the one who wrote: "Very consistent work—has failed every exam so far."

That took me back to my own two teachers—and another of those stories from a droll Buchan loon who insisted that his dog was called Moreover, a possibility which was seriously questioned by the teacher.

But he was adamant and could produce good reasons for the choice: "Ay Miss, it says it in the Bible. 'Moreover the dog came and licked his sores.'"

So there was humour and innocence in those far-off schooldays. And, judging by your warm and spontaneous response to those Northern Lights, they stirred a few memories which helped to lighten a dull day.

TO AUSTRALIA
IN NINETY MINUTES?

I REMEMBER one springtime, many moons ago, driving up a leafy lane by the village of Effingham in Surrey and turning in towards a charming cottage where I was to meet one of the great inventors of this century.

Barnes Wallis is best remembered for inventions like the *R100* airship (the one that *didn't* crash), wartime bombers like the Wellington and later the swing-wing aeroplane—and, of course, the bouncing bomb that finally burst the dams of the Ruhr.

Having seen Michael Redgrave's portrayal of Wallis in *The Dambusters*, it was all the more interesting to meet the man himself, a white-haired gent by now in retirement but still a restless spirit unable to shake off the inventive bug—and suffering badly from migraine.

We repaired to his attic, which turned out to be a shrine of aviation history, so much of it created by himself, and there he talked freely of his remarkable life story.

He was less forthcoming, however, when my attention wandered to his drawing-board. What was he up to now? The gleam in his eye was a clear indication of excitement, but the project was so much under wraps that he politely deflected my curiosity.

It was much later that I learned the truth. Barnes Wallis had, in fact, been dreaming up the next stage in aviation, designed to carry passengers from Britain to Australia in something like 90 minutes.

Roughly speaking, his invention was a cross between Concorde and a moon rocket, which would shoot out through the stratosphere and let the spinning world bring Australia nearer before

139

turning back into the atmosphere like a rocket returning from its mission.

Barnes Wallis died, and I heard no more of his ingenious plans. Was it to be Sydney in time for lunch—or just pie in the sky?

I was discussing the matter this week with one of the world's best-known pilots, Thomas Block of US Air, who assured me the technology to make Wallis's dream a reality was all in place, ready to be implemented whenever we wanted it.

The point is: do we want it? Can we afford it?

Speed comes at a price, and Captain Block was already raising doubts about the advantage of saving two or three hours on the Concorde flight across the Atlantic.

"Isn't it perhaps time we started putting more emphasis on the quality of our experiences?" he asked. "I flew from London to Glasgow this morning on a Boeing 757 along with 220 other people. There wasn't even room to open your newspaper."

It is an interesting thought that while in Barnes Wallis's day the main aim was to get there as quickly as possible, we may now have moved on to another phase in public attitudes.

Thomas Block's journey to Glasgow was in the unaccustomed role of back-seat driver. As one of the senior men among US Air's 6,400 pilots, he is more commonly to be found at the controls on a flight to San Francisco.

A pilot's life, he reminds you, has been described as "years and years of boredom, punctuated by moments of sheer terror."

It was during those years of boredom that he developed another talent, one that would turn him into a high-flying novelist.

"When you are on a long flight and you're into the second hour, you have drunk all the coffee you want to drink and said all you want to say to your co-pilot," he explains. "That's when you have a chance to think about things."

What Tom Block thinks about is his next plot: and much of it has to do with dramas of the air. The result has been a chain of bestsellers, like *Mayday, Orbit, Forced Landing, Skyfall,* and now *Open Skies.* What's more they are extremely popular in airports with people about to fasten their belts.

140

"I suppose I have a captive audience," he laughs. "When you think of the size of the machine and the speed it travels, it is quite natural to be afraid of flying. I think people actually like to be frightened.

"But there are two ways of overcoming that fear of flying. You either have faith and accept it or you understand the technology. Flying has become so commonplace that there is now a generation of people who accept aeroplanes like they do running water."

The pilot likes to feel that he controls the destiny of his passengers, and is prepared for the vagaries of weather or technical fault. What frightens the pilot as much as the public is the new dimension of international terrorism.

By and large, however, flying is much safer than ever. Captain Block can even joke about the pilot who gave his customary calm, reassuring message for passengers before switching to the other microphone, which connected him to the control tower.

"We're in big trouble," he called. "This thing is falling out of the sky!" But his trouble was bigger than he imagined. In selecting his two microphone switches, he had managed to transpose them.

WHAT THE CENSOR SAID ABOUT THE LION

∗4TH SEPTEMBER 1990∗

IN this age of artistic freedom, when anything goes, it must come as a surprise to a younger generation to know that until the end of the Swinging Sixties, every stage play to be performed in Britain had to be vetted by the head of the royal household.

The man with an absolute power of censorship, the Lord Chamberlain, had to apply his own standards of judgment as to what was permissible. While there were no set rules from that Act of 1843, he usually followed a number of parliamentary guidelines which said, for example, that you could not portray on stage any member of the royal family, homosexuality or the Lord above.

In protecting us from bad language and evil influence, he was always liable, of course, to run himself into ridiculous situations. That popular actor, Timothy West, used to tell the story of playwright Robert Bolt, when he wrote *Gentle Jack* for the Queen's Theatre in London. Apparently Bolt went along to the Lord Chamberlain's office to ask why they had taken exception to his passage about a lion "shitting himself with fear". He pointed out that the excretory term had been permitted elsewhere.

It was explained to him that, while that might be all right for other animals, indeed for human beings, it was not all right for the symbol of British supremacy!

The most popular of all four-letter words was invariably cut from play scripts. In seeking a way round the ban, playwright David Rudkin invented the word "firk" for *Afore Night Come*.

But, as Timothy West again pointed out, in a Worcestershire accent the sounds were completely indistinguishable. Honour was nevertheless satisfied.

142

Bernard Shaw was the first to agitate vehemently for the removal of censorship but it took 50 years for it to happen. It came with the mood of permissiveness which governed the 1960s, when persuasive voices, such as John Osborne and Kenneth Tynan, were difficult to counter.

Tynan, as I recall it, was the man who favoured removing all restrictions to the point of allowing intercourse on stage. Of course that indicated a certain naïvety. After all, what actor could really have guaranteed an orgasm at 9.42 on six nights a week and at 4.12 for Saturday matinees?

The point was taken, however, and from the time he became Lord Chamberlain in 1963, Lord Cobbold was making it clear that he thought it wrong for the head of the Queen's household to be carrying out this Act of Parliament. Censorship on stage was abolished in 1968.

It was all the more interesting, therefore, to meet Sir John Johnston, former Comptroller in the Lord Chamberlain's office, who became caught up in those final years of vetting.

Sir John had been a career soldier, a battalion commander in the Grenadier Guards, with vast experience of ceremonial and the ideal chap to plan parades. But helping with the censor's function was something he hadn't bargained for.

Much as he enjoyed the theatrical contact, which he maintains to this day, he was fully behind his boss in pressing for a change in the law. In light of subsequent experience, does he have any regrets?

"None at all," he assured me. "The theatre has found its own level and managements know what the public wants and is prepared to put up with. Curiously, the people who were against censorship being dropped were mainly theatre managers, who felt they were losing the protection of the Lord Chamberlain."

Sir John has put the whole matter into perspective in a new book, *The Lord Chamberlain's Blue Pencil*, in which he reveals the relationship between the watchdog and the theatre.

Not unexpectedly, much of the earlier vigilance centred on that famous temple of nudity, the Windmill Theatre, in the heart of

Soho, which, even at the height of the London blitz, prided itself in the slogan "We never closed!" (sometimes changed to "We never clothed!").

Manager Vivian Van Damm, who stuck rigidly to the rule of static nudes at the Windmill, must have struggled hard to stifle a smile when the man who turned up from the Lord Chamberlain's office to check out the performance introduced himself as Mr Titman!

If the Windmill defied all Hitler's bombardment of central London, it faced a much stiffer opponent in the strip clubs which sprouted in the 1960s. Ironically, with clubs outwith the censorship law, it had become too respectable for the permissive taste and the doors which "never closed" finally did—in 1964.

It was typical of the Van Damms' courtesy that they invited the Lord Chamberlain's staff to the farewell shows. Sir John occupied a box!

Now retired from that second career, he is a director of the Theatre Royal at Windsor, where he lives, and still works for the lady at the castle nearby. She and her family regularly attend their local theatre, happily acknowledging a democratic age in which the public can best act as its own censor.

FLORA GARRY—
TRUE VOICE OF DIALECT

•9TH OCTOBER 1990•

TO speak again to Flora Garry is one of the pleasures of life. To read again her poetry is to catch the full flavour of rural Scotland in generations gone by, to see the great skies of her native Buchan as they stretch towards the Mither Tap o' Benachie.

For hers is a true tongue of Scots dialect, born of everyday usage, unlike so much which seems to have been written in English and translated, line by line, by some academic with more brain than soul of understanding.

I speak to Flora Garry whenever I can, which is not often enough, for the nimbleness of her mind and clarity of her voice are a tonic. The twinkle in her eye suggests the secret of youth yet, when I called last week, it was her 90th birthday.

In the Perthshire village of Comrie she was enjoying a quiet celebration with her husband, Robert C. Garry, wandering back to a heritage shared in uncommon fashion by dint of the fact that they are cousins.

She was once Flora Campbell, the local beauty so envied by girls like my own mother, who recalled her like some goddess.

Flora Garry came late to published poetry, though she had been writing it all along. With sparse beauty, "The Professor's Wife" tells of the country lass who becomes a student at King's College, Aberdeen, while her parents struggle "in a craft at Glenardle".

> They vrocht fae daylicht to dark.
> Fine div I min' on ma midder,
> Up ower the queets amo' dubs,
> Furth in the weestiest widder.

145

> Swypin the greep in the byre,
> Forkin the crap on the lan',
> Treetlin wi water an' aess an' peats,
> Aye a pail in her han'.

So she takes a daaner roun' by a street of professors' muckle hooses and glowers in at curtainless windows where the wife, in a low-neckit goon, is presiding at the table, all candlelight and flowers.

> "Fine," says I to masel,
> "Fine to be up in the wardle."
> An' thocht wi a groo, on the brookie pots
> In the kitchen at Glenardle.

The student ends up as a professor's wife herself, far from her folk in the kirkyard at Glenardle—which is exactly what happened to Flora.

She married Robert Garry, who gained his own fame as a young house doctor at Glasgow Western in the 1920s. Having read about insulin, discovered across the Atlantic, he managed to acquire his own sample and was itching to use it one night when a diabetic was seriously ill.

Phoning his superior at home, he was given clearance. The man lived. Young Garry had thus used insulin in this country for the very first time and was destined to become a distinguished professor at Glasgow University.

His wife hid her own light for too long. But it surfaced in time and, thankfully, she has been spared to gain her place among significant Scottish poets.

She tells a story of her brother, Frank, which I had heard as part of local legend.

A handsome lad, great athlete and fine singer, Frank so tired of the drudgery of the land that he went off to join the Shanghai Police, like many a young Scot of his generation.

Pursuing robbers one day, he tracked them to a house and went

146

in for the confrontation. From under a bed, one robber pulled a gun and shot at Frank. As he fell, he managed to draw his own gun and shoot the robber dead. But he himself died in the ambulance.

Flora Garry remembers that nightmare of 1927, with the news coming in a wireless bulletin when she was at Fairlie in Ayrshire.

"Back home in Buchan," she recalls, "my father and mother were on their way to give a concert at Catterline, south of Aberdeen. They were given the news on arrival.

"But they went ahead with the concert and it was not until the end that my father stepped forward and told the audience what had happened. With his fine baritone voice, Frank had been a member of that concert party which my parents took round the halls."

Sadness clouds the face but not the spirit of Flora Garry, who is soon reviving memories of places like her own poetic Bennygoak:

> It was jist a skelp o' the muckle furth,
> A sklyter o' roch grun
> Fin grandfadder's fadder bruke it in
> Fae the hedder an the funn. . . ."

She came with the century and contemplates the closing decade, the face of wisdom, with its memories of the farm-close and the kye and the cornyard and the strutting cockerel, the moss and the midden, the dry lavvy and the docken leaves; the quiet sing of a summer's day and the wild howl of a dark winter's night. She is the fair complexion of our century.

147

THE SURPRISE I FACED
IN DUBROVNIK

30TH OCTOBER 1990

FOR several reasons, my arrival in Dubrovnik last week was indeed a strange experience; but most of all, I suppose, because it served as a yardstick of this earthly journey.

Could it really have been 37 years since last I touched down in this idyllic corner of southern Europe? What had been happening since that year of the Queen's Coronation when I set out from Paris, on the Orient Express, to seek a first experience of communism at work?

President Tito had kept Yugoslavia independent of the Soviet bloc, and this would be a suitable starting point. Having left the train at Belgrade, I caught an old prop-engined Pionair to Dubrovnik, which is now a leading holiday resort.

In 1953 it didn't even have an airport. We bumped down on a farmer's field, scattering horses and cattle, which knew roughly when to expect the daily flight.

From there I had toured the old walled city before my eye caught the green dome of a handsome residence, with its terraced gardens sloping down to the Adriatic. It bore the romantic name of Villa Sheherazade, clearly a leftover from pre-war capitalism and now, they said, a showpiece where Tito housed his special guests.

The news that Field Marshal Montgomery was currently in residence sparked off a careful negotiation that landed me an interview with our famous soldier. On a balmy evening the iron gates swung open and armed guards marched me down through those perfumed gardens, festooned with fairy-lights, to the terrace in front of the villa where the small, familiar figure of Monty rose in welcome.

148

Having despatched a dark-suited gent to fetch a mild refreshment, he then invited him to put down his silver tray—and introduced him as M. Popovic, the Yugoslav Foreign Secretary! Only Monty could have got away with that.

The conversation ranged widely, even to the casual comments of Winston Churchill when the two men had met at Chequers the previous weekend. ("Winston was telling me what he was backing in the St Leger.")

It all came back in the most surprising manner last week, after the Boeing had touched down on the tarmac of Dubrovnik Airport and screamed its own comparison with the old propeller plane that took me down on that field so long ago.

Dubrovnik has changed, of course, and I had scarcely found my bearings the next morning as I wandered through the hotel gardens, which sloped towards the Adriatic.

Casually I followed a path through an archway that led to the adjacent property, and suddenly I was standing transfixed. Coincidence has dealt me many a hand, but none to silence me more effectively than the sight before me now.

For there, in all its faded glory, stood my Villa Sheherazade, green-domed and aloof and remembering better times. Slowly and nostalgically I began to retrace my steps of 37 years ago, from that iron gate, now chained and without a sentry, down the magnificent slopes where trees and flowers once grew in profusion, all floodlights and fairy-lights and cherub fountains spouting into the night sky.

Now there was nothing but dereliction, gardens overgrown within an eerie silence. What a piece of irony that folk with memories would be casting back to more glittering days of communism before Sheherazade was overtaken by the bleakness of capitalism!

The terrace was still there, looking smaller than it had done in 1953 when Montgomery welcomed me to his table. I stood on the very spot, looking out to the blue of the Adriatic and remembering that I had been in my early twenties then; it could have been yesterday.

Whoever had stolen the time? Consciously I named each one of those 37 years and asked myself for proof that I had lived it. Alas, the proof was there in all its detail.

In 1953 we had never heard of Elvis Presley or Bill Haley. Churchill was Prime Minister and Monty's old boss, General Eisenhower, was President of the United States.

The Suez Crisis was yet to come and the assassination of John F. Kennedy lay 10 years into the future. I had never seen America or Russia or the Far East; the crystal ball had told me little of my career and nothing of my marital future.

Yes, there was accounting for every one of the 37 years. And here I stood alone, in front of a mansion that once had been the occasional residence of Mr Zindin, a Lithuanian arms dealer doing brisk business between the wars. (He housed his mistress along the road.)

Then it was Tito's and now, in the communist reversal, it belongs to the Hotel Argentina next door, with plans to turn it into a casino. Away to the right the old town of Dubrovnik stood unmoved, for centuries past and no doubt for centuries to come.

The Adriatic warbled below and the scents as ever came wafting through the air. The living creatures are what change on this mystifying tapestry. I just stood there on the terrace of Sheherazade, eyes closed against the gentle breeze, and felt grateful that life had been so generous.

THE WONDERFUL VISION OF WILLIAM QUARRIER

• 3 0 T H   A P R I L   1 9 9 1 •

EMOTIONS were in a state of turmoil that June day of 1946 when I walked through the vaulted gateway and bade a premature farewell to my schooldays. I was not yet 15.

Primary years in our local village had so entranced me that the thought of a day's absence could induce tears. But now, at the more impersonal city institution, it had all gone sour and I was leaving with the sound of failure drumming in my ears.

The gloom of the hour was made worse by leaving good friends, not least Wee Joe Mortimer, who had made a particular impression. Joe was a special, caring kind of boy and, as I shook his hand and began that lonely walk into the wider world, I wondered what would become of us.

How would we fare in that bleak period after the war? I knew what I wanted to do, but newspaper jobs for beginners were non-existent in the returning rush of ex-Servicemen. What would Joe be doing for a living?

I lost all track of him and heard only latterly of his movements. But last week I shook his hand again. Over lunch, we filled in the missing years and remembered that, whereas we had been looking outwards to the great unknown on that last encounter, the course had now been covered, the mysteries revealed.

The reason I had caught up with Joe was that he was on the point of retiring, albeit a little early.

As we went our various ways from school, Joe had become a bank clerk in Aberdeen before discovering a route which would lead to something more than a job.

Remembering the nature of the lad, there is nothing pompous

151

in calling it a vocation. For, as we reminisced, we were wandering through the magnificent setting of Quarrier's Village at Bridge of Weir, with its handsome villas, broad avenues, and gracious contours.

As a haven for the orphaned and abandoned, Quarrier's became the biggest children's home in Europe—it housed 1,600 during the Second World War—and was a lesser-known name than Barnardo's only because it didn't follow the more sophisticated techniques of fund-raising.

How little we sometimes know of great works performed on our own doorstep. And they are wrought by people like my pal Joe, who became deputy general director of this remarkable organisation and now bows out after 26 years of dedicated service.

In that time, he has sought to further the ideals of that great Victorian, William Quarrier, a poor lad from Greenock whose mother was left to bring up her family in straitened circumstances.

William helped to ease the plight by becoming an apprentice shoemaker at the age of eight. As a determined young man, he built up a chain of boot and shoe shops in Glasgow but remained appalled by the poverty around him.

With religious zeal, he set about organising jobs and shelter for the young and worked towards his aim of a proper home. A man ahead of his time, Quarrier determined this would not be a huge institution but a place of individual houses, each with a "father" and "mother" to engender the sense of a family home.

He found his land at Bridge of Weir and Dr Barnardo was among those who attended his opening ceremony in 1878. Before his own death in 1903, at the age of 74, Quarrier had pioneered sanatoriums for the tubercular and epileptic.

In the years between, more than 50,000 children found care and love at Quarrier's. But with changing concepts of child care, it seemed that it had outlived its purpose.

In recent years, however, the leadership of Dr James Minto, the general director, who is also retiring, has taken it into a new phase in which spare capacity from falling numbers has been taken up by the elderly and the handicapped.

Some of those magnificent villas are now private residences and land sold for development has boosted revenue.

Whereas the children used to leave Quarrier's at the end of their schooldays, Joe Mortimer made his own mark in matters like starting a hostel where they could remain for the early part of their working lives. He established a system of Foster Friends and a Former Boys' and Girls' Association.

They still come back to see the old place, some distinguished professional people from places like Canada, where many a Quarrier's child would land. The former pupils include the Queen's parish minister in Edinburgh.

Joe Mortimer measures success in those who simply found a steady job and established a family of their own.

In this idyllic setting of more than 40 villas, we walked through avenues with names like Faith, Hope, and Love and up to the magnificent church on the brae, where the Rev. Robert Montgomery ministers to his varied flock.

Inside, the inscription emblazoned for all to see is the appropriate "Suffer little children to come unto me."

It is hard to accept that a lifetime of work has been completed since Joe Mortimer and I shook hands in 1946. But I should have guessed he would spend it in a place like this.

THE SKUNKS WHO CAN STEAL
FROM THE SICK

•18TH JUNE 1991•

WHEN the retiring Chief Constable of Strathclyde has so recently reported on a rising number of housebreakings and a drop in detection-rate, I suppose we are permitted a wry smile to read that the poor man himself has just become the victim of . . . yes, the housebreaker.

When, on the same day, we read that the reigning Open champion of golf, Nick Faldo, can be sitting downstairs in his Surrey home while burglars are at work in the bedroom above, public sympathy is limited by the fact that there are people who can leave £60,000 worth of jewellery lying about the house.

Still on the same day, however, there was another little incident which didn't have the newsworthiness of a chief constable or a famous golfer and therefore didn't reach your breakfast table. But it disturbs me a great deal more.

It took place in a charity shop in Pollokshaws Road, Glasgow, where a wonderful band of ladies give of their time to raise funds for the Prince and Princess of Wales Hospice at Carlton Place, in the city centre.

The hospice needs a lot of money to look after those terminal patients who suffer such fates as cancer and motor neurone disease.

I have seen at first hand what they do for people with a limited lifespan, caring for in-patients in as many beds as they can afford and providing a day-care service for dozens more who turn up for treatment, a bite of lunch and the kind of social contact which adds meaning to whatever life is left.

From the Carlton Place base, those splendid MacMillan nurses go forth to lend support to patients and their families in a manner which goes far beyond the call of duty.

From within those homes comes many a willing worker who wants to express the family gratitude by volunteering her services to the charity shop in Pollokshaws Road.

More than 50 such ladies take it in turn to cover the full week, sorting out donations of clothes and bric-a-brac and selling them to the general public. There are customers who drop in to view the goods, pick up some splendid bargains and stay for a cup of coffee, getting to know the volunteers and feeling the better for their contribution to a worthy cause.

The result is an atmosphere of happiness and goodwill. That is, until the scum of our society get to work. Which brings us back to that morning when the chief constable and golfing champion were counting their losses.

When Edyth Ives turned up to open the charity shop that day, she faced a spectacle which seriously tested her faith in human nature. Her heart sank as she realised that the raiders had been in the night to ransack the place.

And this was no isolated case. In fact it was the fourth time in recent weeks that burglars had forced their way in by bending bars or smashing their jemmies into the door.

The goods in the shop would be of little interest to their pursuit of ready cash and, with a minimal amount of money to be found, you wouldn't have thought it worth their while to come back.

But they had come again and again, smashing collection boxes, stealing the microwave oven and even going away with the kettle from which the ladies make their tea.

Doesn't it make you wonder how low a skunk can stoop? Having cased their joint, they must by then have gathered that they were not entering some prosperous commercial business where they might hope for rich pickings.

This was a life-support for the very sick, the kind of charity which would be freely given to their own wives or mothers or daughters if the need arose. If they have the brains to think, I don't suppose they have the heart to care.

155

What always astounds me about burglary is that, for all the inevitable noise and movement, no-one ever seems to hear or see a thing.

Edyth Ives, herself a young widow from the cancer scourge, could have sat down and wept. From the opening day, she had worked hard for that shop, stirring an interest among business people to donate goods for sale, much of it as good as new.

She could console herself in the generosity of the public who never failed to keep them supplied with items. And weeping would serve no purpose.

Instead, she buckled down to clearing up the mess and trying to find a joiner to secure the premises. None was available. The police were as helpful as possible but they were coping with a bank raid next door, in which shots had been fired that same morning.

Finally, she explained to some joiners working across the street. Their boss released his men to help out in the emergency and refused any reward. Money offered to give the lads a pint was returned to the charity box.

So Edyth Ives began to feel better about the world. Whatever kind of creatures were crawling in the gutters of the night, there was hope for mankind after all.

ALONE BY THE GRAVE OF
GRASSIC GIBBON

INLAND from the sea which raged 'neath Bervie braes, tall trees bowed like ballerinas to the wind and rain that roared and plashed their way through the howe of Arbuthnott in that North-east land of the Mearns.

Face numbed by the on-ding, I was at the grave of my literary hero, Lewis Grassic Gibbon, with thoughts stretching back for more than a generation, to the last time I had stood in similar homage.

Then, I was in the company of a rare witness to Grampian's greatest-ever writer. Alexander Gray was headmaster of Arbuthnott School in the early part of the century when the boy whose real name was Leslie Mitchell came dandering across the parks from Bloomfield.

If Mr Gray sensed genius in the crofter's loon, it was confirmed in an essay he had written by the age of 12: "What an irresistible feeling of power comes when, on a calm clear night, you gaze up at the millions of glistening worlds and constellations which form the Milky Way.

" 'Tis then, and then only, that one can realise the full power of the Creator and the truth of the wild dream of the German poet. There is no beginning, yea, even as there is no end." Wow!

Alexander Gray, then in his eighties, turned out that essay-book which he had wisely kept. It near made you weep that you had not known the man in person.

Working on the Aberdeen daily paper where Grassic Gibbon himself had started, I came across his writing when I was 19. My life was never the same again, thank God.

157

With *Sunset Song* alone, he opened my eyes to the landscape which had been my childhood, 30 years after it had been his. Through the innovative brilliance of his prose he gave that land a voice which stirred the soul, stimulated the mind and made you wonder why you hadn't heard it before. I tried to analyse his construction but genius locks away its secrets.

Leslie Mitchell had gone to journalism in Aberdeen and Glasgow, leaving under a cloud and joining first the Army and then the Air Force, wasteful years except that they landed him in the Middle East, where he could pursue his passion for ancient times.

Settling in Welwyn Garden City, he embarked on a feverish routine, turning out 17 volumes in six years. In 1932 he produced his masterpiece, *Sunset Song*, and followed the story of his heroine, Chris Guthrie, through *Cloud Howe* to *Grey Granite*, forming what became known as *A Scots Quair*.

Old man Mitchell, a cantankerous devil, had ridiculed his son's departure from the land and, even when he reappeared that fine summer of 1934, back in the Mearns with a new motor-car as proof of success, he couldn't resist sarcasm about getting up in the world.

Saddened, the son who had taken his mother's maiden name to become Lewis Grassic Gibbon crossed over to Echt in Aberdeenshire to stay with his old dominie.

Alexander Gray had recalled to me how they sat in deck chairs on the schoolhouse green, where his old pupil scribbled away on a pad. Closing it over, he said to Mrs Gray, a keen admirer: "Well that's the end o' *Grey Granite* but I dinna expect ye'll think as much o't as ye did the ither twa."

In his new Ford, Grassic Gibbon headed south to his publisher, already suffering stomach pains which would need investigation. He went to hospital for what seemed a routine operation but failed to rally from the table.

One of Scotland's greatest literary lights was dimmed before his thirty-fourth birthday. They cremated him at Golders Green and brought the ashes back to Arbuthnott.

And as I stood by his grave on Thursday, I remembered how

158

unfashionable he had become by the 1950s, during my first flush of Gibbon enthusiasm, when his work was so totally out of print that you couldn't find a copy in any Aberdeen bookshop.

I wrote to his publisher, asking about plans for reprinting, but they replied that they had none. Befriending his widow and brother John, I joined in a move to put that right, delighted in the 1960s when he was brought into the Higher Leaving Certificate alongside Scott and Stevenson, where he belonged.

The biggest boost came in 1970 when the late Pharic Maclaren televised *Sunset Song* for the BBC.

Now a new generation comes alive to the power of the man, symbolised at the weekend by the opening of a Grassic Gibbon Centre at Arbuthnott. His son and daughter were there to see their father finally accepted in the parish where he had pricked a few pompous bubbles.

Down by the kirkyard, I called on old Nellie Riddoch, who went to school with the author and still remembers the lonesome lad, reading on the playground dyke, away from the herd.

I read again the words on the headstone—moving words from *Sunset Song*: "The kindness of friends, the warmth of toil, the peace of rest."

And I turned my collar to the wind and wiped rain from my cheeks.

SO YOU'VE NEVER TASTED SKIRLIE?

28TH JANUARY 1992

OF all the things I am not, being a gourmet comes high on the list. Ever since the day I discovered I could scarcely boil water without singeing it, I had resigned myself to the fact that I was a culinary illiterate, best kept at a safe distance from the cooker.

Frankly, my dears, I've never cared a fricassee about what happened in the kitchen as long as the end result didn't stray too far from the staple fare of broth, brose, and mince-and-tatties.

My philistine outlook can be gauged, I suppose, from the fact that I have always regarded smoked salmon as a good fish spoiled (I would rather see it in a John West tin).

In fact, I have paid so little attention down the years to the niceties of *haute cuisine* and all the palaver of posh restaurants that I used to think a commis waiter was a left-wing loiterer.

The language of the larder was destined to remain an alien jargon, unless you could fricassee your stovies or marinate a mealy pudding.

With the palate of a peasant, I have been known only once to utter a coo about cooking and that was when I dined at the Inverlochy Hotel and was tempted to think there might possibly be something in this gourmet business after all.

Quickly regaining sanity, however, I renewed my disdain of those people who are always going on about food, as if they were savouring and swallowing some precious gems which would enrich the rest of their lives.

Instead, and in accordance with the natural law which says that whatever goes down must come out, the plain truth is that 95% of all delicious delicacy is disposable rubbish which will go

160

blootering through the sewers within 24 hours (and faster if it's a curry).

So our own Trencherman can safely eat more than his heart out in the sure and certain knowledge that his job is safe from me.

All of this, of course, stems from a Buchan background in which women couldn't be bothered with menfolk in the kitchen. And they served up good, plain, country fare in the knowledge that a grunt would be the highest compliment they could expect.

My mother's speciality was skirlie, for which I would have entered her in a world championship and bet my bottom shilling that she would win. Since her departure, I have often remembered her skirlie and longed for that crisp and crackling oatmeal texture which could enhance a plate of mince and tatties or stand on its own two feet as a solo accompaniment to the chappit tatties.

In smothering me with love, she failed in only one department of my upbringing: she didn't teach me to make skirlie. Mind you, the prospects of my entering a kitchen with creativity in mind would have seemed to her so remote as to make it hardly worth the trouble.

But circumstances change and there came the day when I was faced inescapably with a kitchen in search of a cook. I might as well have stepped into the control centre at Cape Kennedy. But when needs must . . .

Gingerly, I experimented with boiling an egg. Four minutes, I had heard long ago. But those free-range hens of my childhood must have laid more responsive eggs.

Having perfected the boiled egg, I graduated to the omelette and, purely on the basis of chance, produced a rather delicious creation, complete with grated cheese.

All this was beginning to go to my head as well as my stomach, till I was threatening to share the new-found knowledge with anyone prepared to listen.

One person polite enough to listen was Mrs Violet Reith from Banchory, who was not only my teacher at Maud School in 1939 but also my mother's best friend.

"Good for you," she said, taking a motherly interest in my domestic progress. "But do you remember your mother's skirlie?"

Did I remember my mother's skirlie?

"Well, I'll tell you how to make skirlie which will be as near to your mother's as you will ever find."

This was one of life's more precious moments. Whereas in 1939 I had noted my teacher's instructions on parsing and ana-lysing, the same lady was now offering me something more edibly edifying:

Place the required amount of oatmeal in a plastic mould. Chop in a piece of onion, with salt and pepper, and mix it all into a fine texture with cooking oil. Place it in the microwave oven for a mere three minutes and, hey presto!, you will have your skirlie.

It seemed ridiculously simple. Back home, I couldn't wait for the experiment. I boiled and chappit my tatties, prepared the skirlie and, for good measure, heated some baked beans.

In three minutes, sure enough, I had skirlie as near to my mother's as I could hope to achieve.

I suspect that, for you ladies out there, this is the only signifi-cant piece of culinary information I may ever have to share with you. The recipe comes with my compliments. Go to it, girls!

THERE'S HUMOUR IN
THE KIRKYARD

* 2 N D   J U N E   1 9 9 2 *

IT is a sure sign of age when most of life's acquaintances are to be found in the graveyard, a point that comes closer and closer to haunt me.

There is, I suppose, the consolation of a warm neighbourliness as you traverse the pathways, reading headstones and conjuring up memories of those passing generations.

There are even moments of humour, as in that North-east epitaph:

> Here lies the body of Geordie Denham
> If ye saw 'im noo, ye widna ken 'im!

But more seriously, there is rich history to be recalled, a practical pursuit recently taken up by that lively Glaswegian, Jimmy Black, a retired builder and surveyor, who has been visiting city graveyards with a notebook.

Jimmy has tracked down a remarkable number of notables and dug up (if you'll pardon the expression) some fascinating stories, which he has now put together in a small book, the *Glasgow Graveyard Guide*.

Though I pass it daily, I had no idea, for example, that Madge Metcalfe lay over the wall in Cathcart Cemetery. Even then her name would have meant nothing if Jimmy hadn't told me she was the mother of Stan Laurel, of Laurel and Hardy.

Madge, who died in middle age of "debility", married Arthur Jefferson, manager of the Scotia Music Hall in Stockwell Street, later the Metropole. When Jefferson refused his son a chance to

163

perform, the young Stan went along to the rival Panopticon and asked the owner, A. E. Pickard, for a job.

A. E. Pickard. Now there's a name to conjure with. I remember him well in his Great Western Road mansion, a memorable eccentric, showman, cinema-owner, who once stood in a General Election as Independent Millionaire for Maryhill.

Jimmy Black, who traced his ashes to the Western Necropolis, had personal experience of his stunts. He was working on the cinema building site of one of Pickard's rivals when the millionaire drove up in his limousine and asked a crane-driver to lend him a pound.

When the man hesitated, Pickard said: "Give me a pound and you can have the limousine!" The over-cautious crane-driver lost out on a gift because anyone knowing Pickard could tell you he meant it. With such a good tale, he would be putting one over on his rival.

When Jimmy wandered into St Peter's (Dalbeth) Cemetery in London Road the grave of Sir Patrick Dollan reminded him of another amusing incident, at the Empire Exhibition of 1938, where he was an apprentice builder and Lord Provost Dollan had come to introduce that great Hollywood comedian, Eddie Cantor. Dollan, who could be dreary of countenance, sat unamused as the capering Cantor broke into his song, "If You Knew Suzie", and danced around the immobile provost. The crowd was in stitches.

In the same graveyard Jimmy found the great Labour hero, John Wheatley, whose funeral drew thousands of ordinary folk and an astonishing range of celebrities.

Neville Chamberlain was there to honour his opponent, along with Oswald Mosley, later to lead the British Fascists. The ultimate surprise for an Irish Catholic would surely have been the presence of the Moderator of the General Assembly of the Church of Scotland.

Also in Dalbeth are the graves of the Green family, of Green's Playhouse fame, one member of which married another famous name in that cemetery—the great Jimmy McGrory of Celtic.

164

Wandering on by the Old Churchyard at Glasgow Cathedral, he encountered the Hutcheson brothers, founders of the Grammar School, Charles MacIntosh, famous chemist but best remembered for his waterproof raincoat, and the lady called Mary Hill, who gave Partick Thistle a district to call its own.

In the nearby Necropolis stood the headstone of William Thomson, better known as Lord Kelvin, the genius who was at university before he was 11 and became one of the fathers of physics. There, too, stands a monument to William Miller, who gained immortality as the creator of Wee Willie Winkie.

Coming beneath my own office window, Jimmy Black has good reason to touch on the story of Madeleine Smith, the architect's daughter alleged to have poisoned the passion of her life, Pierre L'Angelier, who came to Glasgow from the Channel Islands to be a clerk.

Though the name on the stone is Fleming, L'Angelier lies in that Ramshorn grave in Ingram Street, supposed to have been saturated with arsenic-laced cocoa. Madeleine, who walked away with a "not proven" verdict, later claimed that she had served cocoa to George Bernard Shaw. (As I recall it, she went to America and is said to have confessed at the end of her long life that she did, after all, kill L'Angelier.)

The Southern Necropolis in Caledonian Road turned up Sir Thomas Lipton, Glasgow's greatest grocer, as well as Allan Glen, who hardly needs explanation.

Sundry surprises include Abraham Lincoln's pastor, the Rev. James Smith, who lies in the Calton graveyard at Abercromby Street, and the notorious Rab Ha', known as the Glesga Glutton. Though his grave is unmarked, it is reasonable to assume he occupies more than his fair share of the territory.

Finally to St Kentigern's in Balmore Road to remember the tragic figure of Benny Lynch, Scotland's first and greatest world boxing champion. The demon drink brought all that to an end when he was 33. I remember his funeral day well.

165

WHO DRIES BETWEEN THEIR TOES?

• 16TH JUNE 1992 •

THERE was no shortage of topics as I drove out of Glasgow with two friends, heading north by Loch Lomond, at the beginning of a weekend which would take us up the west coast, across Speyside and over the hills by Don and Dee to hit the more easterly route back to Glasgow.

No sooner had we left the city than the skies cleared into glorious blue and we were rhapsodising every cliché about Scotland. What a country! Where do you find scenery like this?

On we went by Crianlarich, northwards till Glencoe enmeshed us in her mysteries. We talked of the Campbells and the Macdonalds and sundry adventurers. Conversation spread even to the Romans and we wondered what kind of creatures they must have been to come gallivanting as far afield as Britain—and for what purpose when they could more comfortably have stayed at home and enjoyed all that sunshine.

But Campbells and Macdonalds and Romans were all forgotten as we made our destination for the first night—the incomparable estate of Inverlochy Castle, just beyond Fort William. The rhododendrons were in full bloom, in such clusters of magnificent colour as to take your breath away.

To sit in the dining-room of a summer's evening and gaze out on that terraced landscape, with its loch and rich foliage, is an experience in itself. And when the delicacy of the food tempts even a peasant like myself to consider that there might, after all, be gastronomic life after mince-and-tatties, then you understand why people like J. R. Ewing come all the way from Southfork,

166

Dallas, and Robert de Niro should extend his recent visit, just to savour a heavenly corner of Scotland.

Having lingered with the morning sunlight for as long as time would allow—and taken in the most perfect view of Ben Nevis which, for once, was clear and cloudless—my two Glasgow friends and I motored on by Aviemore and Grantown-on-Spey, striking over the Banffshire hills to the heights of Tomintoul.

From there it was a majestic descent upon Donside and finally towards the royal river and the second night's destination of Craigendarroch.

Yes, there were topics galore. As we walked into Ballater, the Glaswegians were noticing something which surprised them. Every single person, sitting or working in the garden or passing in the street, gave us the kind of warm greeting they had not expected to find in the more reserved North-east of my origins.

So we talked about it over dinner and on Sunday morning drove down Deeside towards Aberdeen, calling on my former schoolteacher from 1939, Mrs Reith in Banchory. John Reith's garden was a picture of perfection, as befits the namesake and relative of the first director-general of the BBC.

Onward to Bieldside, where my friend, Clyne Gall, wanted to visit the childhood home of his late father. We found the house, called *Lauriston*, and were welcomed in like long-lost friends. So much for Aberdonian reserve.

But of all that engaged our attention on this idyllic adventure, there was one topic which came to dominate the weekend, as that reference point of hilarity which can enrich such occasions.

It all arose because of the length of time I took to emerge from the shower. Where on earth had I been, my impatient Glaswegian friends wanted to know.

Well, coming out of the shower, I had to dry myself thoroughly, as my mother had always taught in our Aberdeenshire home—not least between my toes.

Between your toes? they exploded in guffaws of disbelief. Who ever heard of anyone drying between their toes?

Well, I did. Everybody in the North-east dries between the

167

toes, I was saying in defence of my race, no longer in any doubt that I was being regarded as a freak. We were taught it at home, at school; it was part of our upbringing.

And, if they didn't believe me, we would ask other people, seeing we were in the area.

John and Violet Reith confirmed the habit with vehemence. Of course they dried between their toes. It was bad for your feet to do otherwise. What's more, it's uncomfortable.

Now I was feeling a little better of the moral support but still determined to put the matter beyond all possible doubt.

Our next call was on that doyen of Aberdeen insurance experts, the irrepressible Bill Scullion. Surely this would settle it. But consternation! Just as his wife Muriel was saying: "Of course I dry between my toes," the bouncing Bill was exploding like a Glaswegian: "I wouldn't dream of it! Never heard of it!"

But then the revelation—he *is* a Glaswegian! So can this be the basis of the cultural divide between the North-east and Strathclyde? Aberdonians dry between their toes and Glaswegians don't? It's a starting-point for some academic in search of a thesis.

So we drove away back south, contented with our mission of various discoveries.

"You've some funny habits, you Aberdonians," my Glasgow friends were chiding.

That's rich, I thought, remembering my astonishment at a certain social habit which I discovered on arriving here more than 30 years ago.

"By the way," I queried casually, as I curled up in the back seat. "Do Glaswegians still pee in the sink?"

168

WHEN THE HIGHLAND SHOW WENT ROUND AND ROUND

* 3 0 T H   J U N E   1 9 9 2 *

THE farm animals which paraded at the Royal Highland Show on Saturday were an impressive array by any standard—and a tribute to those rural folk who are struggling to cope with bewildering changes on the face of the Scottish landscape.

As the cattle champions ambled round the Ingliston show ring with aristocratic swagger, I had difficulty with some of the breed names which come from the Continent to invade our native strongholds.

But I had no difficulty at all with the breed which led them— solid, weatherbeaten humans who were the sons and daughters of their forefathers as surely as night follows day.

I have known them all my life and witnessed them in that parade ring, kindly faces creased with humour, since I began reporting on the Highland Show more than 40 years ago.

In those days, the show went round Scotland on a rotation of eight different areas, resuming after the war at Inverness in 1948, just as I embarked on journalism.

Dundee set crowd records in 1949 before the show moved to Paisley and then Aberdeen, where a non-stop deluge turned the Hazlehead venue into a quagmire of farcical proportions.

Further disaster struck the Highland Show at Kelso in 1952, with an outbreak of the dreaded foot-and-mouth disease, but my memories of the following year at Alloa are of a different order.

The Coronation had taken place earlier that month and the new Queen was paying her first royal visit to Edinburgh. The occasion, they said, was being televised—and most of us had never even seen television.

169

Suddenly, word went round the showground that someone had a TV set, sparking off a mad dash towards this unthinkable event. There we stood, open-mouthed, little realising that we were absorbing the first moments of a medium which would cut deeply into the rest of our lives.

So the Highland Show followed its peripatetic course by Dumfries, Edinburgh, back to Inverness and on to Dundee, Ayr and Aberdeen. But the cost of annual movement became prohibitive and the directors faced the inevitable decision of settling on a permanent site.

That site was Ingliston, near Edinburgh Airport, and there it has been providing its showcase of Scottish agriculture since 1960. What it gained in cost-saving it lost, to some extent, in the loyalty of local areas, where the farming folk had been stimulated to plan with passion so that their particular show would more than hold its own.

There was an early period of thrawnness from those who vowed they would not be travelling away to that Edinburgh place. Some never did.

But in a bid to retain local involvement, the organising structure circulated responsibility around those same areas of Scotland.

This year it fell upon Aberdeenshire and the full flavour of the North-east was brought to the show by the chairmanship of Jack Sleigh, a gloriously unspoiled character who farms at West Fingask of Oldmeldrum.

The presidency of the Royal Highland tends to range from distinguished Scots to the royal family itself. On this occasion, however, Jack Sleigh introduced a note of originality by seeking to honour Scots who have made their mark abroad.

He was thinking in particular of his fellow-Aberdonian, the late B. C. Forbes, the poor boy from Whitehill of New Deer who started his journalism in Peterhead before emigrating to the United States and founding his own *Forbes* magazine, the world's most prestigious business journal.

Forbes's son Malcolm had accepted the 1992 presidency just a fortnight before he died, two years ago. The invitation was then

170

extended to his son and heir, Malcolm S. Forbes junior, usually known as Steve.

Though less flamboyant than his father, Mr Forbes is rated one of the shrewdest brains in America. He came upon the Highland Show quietly but impressively, spoke at various functions and left a deep mark as he flew out on his private Boeing from Edinburgh on Saturday night.

Before leaving, he donated the historic Pitsligo Castle, near Fraserburgh, to the Scottish nation, complete with endowment. He also delegated his uncle, Wallace Forbes from New York, to host Sunday's parish picnic back at Whitehill, where the family story began.

The original B. C. Forbes himself had started these picnics after the First World War and now Wallace, the last of his five sons, was continuing the tradition. There was tea and bridies, tug o' war and races for all.

There were local families which had endured for generations, their speech and demeanour testifying to the power of heredity.

Yet that changing face of rural life could be detected in alien accents, come now to savour the quieter ways in erstwhile farmhouses, the land given over to bigger units or left fallow to the sinister incentive of a "set-aside" payment.

Across that Buchan soil, once sour and grudging but made fertile by generations of determined people, I could see signs of nature restoring her wilderness. Turn your back on the husbandry of that land and soon it will walk away from you.

So we live in a topsy-turvy world. And that makes it all the more remarkable that Jack Sleigh and his fellow-farmers can still put on a show like last week's spectacular.

With the day of the small man all but gone, you wonder how farming will find its future. Perhaps the native ingenuity, imagination and sheer dogged character will save the day.

AN EXCITING NEW ROAD
TO THE ISLES

I'VE joined in the fire festival of Shetland and strolled on the vastness of Tiree's empty beaches; I've crossed over the sea to Skye, come in to land by Compton Mackenzie's old home on Barra and visited that great Orcadian, George Mackay Brown, in his perch overlooking Stromness harbour.

But all that, and a little more, is still poor apology for a scant acquaintance with that world of myth and magic which stretches into the Atlantic and curves northwards to acknowledge Scandinavia and the Arctic Circle.

My extensive ignorance of the Scottish islands takes in the Cumbraes, Colonsay, and Canna, not to mention Eigg, Rum, and Muck. Worst of all, I have never been to Arran, an omission causing stout friends to back away with open-mouthed incredulity.

But Norman Newton has been trying to correct the cultural flaw, reminding me of what I've been missing down the years, in the hope that I can catch up with a lost romance before it is too late.

Norman, who moved yesterday from Argyll to be a librarian in Inverness, is an authority on the islands of Britain, not just Scotland, and the first of his startling statistics was to tell me that more than 90% of Britain's islands are to be found in the Hebrides. Add in the archipelagos of Orkney and Shetland and the remaining coastal islands are few indeed.

For population, of course, it is a vastly different story. Whereas a total of 100,000 people live off the Scottish coasts, the Channel island of Jersey alone can claim very nearly that amount. Incidentally, there are signs of human settlement on Jersey 80,000 years ago, when it was still connected by land to France.

172

By such a yardstick, the arrival of St Columba to establish his Celtic monastery on Iona in AD 563 is a comparatively recent happening.

But Iona has been pencilled in as part of this resolution to visit the islands of my native land. And so has Staffa. I mean, if that distinguished composer, Felix Mendelssohn, could come all the way from Germany as far back as 1829, find his way to Staffa and feel so inspired by the sound of the sea in an echoing cave as to produce a famous overture, what excuse have I?

I must also remember to reach for Britain's most northerly point, the lighthouse at Muckle Flugga, and to pause with the wonders of Orkney's Skara Brae, the best-preserved prehistoric village in northern Europe, which came to light when a storm shifted sand dunes in 1850.

Curling round by Skye, it would be folly to omit the Kilmuir burial place of Flora MacDonald, whose part in the escape of Bonnie Prince Charlie led her to the Tower of London—and eventually back to Skye, where her funeral, in 1790, was the largest ever seen in the Highlands.

Further south I would wish to see Barnhill, on Jura, where George Orwell wrote his famous novel *Nineteen Eighty-Four* while staying there between 1946 and 1949.

Hearing so much of those evil landlords who drove western Scots from their natural habitat, it is comforting to know there were others of greater benevolence.

Lord Leverhulme, son of a Bolton soap-maker, who gained fame with his Unilever business empire, was ahead of his time when he bought Lewis and Harris in 1918 and tried to establish the kind of local enterprise trust now much in vogue in the 1990s.

Seeking to redeem the islands from poverty, he bought fishing boats, built a cannery, ice-factory, roads, bridges, and a light railway. He planned to use spotter planes to locate herring shoals and created MacFisheries, his own outlet of retail fish shops.

It has to be said that his enterprise met with a mixed reception and ground to a halt with his death in 1925.

Norman Newton, who gives me these reminders of what I have

missed, has put it all together in a splendidly illustrated book, *The Shell Guide to the Islands of Britain*, which by no means dwells with the romance of a distant age.

There is modern excitement in the discovery of oil, with Shetland's Sullom Voe now the largest terminal in Europe. There is the attempt to resurrect an interest in Gaelic culture, from a college of its own and the attentions of the television companies to Sorley MacLean's poetry and the Gaelic rock music of groups like Runrig.

Mr Newton doesn't shirk the conflicts which can arise between native islanders and incomers, including the so-called "white settlers", and reveals that, for many, the dream of escaping a troubled world comes unstuck after the second winter.

There is another, curious, challenge of living on an island. Being surrounded by water for months on end evidently produces a kind of "island madness", which has to be taken seriously. Even native islanders have to get away sometimes.

Economically, there is an intriguing development. Now that the proliferation of potters and mediocre art studios is passing, there is a closer attention to "teleworking", by which people can conduct business by computer from the most remote island.

The Channel Islands have used it to develop their banking and financial services. Now the Scottish islands are establishing "telecottages", being used by individuals and small businesses.

There could be a future, it seems, for all those islands I've never seen.

THE DAY I COVERED A
ROYAL WEDDING

15TH SEPTEMBER 1992

CASTING aside yet another day's diet of royal shenanigans, seemingly guaranteed to put Windsors in the soup, I turned to the chore of clearing out old newspapers from a drawer.

(Strange how the journal of the day, so readily consigned to the fish-and-chip shop, takes on an aura of historic importance when the pages have turned to yellow.)

Suddenly I was faced with a paper of nearly 20 years ago, in which a rather dandyish Webster was all dressed up, as never before nor since, in grey top-hat and tails and stepping out to a special engagement.

Having just read that the Princess Royal is about to announce her second wedding, it was all the more of a saddening experience to find that, on that earlier occasion, I was happily entering Westminster Abbey to describe her first one.

And what a spectacle it was. What a cast for an extravaganza, I was saying in that 1973 report, with all the ingredients of an Ivor Novello musical at Drury Lane.

Swords gleamed, diamonds sparkled and the stirring swell of the music near lifted the roof of the ancient abbey as the glittering Princess Anne came past us on her procession down the aisle of royal blue carpet, chatting to her father all the way.

The wedding language of radiance and bliss and joy unconfined was everywhere. As it happened, it was Prince Charles's 25th birthday as well but nobody remembered. The day belonged to his sister and her handsome soldier in scarlet, watched by 500 million people on television and greeted outside by the seething mob which lined the route back to Buckingham Palace.

175

I had listened as the royal voice said clearly: "I, Anne Elizabeth Alice Louise, take thee, Mark Anthony Peter, to be my wedded husband, to have and to hold from this day forward, for better for worse, for richer for poorer, in sickness and in health, to love, cherish and obey (yes, obey) till death us do part. . . ."

But the joys of a dull November day went the way of so many others. It all turned out to be worse rather than better, as the vows went cascading down the royal plug-hole with a familiarity which makes you wonder why we bother to make them, knowing that about one in three of the charades will end in disaster.

It is the on-going tragedy of the married state, about which this is not a sermon. In fact, Princess Anne has grown immeasurably in stature as a human being and one could only wish that the judgment which seems to benefit second marriage were present at the first.

At least that royal break-up has been handled with a good deal more delicacy than the others which keep exploding around the monarch's crown. No bare breasts or well-sucked toes or conversations which can be picked up by despicable creeps with radio transmitters.

The tabloids have had their field day, self-righteously proclaiming it their duty to inform us about royal indiscretion. Since there is public money—and even, perhaps, the future of the monarchy—involved, I would have no quibble with that.

Where we part company, after this essential information has been duly imparted, is over the hypocrisy of continuing on a daily basis to stretch and distort the material into as many instalments as will keep their circulation increases buzzing at artificially inflated figures.

Sometimes, of course, they take a breather to focus prying lenses on the Minister of Fun, when he is having some, and there again I believe there is a certain justification for keeping us in the picture.

Some would say a man who can cheat on his wife can cheat the rest of us as well. I don't believe that that follows. Where an extramarital activity is a compensation for an unhappy marriage (and it often is), the cover-up may be no more than a considerate protection of partner and children.

My worry in the particular case of Mr Mellor is not only his blatant indiscretions but the fact that a man can consider it a good omen to wear a Chelsea football strip when heading out to score.

When it comes to a man like Frank Bough of television note, the tabloid argument of public duty vanishes completely. That's blatantly gutter. People have all sorts of harmless needs when it comes to stimulation, which may or may not be available in the marital bed.

Whatever Mr Bough may require to fulfil his private aspirations is no more our business than it is to peer through a neighbour's bedroom curtains. Nor does it affect his pre-eminence as a television commentator who happens to sound like a thoroughly likeable man.

My newspaper nose tells me the public are thoroughly sick of it all. They have had it up to the brass-neck of those long-lens snoops. The pity is that they don't follow through with a sanction which would drive home the message where it hurts.

Meanwhile, I see that Sue Townsend, who gave us the *Secret Diary of Adrian Mole* 10 years ago, brings out a new book this week, in which she demolishes the monarchy and commits the Queen to life on a council estate.

Similarly dispossessed, Princess Anne manages to keep a horse in the back close. It certainly makes a change from Westminster Abbey; which reminds me, I never did get that drawer cleared out.

ROMANCE OF THE
OLD STEAM ENGINE

•10TH NOVEMBER 1992•

LIFE is brimful of coincidence. No sooner had I been invited to celebrate the 125th anniversary of Aberdeen railway station—and to christen a locomotive as *The Northern Lights*—than my nostalgia for the age of the train was stirred by a totally unrelated happening.

Almost by the same post came a pictorial booklet put together by my old friend Sandy Murdoch recalling the heyday of the Buchan line, which ran north from Aberdeen to our native village of Maud before splitting into two portions destined for Peterhead and Fraserburgh.

Whatever else we lacked in our rural backwater, we could at least boast that Maud was a railway junction, at the centre of the Aberdeenshire cattle country, taking livestock to the south and bringing back bowler-hatted commercial travellers and assorted oddities to arouse our curiosity.

The station was the very heart and soul of our village life, a gateway to the outside world which filled our thoughts with romantic notions and our nostrils with the pungent yet seductive odours of the steam engine.

The heartbeat of our community was measured in arrivals and departures, the distant hoot as the train came round the Den Wood from Auchnagatt and suddenly appeared with majesty to unfold its secrets.

Our neighbours were signalmen and surfacemen, clerks and porters, who puffed at pipes and thoughtfully studied pocket watches for precise declarations of time.

On Wednesdays they would usher bullocks into trucks or struggle with rearing animals from the annual horse market of Aikey Fair.

178

On the station platform, we had waved our Territorials off to war and awaited the arrival of Glasgow's evacuated children.

Tibby Bruce ran the bookstall and you could enjoy a plate of mince and tatties and a dram at what was known as The Refresh, right there on the platform—licensed premises conducted for a lifetime by Lil and Lena Murison.

It was all part of the permanent fabric of village life; well . . . permanent until Dr Beeching came along with his remit to cut costs on Britain's railways.

Our Buchan Train had been running for 100 years when the doctor applied his scalpel with ruthless dedication. In severing the main artery he cut the heart from our community—and what happened to Maud, and hundreds of villages like it, heralded a major decline in the rural well-being of this country.

It is the sort of thing wise governments would pause to consider. But seeking that kind of long-term wisdom from politicians has the futility of seeking teeth in a hen.

(The Buchan railway, incidentally, had no sooner been destroyed than the discovery of oil and gas created a need for transport routes to Peterhead and St Fergus.)

These memories of a bygone age sprang to life with Sandy Murdoch's collection of pictures. Sandy had gone from Maud School to an apprenticeship with the village chemist, Charlie Anderson, acquiring his first Brownie camera and spending lunch-hours clicking away at passing trains.

Now that he had stirred nostalgia for the steam engine, I happened to glance again at the invitation to celebrate at Aberdeen Joint Station last week.

And there, to my delight, I read that as soon as I had christened the locomotive I would be spirited to a splendid lunch at Inverurie—by that famous old steam engine *Union of South Africa*, preserved by John Cameron, the Fife farmer who is also a member of the BR board.

After a whole generation I would savour once more the thrill of the steam train. I couldn't wait.

So the great day came last Wednesday, when 4,000 Aberdonians crowded into the Joint Station to celebrate a piece of social history. Top brass came from London to join with the Lord Provost of Aberdeen and the Convener of Grampian—and there I was, making my little speech and opening the curtain to reveal that an InterCity locomotive would now bear the name of *The Northern Lights*.

(Just before she died three years ago I had tracked down Mary Webb, the forgotten composer of Aberdeen's anthem, and paid tribute to her in a television film. I secured her old piano for the city and brought her ashes to be scattered to the northern winds of Aberdeen.)

When they cut a huge birthday cake, I suggested, indelicately perhaps, that they should have resurrected Dr Beeching for the task, him with his facility for cutting things.

The naming ceremony over, I found myself surrounded by old friends from Maud, who came to celebrate our childhood days. We stood and blethered on the platform, close by the steam engine, as dignitaries boarded for that Inverurie lunch. My big moment was at hand.

The engine-driver moved his train slowly, for the benefit of the television cameras. But he would stop again, of course. Except that he didn't. As he gathered speed, railway officials on board turned ashen-faced as they spotted their special guest still standing on the platform!

Too late. I had waited 30 years or more for this great moment—and missed a steam train for the first time in my life. As portable phones buzzed between train and station HQ I was whisked to Inverurie by the ignominy of a car, arriving ahead of the party, which was poor consolation.

They say they will raise steam again to celebrate the 150th anniversary in the year 2017. I'll try to catch that one—albeit with the aid of my zimmer.

A NEW HILTON—
AND GLASGOW HAS ARRIVED

♦ 1 S T D E C E M B E R 1 9 9 2 ♦

TO the extent that you can tell a town by its hotels, yesterday's arrival of the prestigious Hilton may finally have marked the arrival of Glasgow itself as a truly international city. To the skirl of pipes, appropriately on St Andrew's Day, Glasgow's Lord Provost opened the doors and the Scottish public walked into a Hilton hotel for the first time on native soil.

That air of excitement was a sharp reminder of how far Glasgow has come since those days, not so long ago, when the choice didn't stray far beyond the railway establishments of the Central, St Enoch's, and the North British. The Albany was first to intrude upon that city centre tradition, underlining the fact that Glasgow was seriously under-served for top-class accommodation.

That the situation has changed so dramatically is merely a tangible reflection of what has been happening since the city washed its grubby face, set native vitality upon the garden festival and the year of European culture and showed it was ready for a role to replace that once-proud title of Second City of the Empire. Germane to all that, I reckon, was the decision to house the Burrell Collection. That more than anything drew the attention of the outside world.

Now that world is beating a path to Glasgow's doorstep, for everything from business and tourism to the lucrative market of international conference, an area in which the new Hilton is already competing with places like the Grand in Brighton. It augurs well for a city which, in attracting large hotel groups, has also been suffering from a bewildering round of name changes.

The Albany became the Forte Crest. The Forum was no sooner

built than it was changing its name to the Moat House International. The Skean Dhu was renamed the Hospitality Inn, confusing the public with its verbal proximity to the Holiday Inn. That was resolved when the Holiday Inn became the Marriott. The Centre Hotel in Argyle Street, constantly mixed up with the old-established Central, has now become the Crest, requiring separation from the nearby Forte Crest.

And as if all that were not enough, the old North British in George Square became the Diplomat and is now the Copthorne.

By comparison, the name of the Hilton is straightforward, though that, too, has had its confusions.

The American founder, Conrad Hilton, branched out from the family inn after the First World War to establish a chain which equated his name with luxury.

The profile suffered not at all from son Nicky's marriage to Elizabeth Taylor (her first) and Hilton hotels spread around the world. But there came a day when the family hived off part of the business, retaining their own surname within the United States and using Conrad's Christian name outside it.

The Hilton International takes the family name beyond the US but turns up as Vista hotels on home soil. At least I think it does!

Whatever the names, I must confess to being a sucker for plush hotels, ever since I downed a gin-sling in Singapore's legendary Raffles and tried to re-live the days of Somerset Maugham.

Indeed, the Far East is hard to beat. The Mandarin-Orientals are counted the best in the world but, having sampled them in Hong Kong and Bangkok, I prefer a Shangri-La.

There is a special excitement in walking into the Willard in Washington or the Waldorf Astoria in New York, especially when you can drop into the latter's cocktail bar and run your fingers over Cole Porter's own piano.

But I wouldn't exchange any of them for the Beverly Hills, which may not rank for size or plushness but has a charm all its own.

So with that kind of interest, I didn't even wait for yesterday's opening of the Glasgow Hilton, wandering around its corridors while the builders were still coping with bare floors and hanging wires.

With only a week to go, you wondered how they could complete the £42m skyscraper. But it would be all right on the night.

While I was there, a platoon of workmen carried in the foyer carpet. Suddenly the lifts sprang into life and I joined general manager David Thompson as he pressed the button for his first self-operated flight to the 20th floor.

From there, the view of Glasgow is spectacular, westward to the airport and eastward across the city. Dinky cars crossed the Kingston Bridge.

Bedrooms and suites costing from £125 to £350 a night awaited their first occupants and a magnificent ballroom lay in silent preparation for anything up to 1,000 diners. There's a Raffles Bar and a Minsky's deli-type restaurant.

Coming home to such a prestigious post, 41-year-old David Thompson must be an encouragement to youngsters entering the hotel business. The son of a grocery manager in Bridge of Allan, he took part-time jobs in local hostelries before deciding on a hotel management course at Edinburgh's Napier College. He worked in the Caribbean then joined Hilton at Abu Dhabi in 1978. That started him on a route, via the Nile Hilton in Cairo, which brought him back to Britain and eventually to manage the Regents Park Hilton in London.

He didn't want to miss out on the first Scottish venture. Nor has he. For this quiet-spoken man is home as the boss, masterminding the glittering arrival of the Glasgow Hilton—and giving this city an even greater chance to flourish.

MY TRIBUTE TO LUIGI ZANRE

• 8TH DECEMBER 1992 •

GIVEN our obsession with the weather, it has never failed to astound me that so many Italians chose to desert the warmth and Mediterranean fragrance of their beloved homeland to seek a better living within these shores.

It tells much about the economic poverty of that beautiful country in the earlier part of the century that they came as an exodus, prepared to exchange those balmy climes for the cold, wet plap of a Scottish winter (and maybe spring, summer and autumn as well) which would most likely offer little but hard graft and bronchitis in some small-town café, making ice-cream or fish-and-chips.

But the choice was theirs and they were evidently glad to take it, all the way from Alloa, which greeted a young Charles Forte, to Peterhead, where the quality of immigrant was typified by the round, friendly figure of Luigi Zanre.

Louis (we never did give him the full pronunciation of Luigi) became one of the heroes of my village childhood. Maud was not big enough for an ice-cream shop so we depended on him travelling the 14 miles inland from Peterhead, two or three times a week during the summer.

I still have a snapshot from 1934, showing the innocent child with saucer and penny, eagerly awaiting the first sight of Louis as he came round the hill from Aikey Brae.

There was no mistaking the yellow motorbike and sidecar, which would no doubt offend the environmental laws of the sophisticated nineties but which did nothing to impair the taste of the finest ice-cream I have encountered, even to this day.

184

Louis's fractured English merely lent enchantment to the warm greeting which came from his round, friendly face, creased with character and good humour. His visits brought colour to our rural isolation.

And when the winter came and I was transported to the Play-house in Peterhead—and to the Hollywood glamour of Clark Gable and Deanna Durbin—my heart would leap at the end of the night as we called at the chip-shop in Queen Street for a fish supper to last us home to Maud. For there was Louis in his other role, still smiling and joking in his Italian English.

But there came that unthinkable, disastrous day when there would be no more ice-cream from Louis Zanre or anyone else. When the childhood dream of the 1930s was turned to the night-mare of Hitler's war, all luxuries were soon removed from our daily lives. No sweets, no bananas, and certainly no ice-cream.

Worse was to follow. Since Mussolini's Italy stood alongside Hitler—and Louis had remained an Italian citizen—he was whisked off in the night, along with 17-year-old son Joe, to a barbed-wire prison on the Isle of Man.

(Among the fellow-Italians he met there was the then-unknown Charles Forte.)

The dismay of Peterhead folk was hardly lessened by the irony that the town was, at the outbreak of war, under the leadership of Provost Max Schultze, a distinguished German exporter who was allowed to go free because he had become a naturalised Briton.

Sanity prevailed in time, thank goodness, and as Louis was released young Joe went off to join the British Army and serve his adopted country with pride. Louis told me later of his prison frustration when he realised he was missing a grand season for selling ice-cream!

While he had flitted across my childhood as a magical figure, it was much later before I knew his background.

When I returned to chart that childhood in books and television films, one of my first stops was at the Peterhead chip-shop, where Louis was still battering up the fish, well into his eighties.

The shape and smiling face were unchanged from the 1930s,

only the mellowing black hair now yielding to time. Back at his house, he told me of coming to Peterhead from Bologna in 1915, travelling 20 miles inland to sell his uncle's ice-cream—from a horse and cart!

He had married Flora Ferrari, from another Peterhead-Italian family, a finely-boned Latin beauty who brought in the coffee and told me she had never seen Italian ice-cream until she came to Peterhead.

In more than 70 years Louis had never missed the annual Aikey Fair, near Maud, and it was there, in 1987, that we preserved his moving image for posterity in my television film, *As Time Goes By*.

Three times in the course of a contented life, Louis went back to visit his native Italy but couldn't wait to get "home", which was now the bare shoulder of Buchan.

Far from the sun and the sweet scents of his birthplace, he had become a true citizen of Peterhead, though he never did become a naturalised Briton.

And there, in the sadness of yesterday, they buried him up at Balmoor Cemetery. For Louis slipped quietly away at the week-end, no pain, no medication. He was 93.

I had to miss the funeral but Robert Mackie, who used to work in his chip-shop and was now his undertaker, read my eulogy, a celebration of a memorable friend.

The aroma of fish-and-chips and the smooth velvet of Louis's vanilla sliders will surely bring excitement to the duller corners of Heaven.

WHAT DID BERNARD SHAW
SAY ABOUT IT?

AFTER a flurry of high ceremony in Washington tomorrow, George Bush goes out to grass on that majestic mall before the White House, leaving the keys to Bill Clinton and his over-ambitious wife, Hillary.

With a late burst of statesmanship, I sense that Bush has won himself a last-minute round of respect and affection, perhaps even stirring a hint of conscience in the American people about the haste with which they discarded him.

After all, the ballyhoo of electioneering is over and it's down to realities from now on. Even before he arrives there are signs that Mr Clinton has quietly forgotten such ridiculous promises as the one about sending a special envoy to sort out Northern Ireland.

Apart from the insulting nature of that hollow nonsense, blatantly designed to capture the Irish vote (and it did), it would take more than the combined brain-cells of Bill and Hillary to find a solution to that.

They are already struggling with lesser problems, like placating the angry host of Hollywood stars, from Kim Basinger and Ali McGraw to Richard Gere and Robert de Niro, who jumped on the Democrat bandwagon at election time and now find them-selves without an invitation to the ball.

In anticipation of their reward, some had even booked them-selves into Washington hotels, which should tell them something about counting chickens.

Like the rest of us, they will have to watch the inauguration on television, a ceremony which forever reminds me of that January

187

day in 1961 when John F. Kennedy was sworn in to America's highest office.

By then a white-haired old man, the great American poet, Robert Frost, was called to the podium to read his laudatory verse and was struggling with the wind and the microphone when a gust caught his notes and scattered them in an embarrassment of directions.

Had we known the shape of things to come, the superstitious would no doubt have been talking about omens. Let's hope for better signs tomorrow.

But as Presidents come and go, there is one departure of this week which is causing consternation among the fraternity of American writers and humorists.

As the breed which depends on public folly for its fodder, they are already mourning the loss of J. Danforth Quayle, youthful sidekick to President Bush, who had a delicious habit of opening his mouth and putting his foot in it. They are even promoting his name for the Republican nomination in 1996.

Though he was never a candidate for Mensa, I wasn't convinced that Dan Quayle was just as daft as he sounded. Mind you, he was certainly daft enough to walk into a classroom in New Jersey last summer and correct a pupil who was writing *potato* on the blackboard.

"There's a letter missing," said the Vice President.

The boy looked at it cautiously and added a final *e*, whereupon he was duly congratulated by the nation's No. 2. The attendant journalists expressed amazement (though what some of them had to be amazed about I really don't know).

It was, I suppose, a minor incident but little things tell a lot and, in a sense, it was the last straw in turning Dan Quayle into a public laughing-stock. There is no saying what harm that did to President Bush's hopes of returning to the White House.

Yet, for all the hilarity, Dan the Dunce might once have found support in distinguished quarters. His compatriot, Mark Twain, once said: "Never trust a man who has only one way to spell a word."

188

And no less a writer than George Bernard Shaw was so critical of our spelling habits that he once applied his mischievous wit to give a plausibly alternative spelling to the very word which snookered hapless Dan.

You can spell *potato* like that, he said. But, by the examples of English usage, you could just as readily spell it like this: *ghoughpteighbteau.*

Still baffled? Mr Shaw explained:

P as in *hiccough*
O as in *though*
T as in *ptomaine*
A as in *neigh*
T as in *debt*
O as in *bureau.*

Shaw may have had a point, though part of the charm of the English language is surely the diversity and subtlety of its forms.

You can see that it troubles foreigners to understand the logic of *plough*, *rough*, *dough*, *hiccough*, and *lough*. But the British themselves are little better at following their own language.

A recent Gallup poll showed that five out of six of us cannot spell everyday words. Only 17% were all-correct with this list: *necessary, accommodation, business, separate, height,* and *sincerely.* Of 1,000 people questioned, one in 10 couldn't spell any of the words! Women beat men hands down and older people were well ahead of the young.

Of course there are those who regard spelling deficiency as a mark of distinction. I have known journalists to call for help with a word, the inference being that, though the spelling may be eccentric, the writing is unmistakably brilliant. I wonder.

The Government is worried about this lack of basic skills and seeks to improve national literacy. But what are we to make of Education Secretary John Patten, who recently signed off in a letter to a colleague with "Yours sincerly"? Let's hope it was a typing error. If not, there may be a future for Dan Quayle after all.

SCOTS WHO FOUNDED THE RAF

• 1 S T   A P R I L   1 9 9 3 •

AS the Royal Air Force celebrates its seventy-fifth anniversary today, the nation remembers a history of heroism stretching from 1918 through to the Battle of Britain and on to those modern encounters in the Falklands and the Gulf.

It will all be acknowledged at a Royal Review in Norfolk, with a spectacular fly-past before the Queen and other members of her family, who will join 10,000 invited guests at a presentation of new Colours.

More controversially, we shall hear again the name of Lord Trenchard being lauded as the father of the Royal Air Force, at a time when historians are questioning his right to that claim.

Hugh Trenchard certainly became the Chief of Air Staff at the end of the First World War, when the Royal Flying Corps took on its new shape and title, and must be credited with finding a new role for the RAF in the post-war years.

But the founding father? A closer look at the origins of the service brings to the forefront the names of two distinguished Scots who had more to do with the foundations than Trenchard and must surely challenge for the title he has so freely enjoyed throughout the years.

One is David Henderson, son of a Glasgow shipbuilder and engineer, who reached the heights in the Army before battling against official opposition to establish the new flying service.

The other is William Weir, from the famous Glasgow engineering works at Cathcart (he was a great favourite of Lloyd George and Winston Churchill), who became Secretary of State for Air at the inception of the RAF—and had to persuade a very reluctant

190

Hugh Trenchard to take on the leading role in the post-war service.

Among those who have drawn attention to the claims of the two Scots is 53-year-old Dugald Cameron, director of Glasgow School of Art, whose famous profile paintings of aircraft come together as a book this week, in celebration of the RAF's anniversary.

"These claims deserve serious consideration," says Mr Cameron. "For someone described as the father of the RAF, Lord Trenchard was a reluctant parent indeed."

The neglected story of David Henderson in particular deserves attention. So what are the facts?

Born in 1862 and having studied engineering under Lord Kelvin at Glasgow University, Henderson decided on an Army career, joined the Argyll and Sutherland Highlanders and was later at the Battle of Omdurman.

By the outbreak of the Boer War he had risen to be Director of Military Intelligence, under Lord Kitchener, enlarging the network of spies.

Wounded and much decorated in that war, he began to write books on the lessons he had learned. By then he had also become a very popular and well-rounded citizen, a pianist and composer who organised theatre shows and designed and painted the scenery himself. He was also the man who set Kipling's poems to music.

A brigadier by 1908 and always interested in new ideas, Henderson was greatly intrigued by Wilbur Wright and his flying achievements. It was then he began to think in terms of aircraft as fighting machines.

But in government and military circles there was no enthusiasm for aeroplanes, the Army attitude being that they would frighten the horses!

Under an assumed name, Henderson was quietly learning to fly, becoming a pilot at the age of 49, when he was described as "a born flyer".

Despite the official coolness, the Government did ask a defence

191

committee to consider the future of aerial navigation and Henderson was part of the three-man group which considered the technical report.

It was the work of that group which brought the formation of an air service in Britain. The Royal Flying Corps came into existence in 1912, when they had to decide on such basics as the size and form of a "squadron"—and even the choice of the word itself.

Henderson was appointed Director of Military Training at the War Office, still with a special interest in the flying developments.

That post made him responsible for training the British Army which would cross to France in 1914. His real work for the Royal Flying Corps, however, began with his appointment as Director-General of Military Aeronautics.

Many Army officers were still suspicious of this upstart service and Henderson had a fight on his hands.

Four days after the outbreak of the First World War, the new RFC gathered at Dover. One squadron flew south from Montrose. As 41 planes made the crossing to France on the first day, including Bleriots, Farmans, and Avros, it was strange to contemplate that it was just five years since Louis Bleriot made the first cross-channel flight.

Henderson, who had now been knighted, and Captain F. H. Sykes mobilised the force with great speed and joined in the crossing, Henderson to be their commander in the field. Back home, Colonel Trenchard was given the task of building up a force from what was left.

From the front, Sir John French, commander of the British forces, was soon reporting on the invaluable service of Henderson and his flying machines, not only in supplying information from reconnaissance but now in fighting in the air.

When the War Office planned to allocate squadrons to Army commands, Henderson declared this as a recipe for disaster since senior Army officers neither knew nor cared about aeroplanes. The plan was shelved.

From that cold start of 1912, the Royal Flying Corps grew so rapidly that the Scot decided he had to get back to his desk, as Director-General of Military Aeronautics. He handed over command in the field to Hugh Trenchard.

Back home, accusations by a Member of Parliament—they were later dismissed—brought Henderson into the limelight for alleged blunders in the construction of our planes. Too many of our machines were being shot down. Germany's Gotha bombers were also launching daylight raids on London.

General Smuts, the famous Boer leader, was asked to examine our defence arrangements and Henderson, who had gained himself some enemies in press and Parliament, proposed the formation of one complete air service, administered by a single air ministry.

Lord Rothermere became president of the Air Council, with Henderson as his vice-president, and Trenchard was recalled from France to be Chief of Air Staff.

But neither Henderson nor Trenchard could agree with Rothermere's policies and both tendered resignations which took effect, rather ironically, on April 1, 1918, the very day the RAF came into being.

Rothermere himself decided to resign—and that was where William Weir came into the picture.

Weir's family firm in Glasgow not only built 1,100 complete aircraft for the war, refusing to take a profit on such work, but later took up the development of the autogyro which led to the helicopter as we know it. The Weirs also gave financial backing to Frank Whittle when others were not prepared to support his idea of a jet engine.

Churchill, who regarded William Weir as a man of exceptional qualities, had put him in charge of aircraft production. But when Rothermere resigned, he became Secretary of State for Air and was soon raised to the peerage as Lord Weir of Eastwood.

All this by the time he was 41 and from a comparatively little-known figure who had no standing in politics. Churchill simply knew that he was a man who could do the job—and who was dedicated to the notion of independent air power.

One of the jobs he had to undertake was to persuade Trenchard to take charge of the RAF. The latter was capable of an awkward arrogance and was spending much of his time just sitting on a bench in London's Green Park.

Behind this front, however, Weir detected the qualities of the man he wanted. Finally, he made it plain he was issuing an order which could not be disobeyed.

It was indeed a curious introduction to a post which would later gain him the credit for being the founder of the RAF.

Meanwhile David Henderson returned to the Army, soon running into the tragedy of his son's death in a flying accident at Turnberry. Nevertheless he took part in the peace talks of 1919 and then became head of the new League of Red Cross Societies in Geneva.

But he had driven himself hard. His health suffered and, when he died at 59, his ashes were buried at Girvan.

The Times called him "The Maker of the RAF". Even Lord Trenchard himself paid tribute to the vision of Henderson. Perhaps it is now time for the rest of us to give these talented and courageous Scots their proper place in the inspiring story of a Royal Air Force which celebrates so proudly today.

GIANTS OF JOURNALISM

•27TH APRIL 1993•

WHEN I came south in my twenties, the warning bells of *No Mean City* still ringing apprehension in my tender breast, I was comforted by the welcome of a fellow Aberdonian who had beaten that same path to Glasgow many years before.

George Ritchie had been a journalist in Aberdeen from the year I was born, an intellectual giant of a man yet so quiet and self-effacing as to pass unnoticed unless you took the trouble to explore the vastness of his mind.

He was the archetypal Scottish lad-o'-pairts, out of school too soon but so well-read and self-educated that he could have taken his place with the greatest dons of Oxbridge.

I recognised him from a dying breed of self-improvers who sought little from life.

But the joy of encountering such a rare human being was tempered by the fact that George, though at that time a man still in his forties, was so debilitated by chronic asthma that we feared for his life. More than once at the sub-editors' desk we received late-night reports that he was gravely ill and was unlikely to see the morning.

But they were discovering new drugs and, if only George could hold out, there might be hope around the corner. His constitution at least was hewn from the granite of his native city.

Can you imagine, therefore, my sheer delight in walking through George Square, Glasgow, last week on the way to a rendezvous with none other than the same George Ritchie? From death's door of more than 30 years ago he had just been quietly marking his 80th birthday, kept alive all these years by the wonders of

195

science but thanking his God just the same for the bonus of time.

And there he was, "still hingin' thegither" as he put it, a wise and wiry figure, gaunt and bearded, who could have been mistaken for a Russian poet or even a prophet deep rooted in Old Testament days.

His eye still sparkled with youthful interest and his memory remained as clear as his knowledge was encyclopaedic.

Not unnaturally we fell to recalling those great characters of journalism of whose generation I merely caught the final whiff. George had known them well.

In Aberdeen he had worked, for example, with old John Sleigh, a legendary reporter who covered the story of the Tay Bridge disaster in 1879! Nobody could trace the origins of his career but one colleague wrote a parody of John Sleigh to the tune of John Peel, ending one particular stanza with this:

> And when the Ten Commandments got their first big shak'
> He gave Moses half-a-column in the mornin'!

Old Gentleman John, always immaculate in black coat, tie, and bowler, was tailor-made for funerals. A society spinster on Deeside had always guarded her age so John was instructed to glance at the coffin lid, which usually revealed it.

Having adjourned as usual to the local hostelry, he was standing near the grave when he heard the minister intoning "earth to earth, dust to dust". Consternation! He had forgotten to seek out her age. Elbowing his way to the front, he was down on hands and knees peering into the grave when John Barleycorn unbalanced John Sleigh and landed him beside her ladyship.

Back at the office he was severely disciplined but, on Deeside, country folk merely sniggered and winked disrespectfully and said it was the first time her ladyship had ever had a man on top of her.

John had finally retired before my time but there were other legends still in harness. We recalled men like Andrew Ingram, brilliant scholar of English though he left the country school at 14, later to be a veteran of the First World War, a formidable figure on the *Times* of India and still thundering about split infinitives in the 1950s.

There was Bill Millar, the news editor who, once when filled with amber, sought to prove his steady hand by firing an air-gun at the reporters' clock. He might have taken lessons from another colleague, Sandy Robertson, who was a brave sniper from the First World War.

We remembered the colourful George Rowntree Harvey, who worked throughout the night as a sub-editor on the *Press and Journal*, studied at Aberdeen University by day and, with a minimum of sleep, didn't even ask a night off for his final exams in which, incidentally, he gained a first-class honours degree in English.

Rowntree Harvey, wayward, dissolute, but brilliant bohemian, went on to become perhaps the most renowned music and drama critic in the land, as well as a playwright of substance, astounding the men of Fleet Street by refusing to leave his native heath.

Rowntree Harvey's boss in the 1920s was George Fraser, another of that brilliant breed, who started writing a column in 1918—and is still writing his weekly column 75 years later. The immaculate English of a man well through his nineties should be compulsory reading in schools today.

George Ritchie knew them all, remembering long hours in the newspaper night, laying down pencils on the stroke of midnight to wish each other a happy New Year, and resuming sweated labour beyond the bells.

As he disappeared in the mists, I gazed after him and knew what a privilege it had been to brush shoulders with such extraordinary people.

REVOLUTION ON THE LAND

15TH JUNE 1993

WHEN I wrote my first television documentary in 1985, about the selling of my father's farm, I intended no more than to focus on the personal dilemma of breaking ties with the land of my ancestors.

For this had been their land over centuries, once the barren wasteland of Buchan, sour and drudging soil, but transformed by generations who bent their backs in sweated toil to clear and dig and manure their few acres of what became known as the great cattle country of Aberdeenshire. It was a heroic story of peasant folk who gained in human value what they lost in sweat, blood, and tears.

And they passed down to their offspring a home and a way of life which became their tradition, the only manner of living they truly understood.

Now and then the lineage would produce an only child who turned out to be a maverick, perhaps a wastrel, interrupting the natural succession. And somewhere within that category I took my place, a sore disappointment to my father, who saw his only possible successor disappearing into the murky unknown of a writing career, whatever that might mean.

How could a decent, hard-working man have sired such worthless ambition? The blame must rest with my more romantic mother, whose genes had dominated.

Out of conscience, I did maintain his beloved acres for eight years after he died but the absurdity of long-distance farming, never in the nature of things, finally convinced me to sell.

So Honeyneuk went under the hammer, and that last day

198

brought the unexpected consolation of an award for my television film.

What I didn't realise as I bade farewell to my patch of Buchan was that I was getting out in the nick of time. The crops we had sown that spring of 1985 became the responsibility of the new owner, in what turned out to be one of the most ruinous harvests in history.

And if nature washed that one away, it matched the devastation with a repeat performance in 1987.

That was not the only catastrophe for small farmers like the men of Buchan. For, just as they had been encouraged by European policy to produce more and more through the seventies and eighties—and to throw themselves into unaccustomed borrowing for the purpose—they were now being deserted by those same bureaucrats, who were pleading mountains of surplus food.

So prices dropped, the value of their farms went into freefall—but the borrowed money still had to be repaid at high interest rates. A proud and worthwhile people had always equated debt with disgrace. Some were unable to face it and, around my native corner within a short time, there were five suicides.

By coincidence, that falling value of land was matched by record property prices in southern England. So, from the proceeds of a semi-detached in Surrey you could easily buy yourself a 200-acre farm in Aberdeenshire, with capital to spare.

Many did—and could be said, I suppose, to have saved even greater financial embarrassment for small farmers. But most of the so-called "white settlers" came as strangers to the ways of the land. Some wanted only a few acres for the children's ponies and promptly sold the rest to neighbouring survivors.

So the small farming of my heritage began to drift into fewer and fewer hands, denying the whole principle upon which a sound tradition of rural life was based.

To compound the farce, the mandarins of Europe are now paying the surviving farmers *not* to farm their land, with a sinister-sounding bribe called "set-aside payment".

But why am I telling you all this when you can see it for yourself

199

in a splendid television film being shown tonight on your commercial channel?

The Grampian production, *Troubled Fields*, has been written by a North-east lass, Frieda Morrison, who even composes and sings her own musical accompaniments.

Here you will witness the kind of personal tragedy I have described. Sandy Jaffrey from the district of Methlick conveys in his native tongue the emotion of having to sell his farm.

"It seems as if I've just got the land rid o' boulders, cleared and ready for plooin—and I have tae walk awa fae it," says Sandy.

He and his wife Isobel place lot-numbers on their belongings and, close to tears, take a last, lingering look at their farm.

"What began as a gentle exodus a decade ago," says Frieda Morrison, "has now become a kind of mass clearance and the silence left in its wake is as much cultural as economic."

Dr Jim Hunter, who has done much to protect the Highland crofter, concedes that the so-called Doric culture of the North-east is more at risk than that of the western Gael.

For in that Grampian corner they have struggled away quietly, without the powerful lobby which convinces distant politicians that you can placate the natives with sops like £10m for Gaelic television. (More people in the world, incidentally, speak the Buchan dialect than speak Gaelic.)

So a voice needs to be raised for the disappearing culture of North-east Scotland. Tonight could be a rallying point.

And my prediction that Frieda Morrison and director Mark Littlewood have created a masterpiece which will tempt awards for *Troubled Fields* has, I swear, nothing to do with the fact that I make a brief appearance!

THE STRANGE TALE OF AIKEY FAIR

◆ 2 9 T H   J U N E   1 9 9 3 ◆

WHEN the splutter of the tractor sounded the death-knell of the Clydesdale horse more than 50 years ago, there would be at least one obvious consequence for the farmer's calendar: the end of those great horse markets which were a mixture of business bustle and social highlight.

As it happened, I grew up within two miles of one of the biggest horse markets of all, the great Aikey Fair, held on a July Wednesday on a hillside between the villages of Maud and Old Deer in the heart of Buchan.

As a child I heard the legend of how it began many centuries before. A packman crossing the River Ugie was said to have slipped on stepping-stones and fallen in and, as he spread out his wares to dry, country folk came along to survey.

He did such uncommon business that he announced he would be back on the same day next year. He was as good as his word and, as the gathering grew bigger and bigger, more people came to sell as well as buy.

Established as an annual rendezvous, a totally spontaneous event, Aikey Fair became the place to sell everything from hair-pins to horses, to settle your accounts, down a dram and savour your day's respite on Aikey Brae (Oakey Brae, taken from the Scots word "aik", meaning oak).

A short corn in the cap or buttonhole became a sign of looking for a "hairst fee" (casual work at the coming harvest).

Travelling showmen turned up with their amusements, and as they set up their stalls on the preceding Sunday, crowds would gather to watch.

201

In 1926 one astute showman decided to defy the Sabbath tradition and set his merry-go-round in motion. Amid cries of desecration, Aikey Sunday was born, running in tandem with the Wednesday horse market until after the Second World War.

But with the tractor endangering the very existence of the workhorse, the days of the real Aikey Fair were clearly numbered.

As post-war crowds of 30,000 flocked to the historic hillside for the Sunday jamboree, I set myself to charting the final days of the horse market. As a local reporter, I was in a good position to do so.

By 1950 the fair, which used to welcome thousands of Clydesdales, was down to a mere one hundred. I was there again with my notebook in 1951 when the numbers had dropped to 60. Another few years would surely see the end of Aikey Fair.

I should have been better prepared for 1952. Once again I was there to record the decline. Peter Grant, the local hotelier, put up his marquee as usual. A few buyers arrived from Maud station. And we waited . . . and waited.

Willie Barber, an Aberdeen horse dealer, turned up with a solitary piebald pony. And that was the last animal ever seen at Aikey. It was bought for £21.10s by another Aberdeen horsey man, George Ross—and in such ludicrous circumstances an age-old institution came abruptly to an end.

The handful of people repaired to Peter Grant's tent and there we drank a toast to the last moments of Aikey Fair. When I recorded this story in my autobiography, *A Grain of Truth*, I ended the chapter by saying: "As I turned to gaze back on the desolate scene, I knew I was witnessing a poignant moment in local history for we would never see its like again."

Well, nature turns some curious cycles. And—would you believe it?—come July 18 there is to be an ambitious attempt to stage a revival of Aikey Fair.

For the Clydesdale hasn't died out completely. There will be around 20 of the breed in a gathering of 200 horses. We'll see how to shoe them and, yes, how to sell them. One of the last horse dealers, Willie Murray from New Byth, will be on hand to demonstrate how bargains were struck.

There will be Romany caravans and riding displays and, despite a threat to the regiment's existence, the Gordon Highlanders' recruiting team will be there, complete with pipes and drums, just as in pre-war days. I remember tales of inebriated farm servants, having failed to gain a "fee", waking up next morning to find themselves with a posting to Singapore!

Ironically, the initiative for this Aikey revival has come from the travelling showmen who replaced the old horse market. With their Sunday funfair losing its appeal, they persuaded a local man, 47-year-old Billy Rennie from Stuartfield, to restore the earlier concept.

So it will run on the Sunday instead of the Wednesday, in a field adjacent to the shows.

Billy Rennie, once a champion showjumper, trained horses in North America before returning to Buchan. With financial help from the local authority, he is taking us as close as possible to the memory of the original fair, albeit with refinements like freefall parachuting.

Strongman Dave Gauder from Birmingham, the man who pulled Concorde 40ft along the runway, will try to stop two Clydesdales pulling him in opposite directions, seeking a place in the *Guinness Book of Records*.

Aikey Fair in the Guinness book? Aikey Fair revived at all? I can hardly believe it.

HERO IN A BLUE SERGE SUIT

• 1 3 T H J U L Y 1 9 9 3 •

LIFE can be a long and lonely furrow, a mixture of joys and sorrows but blessed, thank goodness, with that uncertainty about its outcome.

I remember, for example, a very dark day in the Second World War when our family received the dreaded telegram to say that my uncle, John Argo, had been plucked from the Atlantic after his troopship was sunk by a German U-boat.

The plight of those Scottish soldiers was made worse when life-rafts were thrown indiscriminately from the deck of their ship, adding injury to the dangers of drowning.

My uncle was hauled to safety, alive but no more, and was being taken to Glasgow with serious spinal injuries. My aunt should make her way to Hairmyres Hospital without delay, the implication being that her husband may not long survive.

In the emergency I can still remember my father backing out his little Austin, checking to see if the wartime petrol ration would take him to Glasgow, and bundling my aunt into the car with my mother and grandfather as they sped off into the mystery of the blackout.

I was left to hold the hand of my little cousin, Arthur Argo, bewildered by the news of his father and the departure of his mother. He cried uncontrollably.

With all signposts removed during the war and headlamps masked to a ribbon of light, my father drove blindly into the unknown territory of Lanarkshire.

Out of the inky black night, near Airdrie, came salvation in the form of an air-raid warden called, appropriately, Mr Love. They would never find Hairmyres, he said, so he squeezed into the car and guided them there.

What's more, once they had seen my uncle, this good samaritan took all four back to his own home at Chapelhall, where his wife provided a meal and a bed for the night. Total strangers. That was the spirit which makes people feel nostalgic about the war years.

Meanwhile, back in Buchan, I was anxious for news of a favourite uncle, always so good with children. Would I ever see him again?

His wedding day in 1934 had been my very first memory of life. Because of a recurring illness he had actually been married in bed, after which my aunt, the bride, accompanied the rest of us to the village hall reception.

The gods had given him a poor start but, by the outbreak of war, he was fit to leave with fellow-workers of Aberdeen County Council to form a unit of the Royal Engineers.

The parish had turned out to wave them off, these men whose children were my friends. Johnny Wallace, whose daughter sat beside me at school, was one of the few who could swim.

So, when the Germans sank the troopship, Johnny thrashed about in the water, saving many lives till he exhausted himself and went under, drowned along with his brother. I remember, on the Monday morning, the teacher telling us to be kind to Jean.

It was just the sort of tragedy which struck at individual communities on a daily basis during the war.

My uncle survived his terrible injuries and lived on through a lifetime in which the fates simply didn't let go.

His little son Arthur, whose hand I held that day, was one of the early victims of polio. Yet he battled on to become a BBC producer and leading figure in the folk-song world, acclaimed in America by a young man called Bob Dylan when Arthur hadn't even heard that name!

He helped to foster the careers of Billy Connolly, Barbara Dickson, Aly Bain, and Robbie Shepherd, all of whom pay him the highest tribute. But my beloved cousin was not cut out for long life and was dead by 45.

Indeed, John and Nan Argo not only outlived their son but also their grandson, Martin.

After a lifetime of tilling their few acres in Aberdeenshire, they settled in Glasgow to be near their daughters. Pollokshields was a far cry from the great skies of Buchan and John pined for his native land, accepting the separation as the price of seeing his family.

He kept contact with the North-east through one of Robbie Shepherd's radio shows, on which he was the Doric expert.

City life was not exactly kind to them. In their few years they suffered three burglaries and, just a few months ago, were confronted in their home by three masked men brandishing a knife.

With typical Scottish smeddum, however, my aunt stood up to their cowardly attack—and successfully drove them off!

But time was running out for John. He died in the Victoria Infirmary last week, just another in that great army of ex-Servicemen now slipping away day by day, little noticed by a busy world.

They didn't regard themselves as heroes yet, in their own way, they were heroes every one of them. John Argo reckoned he had had a bonus of 50 years he didn't expect that frightening night of Atlantic drama.

Whenever he attended a wedding or funeral he would point to his blue serge suit and tell you, with that impish sense of humour, it was the same one he bought for the ill-fated wedding day of nearly 60 years ago.

That suit hangs there still, by no means past its best. I don't think they make them like that any more. Come to think of it, neither do they make them any more like its owner, the late John Argo.

FAMOUS SHIPS OF THE CLYDE

23RD NOVEMBER 1993

A DISPUTE at Yarrow's of Scotstoun at least reminds us that they still build ships on the Clyde, a fact which could readily escape the attention of the less observant.

But what a pale shadow of an industry it has become, reduced to a mere three yards where once there were more than 50, making it the greatest shipbuilding river in the world.

Labour practices made their own contribution to the decline. But I leave it to others to examine the nation's folly in abandoning industrial production in favour of the much-vaunted "service" sector.

Instead, I have been looking again at the romance of Clydeside shipbuilding and what it created in the name of craftsmanship and quality.

These elements have been symbolised not only by the famous *Queens* of Clydebank, but right up to the 1990s, with frigates like *HMS Lancaster* from the same Yarrow's yard where the dispute was settled at the weekend.

I have been looking back nearly 200 years, when an engineer called Henry Bell, who helped his wife run a hotel in Helensburgh, dreamed of propelling ships by means of the steam engine, which had been perfected by James Watt from across the Clyde at Greenock.

Watt himself, strangely enough, didn't see a future for the steamship. But Henry Bell engaged John Wood of Port Glasgow to build the paddle steamer which became famous as the *Comet* (named after Halley's Comet, which appeared at the time).

207

Bell ran it for passengers on the Clyde and beyond but failed to interest the Admiralty in the idea of steam. Only Lord Nelson had the vision to support him.

So the Americans came to copy and exploit—and I wonder where we've heard that kind of story before. Bell died a disappointed man in 1830 and is buried at Rhu churchyard.

But the *Comet* is just one of those Scottish vessels which must take their place in the Clydeside hall of fame.

When Samuel Cunard began his transatlantic service he came to the Clyde for his paddle steamer, *Britannia*. Charles Dickens, one of the early passengers in 1842, was to write that his cabin was "an utterly impractical, thoroughly hopeless and profoundly preposterous box", and that the dining salon was "a hearse with windows".

Better reports of those two remarkable clippers, the *Ariel* and the *Taeping*, both built by Robert Shield of Greenock, which took part in a famous race in 1866. Coming home with tea from China, their 99-day race across 16,000 miles of ocean ended with a time difference of just 20 minutes!

So the stories come flowing. The future King Edward VII asked that Glasgow genius, G. L. Watson, to design his royal yacht, *Britannia*, which was launched from Henderson's of Partick in 1893. It passed to his son, George V, who was passionate about the yacht.

But when he discovered his sons didn't share his enthusiasm, he ordered *Britannia* to be scuttled on his death. That order was carried out in 1936 but, in the 1990s, after lying off the Isle of Wight for 57 years, she is said to be in such good condition that there is talk of raising her for sailing again.

Sadly, many a Clyde-built legend has ended in tragedy, not least the *Lusitania*, launched at John Brown's in 1906 as the last word in luxury. Sailing from New York to Britain in 1915, she was torpedoed by a German submarine, sinking in 18 minutes with the loss of 1,200 lives.

A particularly poignant story for Glasgow is that of the *Athenia*, built at Fairfield's and leaving the Clyde just before the outbreak of the Second World War, with many North Americans reaching for home before the trouble started.

The majority of the 1,147 people on board were women and children but that didn't stop a German submarine firing three torpedoes into her side. The date was September 3, 1939. The 112 dead were the first casualties of the war.

Survivors brought into Glasgow were entertained by Harry Lauder and visited at the city's Central Hotel by a young man called John F. Kennedy, whose father was American Ambassador in London.

And who can forget that great British warship, the *Hood*, as she engaged the dreaded German battleship *Bismarck*, said to be unsinkable?

In two minutes of high-explosive action the *Bismarck* split the *Hood* in two, leaving three survivors from a crew of 1,400. The might of the British fleet chased the German battleship and didn't rest until the unsinkable was sunk.

Of the famous *Queens*, I have fond memories of crossing to New York on the *Mary* before she became a hotel at Long Beach, California; sad memories of sailing round the corpse of her sister, the *Elizabeth*, after she was sabotaged in Hong Kong harbour in 1972; and warm thoughts of the *QE2*, which I boarded on the day she left the Clyde in the late 1960s.

With its current theme of ships, the Glasgow Royal Concert Hall asked another legend of the Clyde, Dr John Brown, to choose the 30 most famous ones built on the river. The concert hall's Ken Colville researched the case histories and asked me to write it all into a picture-story book.

That is why Dr Brown and I are preparing to add our autographs this week to those *Famous Ships of the Clyde*.

MY THANKS TO TURRIFF

• 4TH JANUARY 1994 •

DESPITE the ravings of agnostic clerics on both sides of the Border, Christmas somehow managed to survive, perhaps by the kind of miracle in which we are not supposed to believe any more.

To the young at least it is still a time of wonder and joy and for those of us at the other end of the scale it is a privilege to share their emotion, by seeing it through the eyes of a child.

It was a truly white Christmas, high on that Border landscape where I spent the day with a grandson, helping to build a snowman and being reminded once again about the uninhibited rural pleasure of sledging on steep fields under the pale moon of a clear frosty night.

It was the setting for seasonal nostalgia, heightened by a letter from the editor of the *Turriff Advertiser*, asking me to contribute an article to the diamond jubilee edition of the paper on which I started my career 46 years ago.

Diamond jubilee? When I arrived as a fresh-faced schoolboy that March day of 1948 the *Turriff Advertiser* had just passed its 14th birthday. Now it had chalked up 60 glorious years and, without feeling any significant change within the spirit, I had become part of its distant history.

What did I remember from those olden times, when the war was not long past and we were still gripped by a bleak austerity, adding a golden glow to the memory of the 1930s which was probably more than it deserved?

Well, I could still remember the excitement of travelling the 15 miles across Buchan by bus that first Sunday night and settling into my digs, which would cost me £1.15s (£1.75p) from a net weekly wage of £1.8s.1d. It didn't tally. But who cared?

Before the days of Durham's bishop, I put my faith in a providence which already looked after drunk men and children and would surely extend the protection to an impecunious cub reporter. And so it was.

I can still remember looking out from my bedroom window at Woodlands Crescent, Turriff, that Monday morning and nervously wondering what the big wide world would have in store for me. Having left school without as much as a scrap of paper to prove that I had ever been there, would I be capable of doing the job?

Maybe a burning enthusiasm would make good the deficiencies. So I worked as no youngster would dream of working today, often 12 hours at a time, up stairs and down stairs like Wee Willie Winkie, scavenging for news, no item of which was too insignificant to escape my attention.

"It'll make a par" (a paragraph) became a catchphrase of mine which used to amuse my mother no end. With the sure but undeveloped instinct of a journalist herself, she would phone to alert me of some local gossip, invariably adding: "It'll make at least a par!"

There was just an editor and me and when he was sacked I became acting editor of the *Turriff Advertiser* while still short of my 17th birthday. I wouldn't have called the king my cousin.

From morning till night I scoured Turriff and district for news, ending a typical evening at a town council meeting or the weekly gathering of the football committee, where they would consult me on the team selection for Saturday. That way, I couldn't blame anybody but myself if the results went wrong.

In retrospect, I sacrificed a social life through those teenage years, settling for a Friday night dance at St Ninian's Hall, where I would glide across the floor with everything but a number on my back.

Today, the *Turriff Advertiser* has joined the technical revolution and produces itself by computerised magic.

Up that rickety stair in 1948, we were still at the stage of picking individual letters from little boxes, forming words in the way we used to do with printing sets as kids. Not a great deal of progress had been made since Caxton.

Come to think of it, the wages hadn't changed much either. There came a crisis point in 1950 when, in the approach to my 19th birthday, old Willie Peters, the boss, pointed out that, instead of paying me £3 a week, he would make it £2.19s. Well you see, income tax began at £3 and, while I wouldn't suffer, he would save himself a shilling!

Maybe it was time to move on. So in October, 1950, just as Al Jolson died and Princess Anne was christened, I took my farewell of Turriff and headed for the reporters' room of the *Press and Journal* in Aberdeen. I had picked up shorthand and typing and learned the basics of my profession.

A wider world awaited. And now, as I look back down that long and winding road from the wrong end and wonder where the years have gone, I can only be grateful to Turriff.

No wonder I have raised my glass to that diamond jubilee this Christmas and offered a quiet toast to that vibrant little market town in North-east Scotland. To the land of the Turra Coo— thanks for the memory!

WHY CHURCHILL TOOK A SHINE
TO YOUNG JONES

* 2 2 N D J A N U A R Y 1 9 9 4 *

BUSTS of Winston Churchill take pride of place in the home of Professor R. V. Jones of Aberdeen as he reflects on an extraordinary career which brought him fame as a scientist while still in his twenties.

The man who discovered how to divert the German bombers from their wartime targets—and became one of Churchill's blue-eyed boys—now lives alone in Aberdeen's West End, a tall, quiet-spoken man of 82.

His thoughts range from those dramas of 1940 to the personal tragedy of losing, within a month, both his wife Vera and their glamorous daughter Susan, a former Miss Scotland who hit the headlines and the high spots of New York society.

The man who also met Einstein raised eyebrows and incurred the displeasure of daughter Susan when he was found mixing with the Moonies religious sect. But he can explain it all.

So what were the origins of this gifted scientist—and why did he linger in Aberdeen when higher positions were calling?

Reginald Victor Jones was born in the London street which became better known in more recent times as the scene of the Brixton riots. His father's career was split between being a postman and a sergeant in the Grenadier Guards.

But there was a clever streak in the family and young Jones won a scholarship to Oxford in 1929—it was there he met Einstein—and had already gained a doctorate in physics by the age of 23.

"I was going to be an astronomer and my life looked fairly settled," he recalls. But his first scientific paper was on the subject of infra-red detectors, at the same time as radar became a topic.

213

With the rise of Hitler, Professor Lindemann, Jones's superior who became Lord Cherwell and a friend of Churchill, was agitating for the formation of a defence committee. The question in 1938 was: Do the Germans have radar? Our intelligence services didn't know.

Young Jones, who had developed a taste for intelligence work, could hardly have guessed that he would soon be scientific adviser to MI6 and Assistant Director of Intelligence at the Air Ministry.

"I had come to the conclusion," he says, "that the Germans were developing radio beams to guide aircraft on their night-time raids on British cities. Professor Lindemann could hardly believe it but he told Churchill and I was asked to write him a report.

"I had seen Churchill in 1937 when he looked very tired and we all thought he wouldn't last much longer. Now I was called to a meeting and found him at the top of the table with people ranged on either side. They seemed to be talking at cross-purposes when Churchill asked me a question.

"I said: 'Can I tell you the story from the beginning?' He said that was a good idea and apparently I proceeded to talk for 20 minutes."

If Churchill was alarmed by the Jones discovery, he was relieved to hear that something could be done about it. By picking up from German transmitters their pattern of radio dots and dashes, you could jam and paralyse their system and feed in misleading signals. That way, you could divert their bombers to targets in the open countryside where they would do less damage.

Churchill was delighted. From that moment on, he would call young Jones "the man who broke the bloody beam".

Of course it didn't stop all German raids but Jones would include in his claims that it averted at least half a dozen other tragedies on the scale of Coventry's devastation.

It was the beginning of a constant scientific battle, not only to counter the German menace of bombs and rockets but to defeat their own defences against British raids. The Germans would have given anything for a Jones on their side, a fact revealed in

214

post-war meetings with their top men, who were unstinting in their admiration and astonished they had been foiled by one so young.

With all enmity gone, he now counts some of those Germans among his best friends, one of whom sent him a piece of the Berlin Wall!

So Jones became a wartime legend while still very young, credited with being the father of electronic warfare, establishing principles applied as recently as the Gulf War. But, in the peace of 1945, individual genius gave way to bureaucracy and he fell out with the Joint Intelligence Committee.

"I had suffered so much during the war from professors speaking outside their expertise that I thought I had burned my academic boats," he says.

However, an Oxford friend had become a professor at Aberdeen University, passing on good impressions, and Jones himself had visited the city in 1943 to take charge of a German Junkers 88 which came down there.

He and a wartime colleague, Professor Philip Dee, both headed for Scotland, Professor Dee to Glasgow, where he found that one of his predecessors was Lord Kelvin, so venerated that they even preserved broken glass from his attempt to create a vacuum.

Jones, on the other hand, found that one of his predecessors as professor of natural philosophy at Aberdeen was the much-neglected James Clerk Maxwell, whose reputation he set about restoring. In 1946, R. V. Jones settled among his post-war students, many of them returning ex-servicemen intrigued to learn the identity of their professor.

Still in his thirties when I first met him, Jones made Aberdonians feel good to have a man of his calibre in their midst. The obverse of the scientific nature was an impish inclination towards practical jokes and playing the mouth-organ (he wrote a serious paper on *The Theory of Practical Joking*).

Apart from teaching, his scientific work continued at Aberdeen, which became a world centre for creating crystals. Former students also carried his development of mechanical movement into

215

circuit-board manufacture in companies like Philips and Hewlett-Packard (Philips has a plaque in his honour at Eindhoven).

"Aberdeen had a lot going for it when I came here. My wife liked it and we were made very welcome. Over the years I had offers in the industrial and academic fields but I didn't want to become a vice-chancellor.

"I do sometimes wish I were closer to real centres of learning. Aberdeen had the chance to become one of those centres but went instead for expansion at the expense of quality. When I came here there were 23 universities in Britain and Aberdeen was in the top half. Now there are 100 universities and it ranks about fiftieth."

Relations soured a little over his refusal to quit the handsome university house in Queen's Terrace, formerly the Granite City's Harley Street and now prime property for oil-related and financial companies.

There he resides with memories of a lively family. He laments the loss of discipline in society but concedes that he had his own share of problems.

Daughter Rosemary, now a divorcee of 44 with a business in London, once ran away from home. Her elder sister Susan, a glamorous blonde, worried her father by entering the world of beauty contests which took her to the latter stages of Miss Universe.

Susan became the Countess Parente, married to an Italian-American aristocrat who was physician to people like Frank Sinatra and Zsa Zsa Gabor. But high life in Manhattan ended in divorce and she returned to a second marriage in Scotland, acknowledging the frothy nature of her early days.

Indeed she fell to chastising her father, alleging that he had allowed himself to become a respectable front for the cult of the Moonies. The learned professor assured me that, although he is still in touch, he never did have a religious commitment.

They had merely organised some splendid scientific conferences and he had agreed to be co-chairman when there were no fewer than 18 Nobel prizewinners present.

Tragically, Susan's diabetes became a serious matter and she died two years ago at 51, within a few weeks of her mother. Son Robert, 50, is a seismologist.

Professor Jones surveys the various honours around the house but settles on the busts of Churchill, whose determination to be in the thick of the action fascinated him.

He had booked himself a berth for D-Day and stood down only when King George VI said that, if Churchill was going, he was going too. Did I know that Winston, determined to be a pilot, had chalked up 140 flights before the First World War? He gave it up only when his deeply worried wife had a miscarriage.

We were back where the story had started. Back in those dens of top-secret discussion where a young lad from London confronted history—and sowed the seeds of a legend.

THE CHANGING FACE OF RUSSIA

* 24TH MAY 1994 *

A MUSICAL evening in Glasgow last week reminded me what a warm and admirable, not to mention talented, people the Russians really are.

That was hardly the popular impression during those long drab years of the cold war when the image of the Soviet people was one of dull, humourless intransigence, as personified by a man like Brezhnev as he would stand po-faced by the Kremlin wall, saluting the May Day parade.

It was, in fact, during Brezhnev's reign of more than 20 years ago that I paid my first visit to Moscow and saw the regimentation of everyday life at close quarters.

There was something pathetic about the military precision with which large hordes marched to work, reappeared at the end of the day, wheeled towards the universal GUM store, off Red Square, and finally disappeared as one solid mass down the drains of an underground system which would spirit them home to cheerless blocks of badly-built flats.

Among those prepared to talk to a foreigner I found an ignorance of the outside world which spoke volumes for the power of totalitarian control. Yet beneath all that, could so many millions of people really think exactly alike, as well as look alike and speak alike?

With the help of a splendid interpreter I caught an early ray of hope that the shackles of communism might one day be cast off. For those people were anxious to know about that outside world. There was a craving for individual expression and they now had the scent of freedom in their nostrils, even if as yet they could do little about it.

218

Most of all, the sheer warmth and humanity of the Russians came through in their smiles and their handshakes. After all, a nation which could produce people like Tchaikovsky, Rachmaninov, Rimsky-Korsakov, and Khachaturyan was surely not to be judged by the cold face of Brezhnev.

And so it turned out to be. Many years later, when Mr Gorbachev had begun the unwinding process, I returned to find a very different Russian scene. Driving in from Moscow airport, along Gorky Street towards Red Square, I could see them standing on street corners, airing the views which had been bottled up since the Revolution of 1917.

My taxi driver paused to give me a close-up of a man I would be hearing more about, he said. Boris Yeltsin was leading a march up Gorky Street. That new-found sense of freedom extended to Rostov-on-Don, Glasgow's twin city 'way down south on the Steppes, where the warm innocence of the people was a palpable delight.

And it was there that I first encountered the surprise of a musical group called Balalaika, playing those triangular string instruments of that name and producing such a wealth of singing and dancing talent as to astound.

There was a tenor called Oleg Boldyrev who should have been singing in the opera houses of the world. Instead, schooled by the system, he had reached the height of a man's ambition—to be a foreman in the tractor factory. Indeed, he was recently awarded his long-service medal! The singing which should have been his full-time profession was no more than a hobby. And so it was with others like bass singer Nikolai Sevastyanov. The leader of the group, brilliant accordionist Vladimir Skiba, at least had the luxury of being a music teacher.

The next time I met those talented people they had stepped outside their homeland for the very first time and were visiting Glasgow. And whatever the defects of life in this country, anyone with a grouse should have spent a day with those Russians and observed their delight at the things we take for granted—and their disbelief that a people could be so privileged.

Life at home may still be a hazardous business, as Prince Charles has been finding out in St Petersburg, but they are prepared to take their chance on the road to democracy.

That Balalaika group has been paying its own way to come to Scotland on a regular basis, in love with our land to a touching degree. They are here once more, yet so little publicised that countless thousands are being denied an exquisite musical treat.

I would pay my money if only to hear their percussionist, Alexander Krotov, who dirls up the xylophone with every bit as much dexterity as Evelyn Glennie.

I first heard him at a private function in the Carrick Hotel and again when Balalaika were performing for an invited audience of community groups at Glasgow Royal Concert Hall on Tuesday. They make their final appearance at the city's Mitchell Theatre tonight.

Marjukka Fryer of Glasgow District Council has done much to welcome the Russians since that first visit of 1989 and Scott Taylor, manager of the Carrick Hotel, has done the city's business image proud with the extent of his hospitality.

For their efforts, the Balalaika group is grateful to receive enough pocket money to cover their visit. But I cannot help feeling that visitors of such high calibre deserve better recognition in a land which prides itself in a keen musical appreciation, not to mention an unbeatable capacity for welcoming a stranger.

GEORGE ORWELL WAS WRITING
A CLASSIC

• 16TH AUGUST 1994 •

SOME time ago I recalled a particularly dark night in the Second World War when my uncle, snatched from the wild Atlantic, was brought ashore in a serious condition and taken to a hospital near Glasgow. His wife was driven south from Aberdeenshire by my parents, hopelessly lost in the blackout and desperately seeking a place called Hairmyres.

Suddenly, out of the gloom came a saint with a torch, guiding them many miles to the hospital and back to his own home, where he and his wife provided beds and food for total strangers in distress. Those good Samaritans from Chapelhall, Airdrie, were blessed with the name of Love.

That story passed into our family folklore and Hairmyres Hospital, which lies between East Kilbride and the village of Eaglesham, south of Glasgow, became a symbol of our most personal crisis of the war.

I have passed many times since, never failing to glance in gratitude for what it did to save my uncle's life. Until recently, however, when it came into the news as an emerging trust hospital, I knew nothing of the fuller story. And what I discovered merely underlines how little we know about the landmarks which surround our daily lives.

Would I have guessed, for example, that the patients who followed my uncle from the war fronts included survivors from the horror of Belsen? Would I have believed that the nurses who confiscated a typewriter were interrupting the flow of a classic then being written by a tubercular patient called Eric Blair, better known as George Orwell? The book was *Nineteen Eighty-Four*.

221

Perhaps I should have picked up the echoes of wartime dance music throughout the corridors of this secluded hospital. For great bands of the day, like Oscar Rabin, Ivy Benson, and the Squadronaires, extended their Glasgow engagements to play at Hairmyres. And the entertainers who dropped by included singers Rose Murphy and Allan Jones, father of today's popular ballad singer Jack Jones.

But if that was the glamorous side of Hairmyres, there has been a wonderful record of service to a community which now stretches to 190,000 people in the districts of East Kilbride and Hamilton.

It opened in 1904 as the Lanarkshire Inebriate Reformatory, an explicit title which would no doubt be banned today for some loony notion of incorrectness.

In those days, if you were found drunk and disorderly three times in one year you could be detained for up to three years. The first patient was evidently a miner's wife from Shettleston with 41 previous convictions. But patients escaped and those out on licence took to drink once more. The reformatory was in need of reform.

By 1919 it had become a sanatorium, opened on the same June day when John Alcock and Glasgow-born Arthur Whitten Brown set off from St John's, Newfoundland, on the first non-stop flight across the Atlantic.

Though the scourge of TB had dipped from its peak of the 1860s, there were still 5,000 Scots deaths per year around the First World War.

A major stride forward came with the antibiotic streptomycin, discovered in America during the war. At Hairmyres, the first patient to receive the new drug was none other than the man with the typewriter and a headful of ideas which would yet entrance the world.

George Orwell, admitted on Christmas Eve, 1946, under his real name of Eric Blair, had a house on Jura. Every winter since he was wounded in the Spanish Civil War he had suffered chest infections but now it was bilateral pulmonary tuberculosis.

When they removed his typewriter to encourage complete rest,

Orwell bought one of the early Biro pens, then costing £3. Simple surgical procedures were not proving successful so Orwell wrote to his friend David Astor in New York asking if he could acquire some of this streptomycin stuff for Hairmyres.

Astor obliged but Orwell suffered severe side effects and treatment was discontinued. Two other patients gained the benefit.

The author spent the remainder of his stay writing, walking, and playing croquet. He was deeply appreciative of Hairmyres, where he was remembered as a quiet, courteous man who found it difficult to make contacts.

He later complained that he had no-one to talk to. His fellow patients included A. C. Hunter, editor of the *Hotspur* boys' paper, but he found him a rather dull man. Sadly, Orwell's condition deteriorated and he died in London in 1950, still only 46.

During the war, Hairmyres became an emergency hospital and casualties came first from Norway, after the ill-fated Narvik campaign, and then from North Africa and Normandy, arriving by the hundred in hospital trains at Hairmyres station. They came too from the Clydebank Blitz of 1941 and from Belsen in 1945.

Curiously, when they were planning the new town of East Kilbride after the war, Hairmyres was reduced instead of expanded. Better sense prevailed in time, however, and money was spent on broadening its scope.

For putting me right on this worthwhile story I'm indebted to Dr Allan Campbell, a consultant from Houston who spent 25 years at Hairmyres and has now traced its history. I'll feel even more warmly towards it next time I pass.

THE BIG PICNIC

• 1 8 T H   O C T O B E R   1 9 9 4 •

IF you have read some of the criticisms of *The Big Picnic*, the extravaganza about the First World War now running in Glasgow, you will know it is a piece of theatrical schmaltz, weak and inadequate in its story, agonisingly banal in its folk-rock music and a hopeless misrepresentation of that dreadful war.

In fact, having read the Scottish critics (the English ones were far more generous) I'm surprised the doors of the Harland and Wolff engine shed in Govan are not already closed, with Bill Bryden's epic production written off as the flop of the year.

In view of the vitriol, I cannot think what persuaded me to leave the armchair and have a look for myself. Maybe I had been this way before and wondered if the critics and I had been watching the same show.

In any case, I went. And what did I find? I found myself transported into a memorable theatrical experience. I'm no expert, of course. But do I have to be?

Is it not enough that, having read about the horrors of the First World War, I can watch the story fleshed out in stark episodes and feel that I'm perilously close to the reality of the Somme? Pardon my naïvety but is that not good drama?

In common with a houseful of people from all walks and all ages, I was soon caught up in the tale of those boys from Govan as they enlisted in 1914 and marched away to the great unknown in France.

I found truly memorable moments in *The Big Picnic*, the Glasgow humour in the trenches, the fear and the courage—and that wonderfully human scene of Christmas Day when the British and

224

Germans gingerly approached each other across no-man's-land, shook hands, and played football.

It was all true, of course. For some critics, though, I'm sure there wasn't enough political tub-thumping about the evils of war. Not enough John McLeans on street corners.

But is it not enough to open up the hamper of *The Big Picnic* and judge for ourselves, if we don't already know it, what a horrible business war really is? Those flocking to the show in spite of bad publicity include many who are not theatre-goers by habit.

One critic admitted that the playwright has a knack of "convincing ordinary, working-class Scotsmen that the theatre has something to do with them". Well, of course it has. We're not just a herd of cattle who should not be venturing out of the byre.

I left that unique setting with the buzz of an evening which will linger for a lifetime. I also left with two particular thoughts.

One concerned the role of the critic, who can kill a New York show in one night but usually needs longer elsewhere. While the critical faculty must always be exercised in the name of honesty, I wonder if they ever make allowance for the fact that, whatever the artistic failings of a production, they may be driving away people who would actually enjoy themselves.

That does no credit to the critic or the newspaper—and no service to the public they purport to serve. There must surely be a secondary duty to indicate the reaction of an audience, which might turn out to be a better guide for potential customers.

(I have known critics afraid to praise a performance in case some rival, affecting greater perception, managed to find flaws!)

My second thought was even more troubling, linked as it was to the violence which seems to have gained possession of human nature. Hate, hate, hate has become the tribal beat, whether in the war-spots of the world, the demonstrations of Hyde Park or the football slopes of Scotland.

One striking feature of that First World War was that, for all the jingoism, there was little sign of real hate for the individual German. However misguided in their enthusiasm, young men joined up with thoughts of king and country. Some wanted to

225

escape industrial drudgery. And in days before foreign holidays, there were even thoughts of sunny France.

The modern capacity for hate is a different matter—one which I witnessed at close quarters the other day when Aberdeen played Celtic at Hampden Park. I had the misfortune to be close to that small knot of hooligans who besmirch the name of my favourite team.

I'll forget the Celtic part. My own lot were bad enough. Throughout the entire match they rose in unison to point their threatening fingers at the enemy, with all the passion of a Nuremberg rally. There was a football match going on down there but they were not interested. They were there to hate the opposition supporters.

These were "Fenian bastards" here today but any other brand would have done. A former leader of those well-heeled Aberdeen "Casuals", as they call themselves, wrote a book explaining the exhilaration. Kicking in heads was evidently more thrilling than sex.

"My generation didn't have a war," he rationalised, "so perhaps we were inventing our own."

Those young lads from Govan did have a war. They died in it. But they went off to France in a spirit of camaraderie and compassion, even reconciliation. The quality of human nature certainly has not improved since then.

IN FLANDERS FIELDS
THE POPPIES BLOW. . . .

IF there is one voice to encapsulate the mood of Remembrance Day it surely belongs to Tom Fleming, deeply resonant, pleasantly authoritative, quietly sympathetic, Scotland's finest. As he described with simplicity the Cenotaph scene of Sunday morning, the massed bands slid gracefully into Elgar's *Nimrod*, as moving a piece of music as was ever written and itself an indispensable part of remembering the dead.

Their comrades came down Whitehall in waves, every face a story, every poppy a matter of pride.

That same *Nimrod* had been played by the band of the Royal Marines in Holland last week as we stood by the memorial at Uncle Beach in Flushing, where the Scottish soldiers stormed ashore in November 1944 to liberate the Dutch from German occupation.

As I walked alone on that beach I was reminded again of how those Dutch people, often close to starvation, had looked to the skies for the food which might be dropped by the Royal Air Force.

I remembered hearing from Jan de Vries, whose healing powers are now given to the Scottish people, of how he ate grass as a child to survive in his native Holland.

Now the well-fed children of a later generation were playing happily on the beach. Whole families came cycling together along the boulevard at Flushing with such an air of peace and harmony that I wondered if the bicycle has some civilising effect on human beings.

I wondered, too, if there could be any understanding among a generation knowing nothing of war that these Scottish soldiers had come here 50 years ago to liberate their parents and grand-parents and were back now, perhaps for the last time, to honour their dead.

For many of those men from Scotland's farms and foundries it had been the most dramatic moment of their lives, for all its carnage still remembered for its caring and comradeship.

Any doubts about Dutch gratitude, however, were dispelled within hours as I walked through Flushing alongside the wheel-chair of Davie Paterson from Bishopbriggs, a Glasgow Highlander who lost both his right arm and leg in that invasion of 50 years ago but whose smiling face told only of the happiness of survival, not at all of bitterness at a lifetime of severe handicap.

As they took Davie to their hearts, obviously well aware that his sacrifice had been for them, I looked at him in wonder and knew one very good reason why I must never forget to wear my poppy on Armistice Day.

Back home—and throughout this remembrance week—that same thought has been prompted by random events.

By sheer chance on Sunday morning I tuned in to a Radio Scotland programme in which two brothers were discussing their late father. I soon recognised them as the Rev. Michael Mair, now a minister in Aberdeen, who was interviewing brother Colin, a lecturer at Strathclyde University, about growing up in the manse at Netherlee, Glasgow, where the Rev. Stanley Mair was minister for 30 years after the Second World War.

It was frank and fascinating stuff. Stanley Mair was one of nature's more glorious characters, the best Moderator an unim-aginative Church of Scotland never had. What an opportunity they missed!

Son Colin had gone for philosophy, clearly with doubts about the family "business" of religion. There were times when he had even wondered if his father had believed it all. Well, the five Mair boys no doubt knew their father better than I did. But in many a late-night discussion I came to know Stanley Mair fairly well and to realise that he was much more deeply religious than he cared to display.

I also knew about his war, daring exploits in Burma where he dropped in with the Chindits of his friend and leader, Orde Wingate. To me, Stanley Mair came to represent that courage and decency and good humour which so characterised those men who went off to war.

I think of him whenever I buy my annual poppy and how strange that, on this Remembrance Sunday, I should chance upon a discussion between his sons.

That poppy, I discovered last week, is not a symbol of remembrance familiar to the Dutch. To them it is the emblem of socialism, which called for some clarification.

It had all begun, I struggled to explain, on Flanders field in the First World War. A Scots-Canadian doctor, John McCrae, working in his medical post at Ypres, was greatly taken by the rash of wild poppies which continued to grow in the midst of battle.

The ancient Greeks had seen the poppy, with its opium qualities, as a symbol of everlasting sleep. So the 43-year-old Dr McCrae sat down and wrote his famous poem: *In Flanders Fields the poppies blow*. . . .

Sadly he did not survive the war. But the idea was taken up by Earl Haig, the British commander, for his annual fund-raising to help ex-servicemen.

Rounding off my weekend of remembering, I paid a return visit to *The Big Picnic*, that extravaganza of the First World War which ended its Govan run, appropriately, on Remembrance Sunday.

What a stirring finale to a theatrical experience which will linger for ever. That, too, will remind me—lest I forget—that there are a million and one good reasons for wearing that poppy as November days grow near.

PETER MANUEL—MASS MURDERER

• 2ND JANUARY 1995 •

THE distinguished figure who became a legend of Scottish court-room drama straightened himself in familiar posture and recalled with distaste "the most evil man I ever knew". Predictably, he was talking about mass murderer Peter Manuel, the fiend of Birkenshaw, who terrorised the Glasgow area in the 1950s with a catalogue of horrendous slaughter.

And just as predictably, the recollections were those of the great Laurence Dowdall, now in his 90th year but still possessed of that shrewd eye, logical brain, and golden tongue which set him apart in an age when criminal pleading held a special fascination for the general public.

"Get Dowdall!" was the cry of anyone in trouble with the law. It was the cry of Peter Manuel as he faced the Murder Trial of the Century, brought back into focus this week with the opening up of documents at the Records Office in Edinburgh.

In all truth, the Manuel case has long been documented in grisly detail, well-remembered by those who lived through it but emerging no doubt as a surprise to a generation which scarcely knows his name.

"When Manuel's mother came along and said he wanted me to defend him, I explained it was out of the question," said Laurence Dowdall, who now lives quietly in a flat on the South Side of Glasgow. "She was a good and devout lady but I had to tell her I was liable to be a witness for the prosecution."

Indeed, Dowdall was already deeply involved in what would prove to be the most sensational aspect of the whole case.

Long before the public had even heard the name of Peter

230

Manuel, they were caught up in another strange tale, concerning a Glasgow businessman, William Watt, who owned the Deanholm Bakeries in the city's London Road.

In September 1956, Mr Watt left his home at 5 Fennsbank Avenue, High Burnside, for a fishing holiday at the Cairnbaan Hotel, Lochgilphead, leaving his invalid wife Marion with their daughter Vivienne and Mrs Watt's sister, Mrs Margaret Brown.

On the morning of Monday, September 17, the home-help, Mrs Helen Collison, arrived at the Watt home, surprised to find the back door locked. Vivienne usually left it open when she went off to Skerry's College. Mrs Collison peered in at the window and could just see the figure of the girl still in bed. Rattling at the window brought no response.

She went round to the front door and was alarmed to find a pane of glass had been smashed. Just then, postman Peter Collier came whistling up the path. Cautiously they made their way inside together—to be confronted with a house of horrors.

In one room, Mrs Watt and her sister lay dead, shot through the head, with only a trickle of blood from their nostrils to indicate what had happened. In the next room daughter Vivienne too had been shot in the head but was still alive. Before the ambulance arrived, however, she uttered one last groan and died.

Vivienne's pyjama trousers had been pulled off and her top ripped open but she had not been sexually molested.

As William Watt was summoned from his fishing holiday and told of the tragedy, the hunt was under way for the Burnside killer. Ten days later, the police believed they had their man and arrested him. Sensationally, William Watt himself was charged with the murders of his wife, daughter, and sister-in-law.

Discovering that Watt had been unfaithful, the police assumed that he had tired of his invalid wife. The theory was that he had driven back to Glasgow from his holiday hotel in the middle of the night, committed the murders and returned via the Renfrew Ferry and Loch Lomondside before morning, as if nothing had happened.

To make things worse for Watt, the ferryman identified him as the driver of a car which had crossed in the middle of the night. He did, however, insist the car was a Wolsley, whereas Watt's was a Vauxhall.

Now incarcerated in Barlinnie Prison, he issued the familiar call: Get Dowdall!

"That was how I came to meet him," Laurence Dowdall recalled. "Here he was in Barlinnie, charged with killing his own family and distraught at the injustice of it all. So I set about making my own inquiries into the case against him.

"For a start, I took my Bentley car and timed the alleged journey from Lochgilphead to see if it would have been possible for him to do what they said he had done. Yes, it was physically possible.

"Nevertheless, I was soon convinced that Watt had not committed the murders. When I was at the Cairnbaan Hotel, a girl who worked there told me she had seen Watt's car that morning and it was covered in frost, as if it had been there all night. The woman at the hotel was a light sleeper and said she would have been wakened by a car."

Days after Watt's arrest, another man arrived in Barlinnie to begin a sentence for housebreaking. His name was Peter Manuel, who was soon considering an appeal.

Dowdall resumes the story: "I received a letter from Manuel in Barlinnie, asking my advice about an appeal. But that wasn't all. He added: 'I can also tell you that a client of yours who is in here is innocent.' So I went to Barlinnie and asked Manuel which client he was talking about."

"Willie Watt," he said.

"How do you know he is innocent?" asked Dowdall.

"Because I know who did it," replied Manuel, who proceeded to repeat certain things which had already been in the newspapers.

"Can you tell me anything that other people don't know?" asked Dowdall.

"Yes," said Manuel. "My informant told me that, having shot the two women, he struggled with the young girl and had knocked

232

her out when he heard a stirring from the other bedroom. He went in and found Mrs Brown still alive so he put another bullet in her."

"I made inquiries," said Dowdall, "and sure enough, there had been two bullets found in Mrs Brown. When Manuel also gave me accurate details of the Watt house and its furniture, I said to him: 'That leads me to one conclusion—that you did it.' When he denied it I said: 'Do you really think an informant would give you such piffling details of the house as you have given me?'

"Now more and more convinced that Manuel was the murderer, I was in touch with Alex Brown, Bob Kerr, and Tom Goodall of the CID and said this man knew more than he was saying.

"They asked if I would be a witness. I was able to tell Watt in Barlinnie that I believed the real killer was currently in this very prison."

Laurence Dowdall convinced the Crown Office there was no case against Watt and, on December 3, 1956, he was released from Barlinnie after 67 days.

Manuel would remain in jail for another year, during which time William Watt, anxious to get to the bottom of his family tragedy, was making his own inquiries around city pubs.

Having already arrested the wrong man, the police were more cautious in their decisions over Peter Manuel. Though the general public didn't know his name, he was amassing quite a police record. So who was he?

In a familiar pattern, the Manuel parents had emigrated from Lanarkshire to the United States in the 1920s and son Peter was born in Manhattan on March 15, 1927. But they found it tough going in America and returned to Scotland when he was still a small boy.

Nevertheless he would affect an American accent and in later years fantasise that he was once a henchman of Al Capone! He was soon building a criminal life of his own and, by 18, had attacked a woman on the same footpath where he would commit murder 12 years later.

Without paying too much attention, I had actually seen him during a visit to Peterhead Prison in 1951, but the main thrust of his crime was still to come. In 1955, he attacked a woman, and threatened to cut off her head but didn't rape her. He successfully defended himself to a Not Proven verdict, which would be a dry-run for things to come.

Manuel, small, stocky, good-looking, was now on the rampage. On January 2, 1956, eight months before the Watt murders, an East Kilbride girl, Anne Kneilands, was going home to the Calderwood district after being stood up on a date. Passing the golf course, she met a stranger and was found two days later, skull caved in, underwear removed but not sexually assaulted.

Harry Benson, now a world-famous photographer but then working for the *Hamilton Advertiser*, recalls arriving with his camera at the murder spot and hearing from a local policeman: "This is the work of Peter Manuel."

Manuel was indeed in a squad of Gas Board workers, laying pipes nearby, who were interviewed by the police. Asked about fresh scratches on his face, he said they came from a Hogmanay fight. His home at 32 Fourth Avenue, Birkenshaw, near Uddingston, was searched but no evidence was found and he was freed.

Gaining confidence, he now embarked on a two-year reign of terror. Having served his latest sentence in Barlinnie, he was released on November 30, 1957, and within days had gone to seek work in Newcastle. There he hailed a taxi to take him to Edinburgh and, en route, shot driver Sydney Dunn in the head and cut his throat. Motive? A mystery.

The underworld already knew him as a boastful, arrogant psychopath who gained his sexual thrills by terrorising women and who liked to sail close to the wind, as with his revelations to Laurence Dowdall, apparently made because he felt William Watt was gaining the "glory" which he knew to be his own.

Still anxious to track down his family's killer, Watt now came face to face with Peter Manuel at an extraordinary confrontation in December 1957, arranged to take place in the cocktail bar of the old Whitehall Restaurant in Renfield Street, Glasgow.

Laurence Dowdall was the only witness to the meeting, at which Manuel taunted Watt with details of his wife's bedroom. He said the "real murderer" had intended to break into the neighbouring house of Mr Valente, who was believed to have £10,000 in a safe.

On the night before, the Valente daughter was seen going into the Watt house and it had been wrongly assumed that No. 5 was Valente's.

(Deanne Valente had indeed gone in to listen to Radio Luxembourg's *Top Twenty* with Vivienne Watt. Back in her own house before midnight, she could still hear Vivienne playing the No. 1 in the charts. Ironically, it was Doris Day singing "Whatever Will Be Will Be".)

"During that meeting," Laurence Dowdall recalls, "Watt leaned over to Manuel and said: 'If I thought you had anything to do with this, I would strangle you, you little bugger!' He was a big hefty man and could have done it.

"But Manuel sat up straight and said: 'People don't do that to Peter Manuel.' "

Taunting again, he produced a picture and asked if they knew who that was. It was only later that Dowdall realised it was Anne Kneilands from East Kilbride.

The police had received information that Manuel, ever boastful, had been in a pub just before the Watt murders, saying he was going to rob a house where there was money and that he was ready for any obstruction, winking and tapping at a bulge in his pocket.

They were closing in but the psychopath was now in full flight. On December 28, 1957, the attractive Isabelle Cooke left her home at 5 Carrick Drive, Mount Vernon, on the edge of Glasgow, to meet her boyfriend in Uddingston. She didn't get there; nor was there any sign of a body.

Three days later, on Hogmanay night, lights were showing normally at the home of civil engineer Peter Smart at 38 Sheepburn Road, Uddingston. On New Year's morning, his garage doors were open and his car was gone.

But, with the holiday period, it was not until January 6 that the alarm was raised. Peter Smart and his wife Doris were found dead in bed, shot at point-blank through the head, Mrs Smart's nightdress ripped open. In the next bedroom their 11-year-old son Michael also lay dead, again with a bullet.

The killer had spent some time at the house over New Year, even returning to feed the cat, it seemed.

Having taken the car, Peter Manuel also had the audacity to give a lift to a policeman who was about to join the search for Isabelle Cooke. Dropping him off, he said: "They are searching in the wrong place." The policeman paused to wonder.

Public alarm reached fever pitch. Even the hardened underworld was now appalled by the callous killer and the police were informed that Manuel had been spending freely—and in certain pubs. With some good detection, they recovered notes which tallied with those Peter Smart had drawn from his bank at Parkhead.

They swooped on Manuel's house and recovered more notes. When he was taken in for questioning, he tried to implicate a leading figure of the Glasgow underworld, Samuel "Dandy" McKay, saying he had given him the notes.

The police called in McKay and asked Manuel to repeat his accusation. He did—and a shocked McKay told him he had just made the biggest mistake of his life and would swing for it.

Dandy McKay knew a lot about Manuel and was prepared to tell the police about it, complete with dates and times. Manuel began to crack. The case against him was now complete.

At a dramatic meeting attended by the parents he adored, along with detectives Brown, Goodall, and McNeill, his mother set the drama in motion when she said quietly: "Tell us everything, Peter. Tell the truth."

Manuel confessed: "I've been fighting this for years. I have done some terrible things." So the story spilled out—how he had killed Anne Kneilands, the Watts, the Smarts, Isabelle Cooke.

He led the police to Burntbroom Farm, Uddingston, walked around a ploughed field till he stood on a spot and said: "I think

236

she is just about here. I think I'm standing on her." The police dug and found the half-naked body of Isabelle Cooke.

He told of throwing his guns into the River Clyde, near the High Court, and divers went down and found the Webley revolver which killed the Watts and the Beretta automatic of the Smarts' killing.

The trial at the High Court in Glasgow began on Monday, May 12, 1958, Lord Cameron presiding, with a jury of nine men and six women.

Manuel pleaded not guilty to eight capital murders, the taxi-driver's having taken place in England. It would need only one of these charges to send him to the gallows. He put up alibis for all except Burnside, for which he now blamed William Watt.

The courtroom drama heightened when he dismissed his counsel, Harald Leslie QC (later to be Lord Birsay), and conducted his own case, bringing forth the judge's comment to the jury that he had done so with "remarkable skill".

After 16 days, however, it took the jury just two and a half hours to find him guilty of seven murders, the Anne Kneilands one lacking evidence. Lord Cameron pronounced the sentence: "To suffer death by hanging".

Fresh from snapping the Clintons at the weekend, the New York-based Harry Benson, whose father founded Calderpark Zoo, Uddingston, told me of how he developed a journalistic rapport with Manuel and visited him in Barlinnie. On one occasion, Manuel took exception to what a warder had said and made a leap at him, creating a frightening scene of violence.

Benson returned to the death cell and found a different man: "He was now subdued, saying he knew he was guilty and was resigned to his fate."

When his appeal failed, Manuel confessed to three other murders and the police believed there were still more. He did try to commit suicide and even to feign madness, which would have been his only hope of escaping the noose.

Nowadays he would be in Carstairs, aged 67, one of the few survivors of the drama, along with Laurence Dowdall—and

William Watt who, contrary to public belief, is still alive in a Fife village, now aged 87.

On Friday, July 11, 1958, hangman Harry Allen appeared at the door of the Barlinnie cell just before 8 a.m. A priest was saying his last words and Peter Manuel then went smartly to the scaffold. His hands were tied behind his back, a white hood placed over his head and the noose fitted round his neck.

The monster was finally in his trap. At one minute past eight it was all over.

238

THE NIGHTMARE OF LOCKERBIE

• 20TH FEBRUARY 1995 •

AS the prospect of a trial in the Lockerbie disaster reaches dead-lock, the Government is facing a mounting barrage of accusation that it has been responsible for a political cover-up.

With that bandwagon gaining momentum, the gist of the argument is that it diverted police investigation from Syria and Iran because it needed their support against Iraq in the Gulf War of 1991—and preferred to target the Libya of Colonel Gaddafi.

The scramble to uncover a conspiracy and produce "new evidence" in the world's biggest murder case has brought demands for a public inquiry—unlikely to be granted since it would virtually render a subsequent trial impossible.

But now, in the continuing public confusion, the man at the heart of the investigation, former Chief Constable George Esson, has answered key questions put to him by *The Herald*.

Mr Esson, now retired from Dumfries and Galloway and back in his native Aberdeenshire as security adviser to Shell Expro, is still subject to the Official Secrets Act.

But for all the attacks directed at the Government—and the fact that the buck stops officially with the Lord Advocate—the accusations also cast shadows on the investigation by Scottish police who were faced with the biggest murder hunt in criminal history.

So was there a cover-up? Was Esson under pressure to take the heat off Syria and Iran and turn it on Gaddafi's Libya instead?

"There was absolutely no cover-up," he says emphatically. "And I was never at any time under any political pressure. If you look at the facts, we had turned our attention to Libya long before the Gulf War of 1991. Our men were in Malta investigating the Libyan connection in the summer of 1989."

What would he have done if he had been put under political pressure to alter the course of the investigation?

"I would not have gone along with it. It might seem strange to people in other countries but this is the way we operate in Scotland. This was a straightforward police operation."

So what are the facts?

For a start, the manhunt resulted in two members of the Libyan Intelligence Service being charged with the atrocity of Christmas 1988, when 259 passengers of PanAm flight 103 were catapulted from their Jumbo jet at 31,000ft and 11 more died when the wreckage came tumbling down on the Scottish Border town of Lockerbie.

The main thrust of the case is that the two men were responsible for an unaccompanied suitcase being placed on board a plane in Malta, tagged through Frankfurt to London for transfer to PanAm 103, which would be heading for New York. The suitcase is said to have contained an explosive concealed in a radio cassette recorder, programmed to be detonated by an electronic timer. It exploded ". . . and they did murder them".

But the Lord Advocate of Scotland has so far been unable to bring the Libyans to trial. Frustration runs high, in tandem with accusations. Dr Jim Swire, a spokesman for British relatives, whose daughter died at Lockerbie, has gone as far as to say: "I'm beginning to wonder if there is a Libyan connection at all. The evidence seems to be disintegrating by the week."

The picture is also confused by the latest "evidence" which sought to swing suspicion back to Syria and Iran.

This evidence alleges a "confession" by Palestinian terrorist Abdel Ghadanfar that he was part of an Iranian-funded group planning a terrorist attack at Frankfurt. It says that, when he and his group were arrested by the German police before the Lockerbie disaster, one of them, Marwan Khreesat, was in possession of two barometric detonators—"of the type that set off the bomb which destroyed PanAm flight 103".

240

There George Esson claims a fundamental mistake and states that the indictment says nothing about barometric detonators, which would set off an explosive when the plane reached a certain height.

"The indictment says the Lockerbie explosion was caused by a straightforward electronic timer, bought from a firm in Zurich," he says.

Other "new evidence" also claims that Ghadanfar, whose "confession" dates back to 1988, was released by the Germans before the Scottish police had a chance to interview him.

"Baloney," says George Esson. "Our men did interview Ghadanfar in Germany. In those early days Marwan Khreesat was indeed our prime suspect. It would have been grossly incompetent not to have examined this side of it. But all this is caul kail. There was no evidence."

So what compelled the Scottish police to turn their pursuit from a Middle East terrorist cell in Germany to two Libyans with a base in Malta?

The full story of what happened at Lockerbie and the criminal investigation that followed has still to be told.

In the immediate aftermath of the disaster, I remember standing in the devastation of Sherwood Crescent, Lockerbie, and trying to reconstruct in my own mind the passengers' moment of realisation of what was happening.

It was the ultimate nightmare of anyone who has ever been in an aeroplane. Medical experts reckoned all passengers would have lost consciousness within seconds of the explosion but the younger ones would have regained it as they neared the ground.

Incredibly, a man and a child were calculated to have been alive for a time, the man having rib injuries which would not have caused his death if he had been found in time.

After finding the remains of the 259 bodies from the plane, the police then faced a search which eventually produced four million pieces of debris from 845 square miles of winter landscape.

The investigation was led by Detective Chief Superintendent John Orr and the evidence was passed on for examination to

241

Britain's leading forensic experts, Dr Thomas Hayes and Dr Allen Feraday, of the Royal Armament Research and Development Establishment.

For their success against terrorists, both were high on the IRA's hit list.

A watershed in the Lockerbie investigation came when these two men managed to identify a selection of blast-damaged clothing which seemed to have come from the suitcase containing the explosive. The common factor was that the clothes were made in Malta. Neither the police nor the forensic men knew of any Maltese significance, though it would be interesting to find out who bought any of these garments.

Soon after the disaster, John Orr was asking the German police if they could produce a list showing the origins of the luggage which was put on the plane at Frankfurt before it left for London, en route to New York.

For reasons never satisfactorily explained, the German police couldn't produce the list. But seven months after that first request, the Frankfurt company which ran the airport luggage transfer system came up with the full list.

When it was flown to Scotland, George Esson and John Orr couldn't believe what they were seeing. The Germans had failed to pick up the significance of one unaccompanied suitcase which arrived at Frankfurt, tagged for New York—having arrived from Malta!

Valuable time had been lost but, in great secrecy, Detective Chief Inspector Harry Bell led a Scottish police team to the George Cross island to pursue their inquiries. By that combination of skill and luck they not only reached the manufacturers of the garments but found the one little shop on the island which sold them all—to one man.

Shopkeeper Tony Gauci remembered the bizarre nature of the purchase—the customer just wanted a collection of garments, irrespective of size, quality or cost—and he reeled of the list of items bought, from a "baby-gro" to an imitation Harris tweed jacket.

242

That list corresponded precisely to the garments identified by Hayes and Feraday.

In all the current furore about the Scottish police being on the wrong track, one wonders what the critics would have done if presented with that kind of evidence? Would they have ignored it? Wouldn't they have been the first to condemn the Scottish police if *they* had ignored it?

Even that was just the starting point of deeper investigation, which led to the charges now standing. As well as being classed Intelligence men, the accused Al Amin Khalifi Fhimah is described as station manager of Libyan Arab Airlines in Malta and Abdel Baset Ali Mohmed Al Megrahi is said to be head of security for the same airline.

George Esson says: "When I hear what some people are saying I know that they are not privy to the knowledge of those involved in this painstaking and thorough investigation."

Curiously, while the weight of attack on the Scottish lawmen comes from Britain, the American relatives of Lockerbie victims, by far the largest group, are strongly supportive of those men at Dumfries and Galloway, whose diligence, compared to what they know in the United States, astounds them.

The media speculation that an Iranian ayatollah might have paid for the Lockerbie atrocity, in reprisal for an American warship shooting down an Iranian airbus in July 1988, is perfectly plausible, as much so as the idea that Colonel Gaddafi was getting his own back for an American reprisal raid on Tripoli which killed his adopted daughter.

The existence of a Mister Big, whoever he may be, is almost beyond dispute. But in the absence of any proof against such a person—a common hazard in criminal investigation—the Scottish police could not ignore the evidence, which they are ready to bring into open court, against the men they believe to have been the actual perpetrators of the Lockerbie disaster.

WHAT BETTY HADDEN
MEANT TO ME

* 2 0 T H   F E B R U A R Y   1 9 9 5 *

WE not only drank a toast to Robert Gordon at the weekend but wrapped up a corner of my childhood which included a strange and haunting episode. As the nostalgia flowed, the name of Betty Hadden kept flashing before me, as reminder of a grisly murder which has lain unsolved for 50 years and for which I might have had a vital clue.

But I kept pushing her out of mind for this was the night of Robert Gordon, the Aberdeen merchant who made his fortune in Danzig nearly 300 years ago and returned as the great benefactor of education in the North-east.

He opened a haven for poor boys who, in the local dialect, took on the name of Sillerton Loons, after an estate of the Gordon family.

That first building, still the proud focal point of Robert Gordon's College in the heart of Aberdeen today, was soon commandeered by Cumberland as a billet for his troops on the way to and from Culloden in 1746.

But once they had cleared the stench of the objectionable fellow the school resumed its true purpose and became one of the great institutes of education, now including Robert Gordon University.

The day-school remained the continuing link with the founder himself and, in time, the demand from Aberdonians abroad to send their boys home to be educated led to the opening of a boarding house in 1937.

Appropriately, it was called Sillerton House, an impressive grey-granite building at Queen's Cross. So, two centuries after

244

Robert Gordon, there was a new race of Sillerton Loons, the sons of men who had pursued tea in Assam, rubber in Malaya, jute in Calcutta.

Within that mixture of expatriates there was room for country loons like myself, for whom the daily journey to Aberdeen was too far. And that was how I became a Sillerton Loon in the middle of the Second World War, exchanging the brose of the countryside for the greater sophistication of the city.

The overlord of Sillerton was the imposing George E. C. Barton, who opened the doors as housemaster in 1937 and proceeded to give the bulk of his career to that task. I'm not sure they make men like George Barton any more.

But with the changing needs of society, Sillerton House has outlived its day and will close this summer, which explained our farewell toast of Friday night.

Just as there were 13 boys in Robert Gordon's original venture, George Barton too had begun with 13 Sillerton Loons in 1937. Fittingly, there were 13 of us there—his "vintage boys" as he called us—to salute him on Friday.

Now 85, he stood erect as ever and recalled the vision of the 1930s. The memories flooded back and for me there was no escaping that late autumn Saturday of 1945 when a friend and I accepted our pocket money from Mr Barton and headed down Albyn Place for the Odeon Cinema.

At Holburn Junction we were beckoned by a sailor who asked if we would deliver a letter to a certain house, wait to see if there was a reply and bring it back to this doorway.

By skipping the pictures we could earn a couple of bob instead of spending it. Yes, we would do it.

The street, in the Froghall district, turned out to be as much of a slum as Aberdeen possessed. Gingerly we climbed the stair and knocked on a door which opened to reveal a scene of postwar revelry. Sleaze might be a better description.

As I revealed in my autobiography, drunken servicemen lolled in chairs with women on their knees, exposing legs and thighs and goodness knows what. We were innocents at large.

A brittle woman took the note inside but returned to say there was no reply. We duly reported at the appointed hour to the sailor, whose dark, distinctive features I can see to this day.

It all seemed of no significance until a short time later when a man strolling by the foreshore came across a sight which sent him scurrying to the nearest phone-box. He had found a human arm, crudely sawn off, with the fingers arched as if scratching at a killer.

There had been screams in the night but nobody paid any attention. The arm belonged to 17-year-old Betty Hadden, whose mother Kate was a well-known name in Aberdeen. Betty had been seen in the city's Castlegate the night before. She had been seen with sailors . . . her close friends lived in Froghall . . . and the police were looking for a youth who had been known to carry a message to her.

Sailors were eventually traced to the ends of the earth and, trying to recall the name on the envelope, my friend and I felt we might have been able to help the police with a description.

But we were already in trouble academically and any brush with a murder investigation would have been a short-cut to expulsion. We kept our secret and I was many years into journalism before explaining it to the head of the Aberdeen CID.

Whether or not we had a vital clue to the murderer of Betty Hadden we shall never know. It was just an intriguing thought which was bound to filter through the social haze of Friday night.

THE MAN WHO PORTRAYED
MY FATHER

∗ 2 0 T H   M A R C H   1 9 9 5 ∗

AS that talented Scottish actor Bill Riddoch made his debut as an after-dinner speaker the other evening, I was struck once again by his uncanny resemblance, in style and demeanour, to my own father.

In one respect, of course, he was my father—the part he played in the BBC's 1987 drama-documentary *As Time Goes By*, which portrayed scenes from my Aberdeenshire childhood of the thirties and forties.

Though I wrote the film, I left casting to the experts. But I did put in a special request for two of the characters—Eileen McCallum to play the indomitable Lizzie Allan and fellow-Aberdonian Bill Riddoch to play my father.

What I didn't know at the time was that his father, Willie Riddoch, was the same Aberdeen cattle dealer who used to buy his animals at the ringside of Maud Mart where my father was the auctioneer.

In reality, young Bill had never seen John Webster but from the quality of his performance he might have been studying him all his life. Whether he was ploughing the field with a horse, pausing for a word with his son coming home from school or verbally jousting with Lizzie Allan in her village sweetie-shop, the television performance was fine testimony to his instinct as an actor. It could not have come closer to the true nature of my father.

Speaking of whom, it was hard to take in that he would have been 90 on Saturday. At my earliest memory he had not yet reached 30, a bustling personality, the very sight of whose restless

247

activity tended further to drain the more listless disposition of his pallid son, who was often bewildered by the mixture of fiery temper and glorious good humour.

I was less than popular, that day in 1938, when he contracted my dose of measles at the age of 33 and the pair of us lay isolated in one bed. As a restless, impossible patient he received a letter from a kindly old lady who sympathised with the fact that he was suffering from "a measle".

"A measle?" he exploded, his red-spotted face turning purple. "Ah've thoosans o' the buggers!"

On that stage of the Aberdeenshire cattle country he was a central character, powerful performer on the auctioneer's rostrum, unsurpassed as an agricultural authority.

He was in demand as guide and philosopher to many a crofter and small farmer seeking to establish himself with a home and a way of life for his wife and family. He believed in the right of the diligent farm worker to acquire his own bit land and savour independence, however hard that road might be.

He himself had come from a small tenancy at New Deer, his self-reliance put to the test at the age of eight when he took on the responsibility of his widowed mother, his small brother, and their few cattle in the byre.

It forged a man of such judgment and determination that he was well equipped to help others by the time he was into his twenties, scouring the countryside on his motorbike, as the young auctioneer seeking cattle for his particular mart at Maud, just one of three in the village at that time.

It prepared him for that day, in his forties, when he would feel confident enough to borrow every penny required to buy the farm of his dreams. Honeyneuk became his pride and joy for the rest of his life, though he also continued in the role of Buchan auctioneer until retirement age, exactly 25 years ago this week.

Rural life could instil in human beings a peculiar sense of the immortal, a kind of unspoken spirituality in which the dividing line between life and death was not the matter of obsessive concern which creates so much neurosis today.

248

Indeed, it took the premature passing of my mother and a few warning shots to himself before he ever acknowledged, even then in the most oblique fashion, that he might, just possibly, not live for ever.

It was revealed to me in an instruction of what I was to do "if onything ever happens tae me". Once more, his instincts were immaculate. That day came 18 years ago when, with an eeriness of timing, the black crow of death came settling on his window-sill and a silence fell upon the front room.

Dad's immortality had truly ended and we took him to the Hill of Culsh at New Deer, beside so many of his friends and neighbours.

By coincidence, I was back at that same resting place on Wednesday, when we buried my uncle Arthur, and there was time to cast around from that high point of Buchan and remember that my parents had lived their entire lives within a three-mile radius of where they now lay.

Down one side of the brae you could see Backhill of Allathan, where my father grew up, and down another was Mains of Whitehill, the smallholding which was home to my mother. They settled over there in Maud, which became the centre of my universe. And what a tapestry of life we knew.

But all was quiet now on the bare landscape of Buchan except that, in the glory of a fine spring day, you could almost hear the first stirrings of new life.

THE DAY I HOOKED THE GILLIE

• 3RD APRIL 1995 •

AS they made the lucky draw, we were told that last year's prize was a weekend in Paris. What was it this time? First, let's have the name out of the hat. And the winner is . . . yes, I had won it!

A weekend in Paris? Well, not quite. Instead, a weekend in Aberdeen. Now, as most of civilisation knows, I have nothing against Aberdeen. It was the subsequent information which raised alarm.

That weekend at the Copthorne Hotel was to include a fishing trip on an unnamed stretch of water? The River Dee perhaps? Ah well, despite my aversion to the rigorous experiences of life, I might run into the Queen Mother who seems to delight in wading up to her royal oxters in search of Deeside salmon.

The destination was not revealed until I reached the Granite City and the chap arrived at an ungodly hour to convey the two winners to their fishing beat.

"Deeside then?" I queried with forced joviality.

"Na na, man," said the driver. "We're gyan tae the Lake o' Pitfour."

The Lake o' Pitfour? But that's within a couple miles of where I was born—where, more than 50 years ago, I attached a piece of string to an old stick and dug up a garden worm as bait. But Pitfour it was, an estate once boasting a magnificent mansion house and a miniature model of the Temple of Theseus.

Much of the grandeur had gone but, to my surprise, the temple was still there, right by the lakeside, where a little oary-boat was bobbing up and down, awaiting its prizewinners from the south.

Into the boat I jumped, as Mike Morris the gillie supplied the

250

gear and rowed out to the middle of the lake, explaining the rudiments of angling.

I thought you simply cast the line and left it there till the fish came to bite. But it is not that simple. Apparently, at this time of year, the cunning creatures are lying at the bottom, feasting themselves on shrimps. You must skilfully entice them to the surface.

Mike the gillie—a corpulent, hairy, delightful character—demonstrated the repetitive rhythm of casting which leaves you, on a cold day like this, with aching muscles and a freezing posterior.

Wading in the water in search of salmon, he explained, is an even more arduous business, which left me wondering how on earth the Queen Mother achieves her success at the age of 94, when she casts away merrily and up come the fish. Maybe it's by royal command.

Anyway, the regal lady is welcome to her fun, I was thinking to myself as I checked my watch, shook it to see if it had stopped, and wondered how I could possibly endure the full six hours.

Mike the gillie was diplomatic and encouraging. No, I was not the worst novice he had ever encountered. He could remember one who was even more impossible.

Speaking of diplomacy, how could I arrange a tactful form of words to tell him I was planning to quit at lunchtime?

Thus engaged in deep thought, I was suddenly jolted back to reality. Miracle upon miracle! I was straining at the rod.

"Mike!" I cried, "I've hooked something. I've got one!"

"Yes, I know," he replied dolefully. "It's me!"

My glaikit look of discovery confirmed that the poor gillie was carefully trying to unhook my fly from his considerable foliage. The apologetic inquiry as to how I could possibly have managed that was met with another model of diplomatic expression.

Well, that was it. Goodnight Vienna. Back to the Temple of Theseus, where the Copthorne people had laid on a magnificent hamper lunch: smoked salmon, fresh salmon, cheese, celery and grapes, fruit and a whole bottle of Jack McLean's wee goldies.

As my teeth chattered over lunch, the other winner, Ian Cash, a chemical engineer from Aberdeen, arrived with much complaint about the heat. The heat? Yes, he had been so enjoying himself that he hadn't noticed the cold. But Ian was a real angler. Whereas I had just visited hell, Ian Cash was in seventh heaven, drooling over his memorable morning and entering into a fishermen's conversation with the gillie in which they could have been talking Swahili.

They obviously knew the psychology of the species, a couple of Freuds of the fishing world, reaching near-orgasmic enthusiasm in trying to tell me what it feels like to hook the little blighters.

Mind you, it was all right for Ian Cash. With a name like that, he had already hit the jackpot with a whopper of a rainbow trout and was destined to land two more before the day was out.

While he returned to the joys of fishing, I wandered across the road to the ancient Abbey of Deer and privately re-lived the last time I was here, filming my final scene of *As Time Goes By* eight years ago.

Fishing, they say, is the biggest participation sport in the land. But I wouldn't have believed there were so many human nuts in one small nation. On the other hand, they are nice people. Unknown to me until later, Ian Cash had quietly left one of his rainbow trout for my consolation.

Back home, I put it in the microwave for 90 seconds. And it was truly delicious.

252

THE PRIDE AND POVERTY
OF INDIA

INDIA comes at you like a tidal wave, a seething mass of humanity, ground down too often to the lower levels of degradation yet
coming up with a smile on its face to stir the conscience of an
affluent West.

My immediate destination last month was that coastal strip of
Goa, humble enough in its roadside shacks as you drive from the
airport, yet ready to cosset you in little pockets of paradise, with
the Arabian Sea lapping sandy beaches and the swaying fronds of
the palm tree shading you from a generous sun.

But you know that the unbroken luxury of Cidade de Goa will
give only a limited impression of India so you call your friendly
local agent, who glories in the name of Wringo ("The fourth
Beatle," he insists!), to see what he can do about interrupting the
idyll.

Soon you are being spirited a thousand miles northward to
Delhi, a capital of nine million people, where you begin to gain
the flavour of this extraordinary nation. Old Delhi has streets so
narrow that no ray of sunshine ever penetrates.

But if the colonising British did nothing else for India, they can
at least claim the splendour of the adjoining New Delhi, with the
spacious heart of a Hyde Park and the radial contours of Paris,
complete with Arc de Triomphe.

At Gandhi's memorial, on the spot where they cremated his
body, I was struck once more by the speed with which the events
of the day, still fresh in the memory, become established
history.

Wasn't it only yesterday that the frail little figure, all loincloths and fasting unto death, a thorn in the flesh of some, heroic visionary to others, was battling for India's independence?

He gained that freedom in 1947 but was no sooner coping with internal religious troubles than a Hindu assassin brought his days to an end in January 1948. Now the pilgrims flock to his memorial; and from that eternal flame I cast an eye around this teeming land and wondered how long it takes, even with the incentive of home rule, to bring some order to a nation of nearly one billion people.

Almost half a century later, amid the poverty and squalor, there is still no compulsory education; people in desperate need of help queue endlessly outside hospitals.

Close by Gandhi's memorial, limbless children vie with blind beggars for the crumbs of your wallet. It doesn't ease the pain to know that some of those children were maimed deliberately at birth to ensure a future beggar in the family; or to know that their efforts are well orchestrated—and quite lucrative compared with the meagre wages of the workers.

So you tackle the five-hour drive to Agra, city of the Taj Mahal, and gain the fuller sense of what India is about, from shanty town to harvest field, stately women bearing unthinkable loads on noble heads, poor and primitive but proud—a nation moving with ant-like purpose, clinging precariously to overcrowded vehicles being driven with suicide in mind. (They still manufacture—and export—the old Morris Oxford!)

Through it all comes the smiling face, prompting much wonder that the serenity and contentment of the human race seems to exist in such inverse ratio to material wealth.

Running the gauntlet of beggars and lepers, you finally emerge from the squalor and catch that first glimpse of the Taj Mahal, the memorial erected 350 years ago by the emperor Shah Jahan for the wife who died after her 14th reproduction in 17 years.

Initial disappointment soon turns to appreciation as you close in on the sheer scale and craftsmanship of the place. Mind you, when the old emperor was planning to squander the family shekels on a second mausoleum, his son and daughter had him locked up in the nearby fort. And quite right too.

254

Onwards to the Deserted City, dodging the depressing sight of tethered bears sent dancing out on the roadway to solicit your patronage; listening to a tour guide making much of a particularly eccentric queen who had a passion for keeping pigeons.

He went on at such length that I was tempted, in a moment of mischief, to ask if her last and most sluggish pigeon was, by any chance, "a Hindu". Doubting his appreciation of a Scottish pun, however, I thought better of it.

So it was back to Delhi and another 1,000 miles south to Goa, which now seemed like the very heart of civilisation by comparison. That visit to the capital at least lets you into one of the guarded secrets of athletics—how to run faster than Linford Christie!

But all is eventually well and you lap up the sunshine of glorious Goa before facing that round-the-clock flight to Britain via Bahrain. On the last lap from Manchester to Glasgow, we struck an air current more violent than I have ever known, throwing cups in the air and spilling tea and coffee in all directions.

The stewardess was giving her calmly-scripted announcement about fastening our seat-belts because of turbulence when the plane took its biggest lurch of all. With exquisite spontaneity, the dear girl blurted out an unscheduled "Bloody hell!" and defused a most alarming moment.

We all laughed, nervously but heartily—and knew we couldn't be far from Glasgow.

A NIGHT WHEN EDEN WOULD HAVE ENJOYED HERSELF

* 3 1 S T   J U L Y   1 9 9 5 *

AN invitation to the reunion was not, strictly speaking, for me because I was not a member of that class of '55. My own academic career, if I can so enhance the description, had ended miserably almost a decade earlier.

Yet this collection of classmates, now planning to mark the fortieth anniversary of the day they left Fraserburgh Academy, did indeed bear relevance to my own life. For, as the young man-about-town, reporter for the local daily paper, trench-coated in a fair imitation of Humphrey Bogart, I had caused a bit of a stir at that academy by settling my attention on one of its pupils.

On the very first date I had even proposed to the young Eden, who turned up at school the following week, flashing an engagement ring and announcing that she wasn't coming back. Amid the shock-waves, they didn't know what the world was coming to.

So I married the child bride and, 40 years later, her classmates were reaching the upper-fifties and looking back on those good old days, concluding it was time to hold their first reunion.

Sadly, Eden was one of three who did not survive to anticipate this gathering of old friends from the Aberdeenshire fishing port. It was not an occasion for partners, except for the next-of-kin of those no longer with us.

So, accepting the invitation by proxy for Eden, I drove north with some trepidation, knowing in advance that I would have to say something. Would my nerve hold on the night? For this was a time of joyous reunion in which any mention of absent friends would have to be handled with care.

Though all were younger than me, I had come to know many

256

of these people during the years. So I wasn't a total stranger. Yet I realised I was somehow on the fringe of this gathering, more in the role of observer, just as I had been 40 years earlier.

I did not share their immediate memory of teachers and escapades, though much of it had come to me secondhand down the years. But they had fond memories of Eden and wanted to include me.

My own upbringing took place 15 miles inland, but this town had always held a special place in my affections. From 1936, Maud School had taken its annual picnic to those magnificent golden sands at Fraserburgh. (Given the weather, is there a finer beach in all the world?)

With the dark clouds of war, I remembered that Guy Fawkes Night of 1941 when a blaze at Benzie and Miller's shop lit up the night sky over Buchan and diverted German bombers from attacking the Forth Bridge.

I remember cowering under the eaves of our village house as the enemy planes went bumbling towards their new-found target of Fraserburgh. Then came the thud-thud-thud which left 35 dead that night. I remember seeing a fleet of lorries taking the coffins to Kirkton Cemetery that Saturday, a harrowing sight which bound me emotionally forever to this community.

Making my way as a journalist in the early 1950s, I covered the Buchan beat from Fraserburgh, chugging along in the battered Ford Anglia to record such events as Coronation Day, the Great Gale of January 31, 1953—and the Fraserburgh Lifeboat disaster which followed nine days later.

These were events I could recall to the audience at the Alexandra Hotel that evening, dramas from their schooldays in that post-war period when society had not yet worked out its future.

Looking back to 1955, I suggested that that year, in which they left school, had marked a watershed in social history. Bill Haley and Elvis Presley had sprung on the scene with rock 'n' roll, heralding a whole new culture which had dominated the rest of our lives.

At that precise point, they had gone their separate ways, some

257

still living in the Fraserburgh district, but many now domiciled in distant parts and returning to greet old friends and classmates, mostly for the first time since 1955.

Bill Maitland, a businessman in Fraserburgh, and Sandy Campbell, a chemist in Dundee, had rounded up the exiled Brochers with admirable diligence and found that any element of risk which attends such gatherings was quickly swept away in a tide of uninhibited warmth and joy.

I looked around that company, last seen so long ago, and stripped away those flecks of grey and lines of experience to remember fresh faces of youth which seemed now, in retrospect, to have belonged to a distant age of innocence.

By coincidence, that class of '55 had brought together Ronald Benzie, now a businessman in the south of England, and Ian Miller, registrar of Edinburgh's Napier University—the two direct descendants of that Benzie and Miller business which went up in flames on Guy Fawkes Day of 1941.

Both were there on the night. And so was Norah Richards, who had been bridesmaid at our wedding all those years ago. We ate and drank and danced—and I managed, with some difficulty, to cope with my speech.

Yes, Eden would have been in her element on a night like this, I was thinking to myself as I drove off south, wondering where on earth the years had gone.

GEORGE FRASER—
STILL MASTER WORDSMITH AT 100

∗6TH NOVEMBER 1995∗

AMID the glam and glitter of an Oscar-style occasion, we celebrated far into the night at Aberdeen's Beach Ballroom on Saturday, as the biennial bonanza of the Bafta Awards spread honours throughout the realm of film and television.

Recorded and beamed to the nation last night, it was one of those rather special events where the so-called media was much in evidence.

And when it was all over, in the grey dawn of a Sabbath day, I kept an appointment with a very special gentleman for whom the word media would have very little meaning.

In George Fraser's early days, that plural word had nothing to do with the spreading of news and information. There was only a medium, and that was the newspaper, which was so well read throughout the population before the days of radio and television that people were remarkably well informed on what was happening around the world.

For George Fraser entered journalism in Aberdeen during the First World War and edited the news of those ghastly battles on Flanders field, as well as the story which brought the welcome relief of Armistice.

Before that war was over he was writing columns for his northern readership, and the delightful news for those who value the continuity of things is that he is still writing his weekly column 77 years later.

And what a model of journalistic perfection it is, a Saturday morning gem which should be compulsory reading for anyone aspiring to the role of writer.

259

He was telling readers last week of the man who once promised he would paint the outside of his house if he lived to be 100. Well, my good friend George will reach that milestone on Friday and, true to his word, the painter turned up the other day and gave him a shining exterior.

With similar brightness, George Fraser's clear mind is reflected in his weekly writing, conjured up nowadays from a more restricted lifestyle but benefiting always from that deep well of experience and imagination which the gift of the natural writer can mould to high craftsmanship.

Such a man is George Fraser, who was my editor when I joined Aberdeen Journals in 1950. He was then a very youthful 55, with a lively intellect to match the briskness of his walk, the speed of his turn. I suppose you could have speculated that, given the good luck of a sound heart and clear arteries, he would survive longer than most of us.

When I visited him yesterday there was a chance to recall that he had started life in 1895 at the village of Newmachar, north of Aberdeen, where his father was the railway signalman.

This clever lad-o'-pairts went on to Aberdeen University with thoughts of teaching but a chance meeting in Union Street with a fellow graduate (later to be the distinguished author, Alexander Keith) diverted him to the Broad Street office of Sir William Maxwell.

Thus George Fraser joined the old *Daily Journal*, one of four sub-editors handling the war news from France as well as writing his own column. At the end of that war he was working with a journalistic colleague by the name of Leslie Mitchell, who became his rival for the hand of a girl called Peggy in the cashier's office.

Peggy eventually married George but always kept the loving poems which Leslie Mitchell had penned for her. Mitchell was, after all, the real name of that greatest of North-east writers, Lewis Grassic Gibbon.

So here is a man with a clear recollection of the century in its entirety. I have said before that we Scots do badly at acknowledging the real worth in our midst.

260

But one lady who has not failed in that respect is Queen Elizabeth, the Queen Mother. On her regular and lengthy stays on Deeside, I happen to know, she is an avid reader of the Scottish papers—and a longstanding admirer of George Fraser's writing.

Nevertheless, it was with surprise the other week that George received an invitation to come to have tea with his royal admirer at her Birkhall home, near Balmoral.

He was a bit wary of such an occasion but was able to tell me yesterday of how pleased he was that he had gone. Imagine the charming scene of those two special human beings discussing an age to which there are now few witnesses.

George had remarked on the fact that he was a Victorian. "But so am I!" the Queen Mother reminded him. And, of course, so she is, albeit by a narrow margin. So they talked with great warmth and affection in an encounter which put the royal seal on the distinguished career of a truly worthy Scot.

The omens had not been too auspicious when childhood illness left George with the weakened heart which kept him out of the First World War. They improved when Sir William Maxwell had welcomed him to newspapers with the quip: "Journalists live to be a ripe old age."

And these turned out to be prophetic words indeed. As George Fraser opens his house for a centenary buffet this week, knowing he is the oldest working person in Britain, we'll raise our glasses for a very special toast—to our Grand Old Man of Letters.

THE LEGEND OF OL' BLUE EYES

* 1 8 T H   N O V E M B E R   1 9 9 5 *

MILESTONES gain in significance the longer the journey lasts: more experience gained, less time to go. So it is with Frank Sinatra, surely the greatest entertainer the world has ever known, who will complete his 80 years on December 12.

Daughter Nancy, herself no mean singer, wrote a loving book for his 70th birthday and has now updated the story, this time in the rather different form of a month-by-month diary, with a patchwork splattering of pictures and quotes which makes it look a bit like a family album.

It is, of course, the very subjective view of Sinatra's adoring daughter but, considering the singer's longstanding conviction that he would never write his own story, this is the closest we are likely to come to an autobiography. To her credit, Nancy does not gloss over the allegations that Sinatra had Mafia connections, albeit if only to mount a defence against the rumour-mongering for which she blames a succession of journalists.

There was at least one occasion, however, where her father could have shown more sense. She tells the story of how Frank Sinatra played a vital role in putting John F. Kennedy in the White House.

Needless to say, it began with the future President's father, the ruthless and despicable Joseph Kennedy, who would stop at nothing. If he were to gain the Democratic nomination, John F. Kennedy simply had to win the primary election in West Virginia. So crooked old Joe approached Sinatra and suggested he should seek the co-operation of notorious mobster Sam Giancana. And that's what Sinatra did. Sam sent one of his henchmen to ensure that local sheriffs and powerful coal-mining unions would deliver the necessary 120,000 votes for Kennedy.

However, deeds come back to haunt you. Kennedy eventually shunned Sinatra. And if the great singer was having his own private thoughts at the time of the 1963 assassination, he didn't have long to dwell on them. Two weeks later, he was caught up in the personal crisis of his own son, Frank junior, being kidnapped. After the ransom was paid, young Sinatra was released and two men given life sentences.

Darker incidents should not, however, detract from the warmth and compassion which are so much at the heart of Sinatra's character. And he does, after all, remain the most popular single artiste the world of entertainment has ever known.

It has been a remarkable career, all the way from Hoboken to Hollywood—the working-class home in Hoboken, just across the Hudson River from Manhattan, where his Italian father Marty was a prizefighter and dock labourer before working for the local fire department.

Sinatra himself worked in the shipyard but sang at school and liked the applause. His early heroes were Russ Columbo (killed in a 1934 shooting accident) and Bing Crosby. It was when he took his girlfriend Nancy to hear Bing in downtown Jersey City that he decided, there and then, he was going to be a singer.

He formed the Hoboken Four, later gained a radio spot with another promising youngster, Dinah Shore, and finally got the break of an engagement with that great band-leading trumpeter, Harry James. In 1939, the year he married Nancy, he cut his first record, "From the Bottom of My Heart". The career, now well documented, took him on to the orchestra of Tommy Dorsey, with whom he eventually fell out, and thereafter towards the heights of show business. Here was The Voice, the man with expressive hands, soft speaking tones and that hungry and vulnerable look which stirred the girls, by now bereft of their boys at war, to swoon over him, to want to take care of him, make love to him. Ironically, that wonderfully musical ear was a perforated one, damaged at a forceps birth, which was to keep him out of the forces.

It didn't stop him becoming a film-star with MGM, appearing in *Anchors Aweigh* with Gene Kelly, who taught him how to move. He would win an Oscar for his part in *From Here to Eternity* but felt he had given his best performance in *The Man With the Golden Arm*.

Meanwhile, he and Nancy were divorced and his magnificent obsession with Ava Gardner led to marriage in 1951, Ava having already been married to Mickey Rooney and bandleader Artie Shaw. In that immediate post-war period, the unknown name of Las Vegas burst upon public consciousness as the dream of mobster Bugsy Siegel to make it the mecca of the gamblers' world. In helping to shape its reputation, Sinatra became King of The Strip and has never lost that sense of belonging there.

Daughter Nancy traces her father's ups and downs from the wild days of the Rat Pack, through his marriages to Mia Farrow and Barbara Marx (Zeppo's widow) to those sadder moments when his contemporaries began to melt away. The name of Nelson Riddle will forever represent the greatest orchestra to bring out the best in Sinatra. Yet, on the day of Riddle's funeral in 1985, Frank was attending the New York funeral of that other friend, Yul Brynner. Frank junior did the honours in California.

And on that very same day, the death was also announced of one of the singer's closest buddies, the great Orson Welles.

Nancy's book, incidentally, includes a compact disc covering some rare moments in her father's life.

Inevitably, there would be other books to mark Sinatra's 80th birthday. Ray Coleman, who specialises in showbiz biographies, has come up with *Sinatra: Portrait of The Artist*.

This is a more coherent narrative from a professional writer, again lavishly illustrated and doing full justice to the man who has won his way to so many hearts—the legend we know as Ol' Blue Eyes.

ON THE LONELY SHORE

✦ 2 9 T H   A P R I L   1 9 9 6 ✦

IN the early days of this column I devoted the entire length to a man I admired above most—my old friend and colleague Don Whyte, one of the finest wordsmiths this country has produced.

"There will no doubt come a day of great eulogies," I wrote, "but I would rather tell you about the old devil now."

So I did, because I am constantly appalled to read obituaries of people whose stories are so fascinating that I wonder why on earth I have not heard of them before.

As it happened, the day of Don's eulogy was postponed for longer than he might have expected, considering he had to endure a lifetime's struggle with the crippling effects of polio, which felled him one day in 1938 when he was 12. But the day did, inevitably, arrive and it was my melancholy task last week to deliver that eulogy at Clydebank crematorium. It was nevertheless a privilege to speak of such a man.

When we first met, in the spring of 1960, he was coming to terms with the last days of his own distinguished father, Ian Whyte, founder-conductor of the BBC Scottish Symphony Orchestra.

Now it was his own turn. And as I sat by his bedside at Gartnavel Hospital, Glasgow, we recalled, for as long as his oxygen mask would permit, some of those experiences from the early days of our careers.

Don loved to tell a story linking his affliction of polio to my own longstanding problem with a stammer. His recollection of it was better than mine but it makes a good story nevertheless.

Apparently, in the rush of our newspaper's edition time one night, when all hell was breaking loose, Don became impatient with my stuttering as I persisted with a question.

Apologising later for what now seemed like rudeness, he was leaning heavily on his walking-stick when it slipped and he fell full length on the floor. Hoisting him into my arms, I apparently said: "Ay, there's just one difference between my problem and yours."

"What's that?" asked Don.

"Mine doesn't land me flat on my arse!"

But then Don Whyte was full of fascinating memories. When his father was organist to Lord Glentanar at Aboyne, he remembered Deeside summers like this: "Summer was a rhapsody of warm lawn grass and the smell of ripening strawberries. Summer was when honeysuckle clung to our porch of spaniel brown, and its scent clung to my nostrils. Summer was a plethora of sweet peas and peonies, a nuzzling of bees, a guzzling of raspberries and farm cream, and gooseberry fool."

Nature was his inspiration and, from an early age, he showed a rare faculty for absorbing its beauties into the very marrow of his soul and reproducing it in word pictures which were a joy to behold.

I'm sure that wonderfully gentle landscape of Deeside helped to forge this wonderfully gentle man, just as the musical genius of his father was encouraged by childhood lingerings in the family smithy in Fife, where he was introduced to the rhythms of music by his grandfather's hammerings on the anvil.

As Ian Whyte moved back south from Aberdeenshire, emerging as the distinguished conductor and composer he became, there was a whole new world opening up for young Don. His father was mixing with idols of the day, like the great Toscanini. Don used to tell the story of his mother answering the door of their Edinburgh home, on a day when she was expecting the piano tuner. The shabbily-dressed little man went straight to the keyboard and announced it would take about two hours. Two hours for a well-kept Bechstein? It seemed ridiculous and Mrs Whyte, who intended going out but couldn't, did not disguise her displeasure.

What's more, he now seemed to be entertaining himself to Beethoven instead of tuning the piano, though she had to admit it was pretty good-quality Beethoven. No wonder.

When Ian Whyte arrived home he was full of apology. There had been no time to warn her that John was coming up to study before conducting that evening. The "piano tuner" was Sir John Barbirolli no less!

To browse again through Don's autobiography, *On The Lonely Shore*, is to be reminded of what a fine writer he was. Even in his crippled condition he went out reporting for the *Express*, once pursuing the incident of a bull which ran amok in Duke Street, Glasgow.

He told the chilling but hilarious tale of how the bull "lowered his handlebars, pawed the ground, and charged", choosing as his soft target the reporter with sticks and caliper!

A generation of journalists will recognise his description of his chief reporter, Jack Coupar, "a lean man with shrewd blue eyes and a mouth set like a rat trap".

But Don Whyte felt something of a prisoner at a desk in the grey heart of a city. Like Yeats, he could always hear the lapping waters of the countryside. So he would strike out, to fish or sail or climb, anything which would take him close to nature.

As I said at the funeral, he never stopped marvelling at the wonders of the Universe and will no doubt be seeking more of its glories, even now, as he wanders by himself, on that lonely shore.

SIR FITZROY—
REAL-LIFE JAMES BOND?

•24TH JUNE 1996•

MORE swiftly by the day, the unrelenting hand of time bears away that generation of Grand Old Men who were daring young heroes of the Second World War.

If there is anything at all to be said for that war, it is that it revealed the potential for heroism in apparently ordinary human beings. Not that Sir Fitzroy MacLean was an ordinary human being.

Indeed he always struck me as a rare specimen who might well have been an even greater figure if he had lived in an earlier period of Scottish history. On the last occasion we met, for example, there arose the question of Bonnie Prince Charlie's march towards London and his disastrous decision to turn back at Derby.

"It wouldn't have happened if I had been there!" he boomed with great good humour. And you could believe it of the man who died last week, a broadly based giant in every sense of the word, to whom well-deserved tributes have been paid from all over the world.

He and his distinguished brother-in-law, the late Lord Lovat, are just two of that wartime breed who proved their worth within a broad scope of adventure which, hopefully, will not present itself again. The world now seems destined to a different, if hardly less sinister, way of settling human conflict. Legend has it that Sir Fitzroy was Ian Fleming's model for the fictional James Bond, a romantic story which will no doubt persist whether it is true or not. What is much more certain is that he became a real-life legend in the Yugoslavian land which has been tearing itself apart in recent years, gaining Britain's support, in the Second World

268

War, for the leadership of Marshal Tito, with whom he formed a close personal friendship.

I picked up on that liaison during a visit to Tito's sumptuous mansion in Dubrovnik 43 years ago. Such was the standing of the distinguished Scot in Yugoslavia that he became the first foreigner allowed to own a house within the laws of that post-war communist state. The legislation which allowed it became known as MacLean's Law.

Sir Fitzroy and Lady MacLean duly took up residence on the Adriatic island of Korcula, as an alternative to their main home at Strachur in Argyll. And it was in that idyllic setting on the Dalmatian coast that coincidence was to weave a subsequent strand.

For just to the south, in that charming city of Dubrovnik, another member of the clan had come to take up residence. Indeed Alistair MacLean, by then one of the world's biggest-selling novelists, was to spend the last eight years of his life in a villa overlooking the Adriatic.

It could then reasonably be said that the two best-known of the clan in the world, both with family roots at Strachur, were living within a short distance of each other in an unlikely corner of Europe.

In the light of a tragic incident to follow, it was to prove a lucky coincidence for the man who wrote books like *HMS Ulysses*, *The Guns of Navarone*, and *Where Eagles Dare*.

In 1984, Alistair MacLean's son Ali had just arrived to visit him in Dubrovnik when he reversed the Mercedes from the villa gates into the path of a bus. The driver swerved towards a solid wall of rock and when the novelist rushed out to see what had happened, he found the bus-driver and three of his passengers lying dead.

Held responsible for the accident, young MacLean was sent to prison for a year. And that was when Alistair, believing his son had been unfairly accused, turned in desperation to Sir Fitzroy, a man he had never actually met. Over dinner in Dubrovnik, they discovered the further link that Lady MacLean came originally from Inverness, while Alistair had grown up at the manse of Daviot, a few miles away.

269

As to the plight of young Ali in prison, Sir Fitzroy would do what he could for a fellow-Scot. With Yugoslavia's annual freedom celebrations at hand, there could be a pardon for prisoners. So it was that the lad was released, his sentence cut from a year to a few weeks, earning Sir Fitzroy the undying respect of one grateful family.

But as we bid farewell to one of Scotland's Grand Old Men, there is cause to rejoice over the latest news about another. In my pursuit of recognition for worthwhile Scots, I have told readers about George Fraser, my former editor in Aberdeen, who was writing columns before the end of the First World War. Now in his 101st year, dear George still writes his delightful weekly offering in the *Press and Journal*, a model of how to handle the English language. So imagine my delight as I turned on the wireless for the 1 a.m. news the other morning, in time to hear that the Queen had honoured George Fraser with the MBE. I let out a whoop of joy.

In the morning, the phone at his King's Gate home was constantly engaged. But eventually he answered—and confessed to a feeling of unbridled happiness. Having to enter your second century before recognition may seem a long time to wait. But justice has been done.

And if the medal had not represented a royal award, its initials could just as well have stood for Master of Better English.

REMEMBERING ARTHUR ARGO

THAT massive pop party at Strathclyde Park last week produced a statistic which prompted a query. My surprise about T-in-the-Park was not so much that the clean-up men found 5,000 used condoms in the aftermath of what was obviously a bit of a bonking bonanza. No, my question is this: Who bothered to count? And for what practical purpose?

While all that effort was being expended I was, simultaneously, enjoying an ecstasy of a different sort. Not being one to rave about parties, or even to show suitable pleasure over birthday and Christmas presents, I have to say the recent birthday celebration was a matter of exquisite delight.

It lasted for not so much a day as a week, greatly enhanced by the flood of good wishes from out there in the readership and culminating in the kind of family gathering which can be rare when your offspring are scattered.

So the day began with a Grampian Television crew arriving from Aberdeen to film the Glasgow end of a 30-minute documentary, which will round off my 48 years as a staff journalist.

I strolled with memories up Buchanan Street and through George Square and came back to the *Herald* office to sit by this computer screen which will serve me for the next two weeks. The television crew then followed me home to the South Side of Glasgow and captured early stages of the family gathering.

Thereafter I was in for such a night of touching surprise and sheer delight as to make you realise the worth of the people around you. In the midst of a heady night, it fell to the eldest son, Geoffrey, to say his piece about the "old man", for that is what

271

I have always been, even when I was a young man. The old man hadn't been such a bad stick, apparently leaving some reasonably good impressions (even when I thought I was being rather neglectful of three growing lads with my various gallivantings in the name of journalism).

Geoffrey, Keith, and Martin, who all became journalists, knew that, for all the old man's joy in writing over the years, he was still stuck deep in the dark ages of the typewriter, producing books by a technology which is already synonymous with the Ark.

They themselves belong to the new age of computers, with its jargon of gobbledygook, which sends old-stagers like me scurrying for shelter. But if I intend to ward off senility in the twilight years by continuing to write in some form or other, then it is clear that this modern mystique must be unravelled, the illiteracy must somehow be resolved.

I was due to see a specialist the other day but the 65th birthday party put a different complexion on all that. In the big surprise of the night, I was led to a spare room, told to close my eyes, then open them.

And there, laid out in all its mystifying glory, was the array of gadgetry which will see me towards the new century. All I need to do now is learn how to use it.

So we cut cake and drank champagne and celebrated into the early morning, keeping in mind that I had to be in Stonehaven by midday for the big folk festival. It was a longstanding engagement to talk about the Scottish rural life which produced those folk songs in a bygone day, as a lead-in to the Arthur Argo Memorial Concert.

Arthur Argo spearheaded a folk revival in Scotland nearly 40 years ago, as a performer and organiser, gaining in influence through his position as a BBC producer. He discovered artistes like fiddler Aly Bain from Shetland and was well placed to give such people a proper exposure on air.

Others who would give him credit for playing a part in their early careers included Barbara Dickson and Billy Connolly.

Indeed, as I arrived at the St Leonard's Hotel in Stonehaven, on a gloriously hot day, the festival folk were sunning themselves on the lawn, with its elevated view of a calm blue sea. And among those enjoying the idyllic setting was the same Billy Connolly, whose professional career grew very much from that background of folk music.

He was there as a spectator and came to hear my talk, no doubt with his own memories of Arthur Argo. For Arthur was one of those boyish enthusiasts who knew everyone and was loved by all.

As it happened, he was also my younger cousin, both of us growing up in the village of Maud and following the same route into journalism via Turriff and Aberdeen. Though both great-grandsons of Gavin Greig, world authority on folk song, it was left to Arthur to carry on that part of the family tradition.

He did so to great effect, even if his own life was cut tragically short at the age of 45. He died on Good Friday of 1981, and the concert is an annual memorial to a lively spirit.

They are currently writing his biography, which is no more than he deserves. But as I spoke of him at Stonehaven last week, I remembered that he would have been at my birthday party on the previous evening. And how he would have enjoyed himself! If only the fates had dealt a better hand.

MY FRIEND 'MAD MITCH'

* 2 9 T H   J U L Y   1 9 9 6 *

THIS would have been the moment of farewells. But I'm delighted, instead, to say the old horse is not going out to graze quite yet. In fact, the weekly column remains—and a broad selection from the past 10 years is due to be published in book form in the autumn, under the title of *The Herald Years*.

Otherwise, it would have been a doubly sad day, saying goodbye to so many friends and paying tribute to one of them who died last week.

That colourful soldier, Colin Mitchell, who gained the soubriquet of Mad Mitch and became a Scottish hero, seemed like the durable dynamo who would live long to tell hair-raising tales of adventure.

Instead, he is gone at the precise point of the allotted span, not from the ravages of malignancy or the sudden flash of a heart attack but simply, I'm told, from exhaustion.

The hero of the Aden encounter of 1967, whose career was ended prematurely through petty bureaucracy, may have vanished to obscurity, a sometimes sad and forgotten figure, but in fact the trained killer had turned his energies towards the saving of life by founding a wonderful organisation.

Appalled by the vast amount of explosive debris left by wars around the world, he set out, with his wife Sue and a friend, to do something about it. Colin Mitchell trod the path from Afghanistan to Cambodia, Mozambique, and Angola and wherever there were land-mines posing a threat to millions of civilians.

Unlike his daring recapture of the Crater district of Aden, he avoided publicity and simply went ahead with a humanitarian

274

crusade, enrolling an army of volunteers and achieving wonders which saved countless thousands of lives. Back home, at his flat in London's exclusive Dolphin Square, just round the corner from Westminster, he would reflect on a life as it might have been.

I first met Colin Mitchell on the day he left Aden. As Mad Mitch of the Argylls, he was hot news. In those recent months from July 1967 he had given the British Army a new sense of public relations by coming on television, as soldiers had never done, to capture public imagination with nightly explanations of what he was doing.

And what he was doing in Aden was nothing if not dramatic. Before the territory was due to be handed over to its people, the town of Crater, built in the shell of an extinct volcano, had grabbed its own independence.

British soldiers were being freely massacred as police mutineers ran riot. On the day Mitchell arrived to take command, he hovered over Crater in a helicopter and witnessed a slaughter, which included men of his own Argylls. The fate of those Scots lads is too gruesome to recall but Mitchell was so incensed he vowed this would not be repeated while he was in charge. Nor was it. A few days later, he took matters into his own hands and, in the dead of night, marched his Argylls back to the no-go territory of Crater, pipes a-skirling.

He so stunned the Arabs that British authority was soon re-established—and that was how it remained until Harold Wilson pulled out the troops.

While Britain ruled, Mitchell was showing who was boss. Press and television went with him and people were fascinated by this straight-talking young colonel of Glasgow background, who shared a birthday with Montgomery, fought bravely at the end of the war, and escaped death by seconds in 1946 when he was about to enter the King David Hotel in Jerusalem at the moment of its destruction by terrorists.

This final fling of British Empire would soon be out of date but there was a lingering admiration for men of Mitchell's calibre. He was the archetypal tough-guy, handsome in a film-star mould, born leader of men, full of good humour and irresistibly likeable.

But it soon became clear he had done the unthinkable. He may have restored order but he had gone further than his superior, Major-General Philip Tower, had sanctioned.

I was now close enough to Mitchell to know what was happening. Through the old-boy network he was being given the hint that it was time to go. He would not get the decoration he was due. Worse still, his beloved Argylls were under threat from the Labour Government.

He promptly resigned from the Army and campaigned to "Save the Argylls". The campaign was headed by my newspaper and culminated in George Younger (Scottish MP and former Argyll) and myself carrying 1.5 million signatures into the House of Commons.

The Argylls were saved by the incoming Tory Government, which Colin Mitchell joined as Member for West Aberdeenshire, gaining the seat from the Liberals, who were represented by Jo Grimond's wife Laura.

Colin Mitchell had a job for life. But redundant colonels are a restless breed. He stood down in 1974 and from then until he founded his Halo organisation for clearing mines, there was a lack of fulfilment.

I hadn't seen much of him recently but between foreign sorties, I'm told, you would find him walking around London for hours on end, his little pork-pie hat perched on thick grey hair.

I can't help feeling a sadness that we didn't make the most of an extraordinarily brave and gifted Scotsman.

THE GENIUS OF
FRANCIE AND JOSIE

∗5TH AUGUST 1996∗

THAT last day at the office was a weird experience. Clearing out the desk, separating the junk from the bits which might come in useful again—and measuring out the countdown to the teatime presentation.

Hour by hour the ties were loosening as you realised that, very soon now, you would no longer be part of this place. Someone else would sit here and grow to know it as you had done.

I toyed with the screen in front of me, considered the 48 years and four months since I began in Turriff, and keyed in a last sentence: "Well, that's it folks!"

The editor made a generous speech over the wine buffet and it was down to Tom's bar for the rest of the evening; the morning hangover could have been much worse. So to the life of a free-lance writer and, as an antidote to any threat of brooding, where better to turn than to that genius of the comic art, Rikki Fulton.

A session with the Rev. I. M. Jolly was sure to cheer me up. And it did. I had been delighted to see from the billboards that Rikki and his sparring partner, Jack Milroy, were making a come-back in their incomparable roles as Francie and Josie.

Retirement had always been threatening for those lovable layabouts but, like Frank Sinatra, they just can't stay away. So, for the first three weeks of October we are in for a treat at the King's Theatre, Glasgow, with *Francie and Josie's Brand-New 19th Farewell Performance*.

What I did not know until I settled down with Rikki Fulton was that this column played a major part in bringing the pair of them back to entertain us. It all happened in March of last year when

277

I joined the audience at a charity show in the King's Theatre and came away with muscles aching. Francie and Josie had come out of retirement to raise money for a good cause. But in this column on the following week I raised the question: why, outwith a charity night, is there no commercial theatre catering for this kind of audience?

The answer I could have anticipated was that it costs around £100,000 per week to stage an extravaganza such as we had on that memorable evening. But surely it could be done, I argued: "Could they [Francie and Josie] be prised out of retirement even once a year for a week? In the name of sheer unadulterated joy, let us hope so."

Rikki Fulton read the column and generously gives it credit for having been the catalyst for what happened next.

Of course, as they drew breath after that hilarious night, he and Jack Milroy were well aware that they had been through a very special experience. More precisely, Rikki Fulton admits he could not recall a reception quite like it. "I was taken aback by that night," he told me. "And there is no way to describe the feeling. It is the most joyful, glorious experience that any human being can have."

Fulton let me into the secret of a routine which he and Milroy follow just before they go on stage. Once the make-up is on, the adrenaline is flowing, and the safety screen has been raised, they wander down to the stage and listen from behind the curtain. As seasoned professionals, they can tell from the chatter and general buzz what like an audience it is going to be. Well, Rikki Fulton turned it all over in his mind and he and Jack came to the conclusion that maybe, as I had implored, they could be prised out of retirement.

The mechanics of what happens next is a side of showbusiness which always fascinates me. Who makes the move? How does it all come about? On this occasion, naturally, the initiative had to come from the two stars themselves. They had dinner at the Country Club with Billy Differ, then manager of the King's Theatre, and broke the news that they were ready to do it again.

278

With a fine sense of melodrama, Billy literally fell off his seat! Absolutely wonderful!

So Fulton, who writes the scripts as well as playing the part of Josie, got down to the task as soon as possible and the booking office is already buzzing with anticipation of that opening night on September 30.

What we are promised is a night of fun and nostalgia, straight from the tradition of good old variety, complete with a line-up of dancers, a magician, and the talent of singer-comedian Dean Park.

Jamie Phillips, the former Glasgow opera singer who now runs his Trends agency in London, is producing the show, which will certainly need all of that £100,000 a week to cover itself.

But if Francie and Josie can't do it, who can? In the light of some pretty dreary entertainment around these days, I suspect they will prove that variety is far from dead. Meanwhile, the two characters are rehearsing their lines in the spaciousness of the Fulton house. They live not far from each other in Glasgow's West End and twice a week you will see the eccentric Milroy stepping round to Rikki's place, more than likely talking to himself about the joys of being alive. But no sign of senility here. For a pair of septuagenarians, their memory for a script is remarkable. What a joy that comic genius of this calibre is still with is.

THE DAY I CONDUCTED AT THE ROYAL CONCERT HALL

THAT recent Saturday feature in which I was seen, complete with white tie and tails, on the conductor's rostrum of Glasgow Royal Concert Hall, was evidently taken by the more sceptical of *Herald* readers as a piece of photographic fake.

But not a bit of it. Well . . . the photograph was genuine enough, taken to illustrate an article about my love of music. I was definitely standing on the podium where conducting greats have stood before.

And if you had been there with eyes closed you would have heard such a magnificent swell of quadrophonic sound as to raise hairs on the back of your neck. The technical people did me proud.

Only when you opened your eyes might you have been less than impressed by the numbers obeying the command of my baton. And apart from a few cleaners, flower arrangers, and odd-job men, no doubt muttering obscenities about that heid-banger up there, the audience wasn't up to its usual standard either.

But I was away on a cloud, oblivious of their scorn, launching myself into the role of orchestral conductor, knowing I might as well make the most of this opportunity since it was unlikely to arise again. I had long dreamed of indulging this fantasy and now the moment was here.

So I was not only dressed for the occasion but the state of mastery over my repertoire was a clear sign that I had not come unrehearsed. On the menu at the Royal Concert Hall that day was Elgar's sombre but deeply-moving *Nimrod* and that most rollicking of American show-stoppers, "Hooray For Hollywood".

280

They don't come in greater contrast than that—and I was fair giving it laldie.

But if the performance raised a modicum of self-consciousness in myself (and some doubts about my sanity in others) I need not have worried too deeply. I knew that Richard Wilson played out such a fantasy when he didn't have *One Foot In The Grave.* But now I have discovered that our little peccadillo is shared by so many frustrated conductors that there are actually some books on the subject.

It is the discovery of one such book which brings me more fully to the topic today. In *The Armchair Conductor,* a couple of chaps called Dan Carlinsky and Ed Goodgold take you through the steps of how to lead a symphony orchestra in the privacy of your own home.

Amid the tongue-in-cheek fun there is some good practical advice, from what to do with your baton (polite version) and what to do if it flies out of your hand (grab a carrot, for example) to the basics of conducting Beethoven's Fifth—and how to pronounce Mstislav Rostropovich.

So to the stories, apocryphal or otherwise, about famous conductors, who can be as eccentric a breed as football goalkeepers. The first one I ever saw was Sir John Barbirolli, when we were taken on a wartime school outing to hear the Halle Orchestra at the Music Hall in Aberdeen.

The great Barbirolli claimed he didn't need a timer when boiling his breakfast egg. He just stood in the kitchen and conducted the overture to *The Marriage of Figaro.* Three minutes exactly!

At a rehearsal of his opera *Elektra,* Richard Strauss was landed with a soprano who was not his favourite. "Louder, louder!" he roared at the orchestra. "I can still hear her!"

Otto Klemperer could be a crusty old devil, niggardly with praise. But when he shouted "Good!" at the end of one difficult piece, the orchestra burst into the applause of relief. Klemperer turned, scowling. "Not that good!" he roared.

Poor old Klemperer should have been kinder to people. In

1933 he fell off the podium, landed on his head, and had to have brain surgery; in 1951 he fell from an airport ramp and broke his thigh; in 1959 he set fire to himself while smoking in bed and was seriously burned. He still managed to survive to 88.

One of my favourite composers, Antonin Dvořák, had conducted one of his pieces so often he once fell asleep on the podium.

But when it came to ego, there was no-one to beat Sir Thomas Beecham, whose family gave us those famous powders and little liver pills. Congratulated by Fritz Reiner for "a delightful evening with Beecham and Mozart", the conductor replied "Why drag Mozart into it?"

He was rivalled for ego by Herbert von Karajan, one of the most popular of all conductors. Hailing a taxi one day, he pondered the driver's question "Where to?"

"It doesn't really matter," waved von Karajan wearily. "I'm in demand everywhere."

The energy expended by conductors has been calculated to exceed that of the fittest baseball players in America and must explain the good health which keeps so many going to their eighties.

The memorable Arthur Fielder, for example, was still conducting the Boston Pops Orchestra at 85. And that brings me back to my own appearance at the Royal Concert Hall, when the music of "Hooray For Hollywood" was recorded by Fielder's old band—and there I was, dreaming about conducting it.

Well, do you know what I have discovered? For anyone who comes up with a contribution of $5,000 towards Boston Pops orchestral funds, there is an open invitation to turn that dream into a reality. Will you pardon me while I check the piggy-bank?

CALIFORNIA—HERE I COME!

23RD SEPTEMBER 1996

WHEN you fly away to the sunshine, managing en route to catch a streaming cold which settles into the chest, the least you expect on return is to hear that the folks back home have been suffering a dose of predictable Scottish weather. Well it didn't happen, did it? Sporting the glorious tans of an Indian Summer, they were able to tell me about balmy days in the back garden which didn't cost them a brass farthing.

Ah well. There were certain compensations in California, where I divided the time between my favourite ship, the *Queen Mary*, and my favourite hotel, the Beverly Hills.

To reach the *Mary* from Los Angeles Airport you drive 20 miles south to the city of Long Beach, where she floats in regal splendour as a hotel and tourist attraction, welcoming on board more than a million people every year. Suddenly those three famous funnels loom large in the distance and your heart beats faster at the sight of them.

Close up, you still marvel at the sheer scale of this magnificent lady, pride of Clydebank, as you soar in a lift to the reception area.

This time I had the Churchill Suite, presided over by a portrait of the man himself, who was sailing on the *Queen Mary* from the Clyde, to meet President Roosevelt, when he was given the plans for D-Day. They have even named the main restaurant after him and from the comfort of Sir Winston's you have a spectacular view across the bay to Long Beach, a city about the size of Edinburgh.

Early evening cocktails are in the Observation Bar, where a

283

pianist ripples the arpeggios in a reminder that this is a ship of the 1930s. Tuesday lunchtime brings two hours of ballroom dancing, when former GIs from the Second World War can turn up with the aid of sticks, even zimmers—and promptly discard them when the Big Band glides into action. The healing powers of Glenn Miller are worthy of medical research!

Beyond that, I can simply wander the decks for hours, recalling days of luxury travel on the Atlantic before jet-planes put them out of fashion. Enlarged photographs remind you that this was the playground of the rich and famous, from the Duke and Duchess of Windsor to every major star that Hollywood produced.

From these decks, too, you have a grandstand view of the neighbouring dome which once housed the world's largest aeroplane, Howard Hughes' famous *Spruce Goose*, now gone elsewhere.

That dome has become a spacious film-set, a godsend to producers who don't have far to come from Hollywood. Last week's attraction was Arnold Schwarzenegger, who was there to star in the latest Batman film.

So I waved the *Mary* goodbye and headed for Beverly Hills, with its broad, quiet avenues of magnificent villas, home to so many of those Hollywood stars. The hotel, built in 1912 and uniquely giving its name to the city which developed around it, is back in business after a renovation costing its owner, the Sultan of Brunei, upwards of $100m. Popularly known as the Pink Palace, the Beverly Hills must now be, surely, the most tastefully beautiful hotel in the world.

The famous Polo Lounge reeks of Hollywood history and is still the scene of the Power Breakfast, where film moguls thrash out early-morning deals. The private bungalows in the garden remind you that this was where Marilyn Monroe had her passionate affair with Yves Montand when they were making *Let's Make Love*. That's exactly what they were doing, until Montand's wife, the gorgeous Simone Signoret, put a stop to it.

For long spells last week I was by the poolside, remembering that Irving Berlin once lay right here, under a sweltering sun which prompted him to start dreaming of a white Christmas. He took out his pad and pencil and promptly jotted down the words and music which became Bing Crosby's greatest hit. In the cool of the evening I was strolling round those quiet streets, saddened by the number of residents now disappearing. Since my last visit Gene Kelly has gone, his home in Rodeo Drive looking forlorn.

I passed Dean Martin's last house, modest by comparison to the mighty mansion of his hell-raising days, now owned by our own Tom Jones. George Burns's villa is under renovation by the new owner. And saddest of all, the "For sale" sign is showing at Ella Fitzgerald's secluded home in Whittier Drive.

Seeking out the living, I passed Elizabeth Taylor's mansion and, close by, that of the Reagans, who are known to be at home when the security cars are drawn across the gateway.

On North Roxbury Drive, James Stewart's dining-room was set for his evening meal. And on that same street I paid customary homage at the old home of George Gershwin, now owned by Rosemary Clooney.

I hadn't realised that another of my composer idols, Jerome Kern, lived so near to Gershwin, just round the corner—and across the street from Ella Fitzgerald. With Kern very much in mind, I strolled back to the Polo Lounge. And what met me but the strains of "Can't Help Lovin' That Man o' Mine". When I told pianist Douglas Amster where I had just been, he launched into an evening with Jerome Kern. And my visit to California was rounded off to perfection.

WALKING BACK TO HAPPINESS

• 14TH OCTOBER 1996 •

THE train journey to Aberdeen was a pure delight of early autumn. In a week of uncertain weather and even more uncertain forecasts, the day improved the further north and east we sped, till the sight of Aberdeen's granite glinting in the late afternoon sun would have lifted the heart of a total stranger, never mind a dyed-in-the-wool Aberdonian who, in his early days in Glasgow, could be found at the barrier of incoming trains from the north—just to see if there was anyone he knew!

I have grown up since then; but that return to the North-east is still a cause for quickened heartbeats.

And the mellow colours of autumn which turned the journey into an artistic joy took on an even richer hue on account of the fact that my round trip to the Granite City cost a mere £8. That was enough to put a smile on the face of any Aberdonian.

The railway company (whatever it is now called) was apparently offering this concession for any return journey within Scotland for those who could prove they were over 60.

As I fumbled to provide proof of age, the girl at the Queen Street Station counter waved aside my attempts with a gesture which meant, unmistakably, that I was dabbling in the superfluous. When she then realised that she might possibly be causing the old boy some offence, she corrected herself to a more diplomatic comment about knowing an honest face when she saw one. At that point I caught sight of my reflection in a mirror and, as a realist, conceded that there was definitely more wear-and-tear than honesty in that face—and that the girl had been right in the first place.

286

So to Aberdeen and a night's rest before starting out on the meticulous task of fitting a voice-over to the half-hour documentary I have just written for Grampian Television.

Centring on my recent retirement, it begins in the throbbing heart of Glasgow, the city which is now my home, finds its way to the North-east, back to the house where I was born, and the village school at Maud where I first went that spring day of 1936. Circling around my childhood scene, I end up at Honeyneuk, my father's old farm, which figured in the 1985 documentary of *Webster's Roup*. Jim Muir and family are now well settled in there, far from their Orcadian origins, and enjoying the Buchan countryside which was my childhood.

The new documentary drifts back to Glasgow, to my last day on *The Herald*, followed by the 65th birthday party which took me into so-called retirement. In writing the script to match the pictures, I became more and more conscious that I was revisiting the mood of the award-winning *Webster's Roup*. More than 10 years later, people are still haunted by that film and write to ask where they can acquire the video. Sadly, it doesn't exist.

So, in a soundproof studio at the Grampian TV headquarters in Aberdeen, I grappled with the voice-over of *Walking Back to Happiness*, measuring my flow of language on the regular basis of three words per second. Yes, that's the speed we speak on television.

You must regulate the voice to hit the right tone and inflection. And, in the end, you must be sure that you have presented a clear and logical account of what you are trying to portray.

It is much more complicated than you would judge from the final result. But now it is in the can, as they say, and I'll await the outcome on December 11, with one regret: that so far as I know, it will be seen in the Grampian region only, whereas I think it would be of even greater interest in the central belt, where the majority of *Herald* readers are to be found.

So I caught the train back to Glasgow, completing the budget trip, in time to deck myself out in morning wear for the wedding of an eldest son. It was back to the realms of the media, with

Geoffrey emerging from his studio at BBC Scotland to prove that it is not impossible to effect substantial links with the opposition at Cowcaddens.

For, in the most harmonious of circumstances, he was marrying Louise White, a presenter at Scottish Television. We sped from Broomhill Church in Glasgow to the idyllic setting of Lochgreen at Troon, to a champagne wedding breakfast with the mellow tones of Terry Martin at the piano.

It was all very pleasant and civilised, with speeches at the minimum. Geoffrey was born in Aberdeen, of North-east parents, so had little chance of escaping the customary ribbing about the mean Aberdonian.

I offered the explanation that we of the North-east belong to the Pictish breed, a characteristic of whom was that they were slightly short in the arm. So was it really our fault if our hands didn't reach our pockets?

As an afterthought, I suggested that at least we couldn't be branded as Pict-pockets! I knew I would get a roasting for that. But on such a delightful day, it was more than worth it.

MY GLITTERING NIGHT

THE revival of a two-minute silence on the 11th hour of the 11th day of the 11th month reminded us that we were talking about 1918 and the horrors of the First World War.

This, in turn, brought back memories of that generation of poets, some of whom scarcely survived the conflict.

Robert Graves, given up for dead at the Somme, crawled back to life in time to escort fellow-poet Siegfried Sassoon to Craig-lockart Hospital, Edinburgh, suffering from a nervous breakdown.

That was where they met Wilfred Owen, who recovered his own nervous balance and returned to France, only to be killed in the last days of the war. Robert Graves did not see Scotland again for well over 50 years. With various love involvements, he fled to Majorca, where guide books would mention him as a historic monument and coach drivers stopped to point him out!

When he eventually came back for one last look at Scotland, he stayed at the Central Hotel in Glasgow and there, as he mounted the staircase, he paused to look around and told me he had quite forgotten the grandeur of the old British hotel, its marble pillars and chandeliers.

We wandered into the grand banqueting room and ran a hand over the famous Adam fireplace which even then was insured for a million. And we discussed the history of this building.

That rendezvous with one of the century's great poets came vividly to me last week, rather like a flashback in a Hollywood movie. There we were in the same banqueting room. And, if Robert Graves had forgotten the grandeur a generation ago, I too had rather overlooked it in the years between.

289

But what a setting it proved to be for one of the greatest nights of my life. I was glad so many *Herald* readers were there to share it.

For this was the night I would step up to receive the nationwide award as Speaker of the Year, following in the footsteps of Peter Ustinov, John Harvey Jones, Edwina Currie, Kate Adie, and last year's winner, the Speaker of the Commons, Miss Betty Boothroyd.

On this glittering gala night, national president Ken Sharpe handed over the Caithness Glass and the standard of oratory was set by Murdo Morrison from Wishaw, world leader of the Burns movement, Joe Campbell from Ayr, coincidentally the man who masterminds the biggest Burns Supper in the world, and the presiding Margaret Hunt from Carlisle.

Then it was my turn for what would have to be the best speech of my life. Well, I was determined to absorb my surroundings and controlled the adrenaline until the last moment. Then the flood-gates flew wide!

Never had so many strands of my life been drawn into one company. Outwith family, there were old friends like Lord and Lady Macfarlane, Margie and Jim Moffat (founders of A. T. Mays), Kate and Rikki Fulton, and John Brown, who started designing the *Queen Mary* in 1926 and was resplendent in white dinner jacket at the age of 95.

Among the surprises of the night, my teacher from Maud School in 1939, Miss Morrison, was somehow spirited to Glasgow. Linda and Alan Bain flew in from New York, where Alan is a prominent lawyer as well as president of the American-Scottish Foundation.

And they met up with Mary and Calum Bannerman, Alan and Calum having been friends at Cambridge.

From this sea of faces came a tide of memory and emotion and the biggest buzz of atmosphere I can remember. I was able to tell them, as I had told Robert Graves a generation ago, about the history of our surroundings.

In the days of the Glasgow Empire, when every Hollywood star from Laurel and Hardy to Bob Hope stayed at the Central Hotel,

Roy Rogers walked Trigger up that staircase—and booked a room in the name of his horse!

It was from a bedroom on the fourth floor, on a famous night in the 1920s, that John Logie Baird transmitted his first television picture down the line to London.

I recalled the day war started, when the passenger ship *Athenia*, two days out into the Atlantic, was sunk by the first German torpedo and the survivors were brought back to Glasgow, back to this hotel.

To greet the many Americans on board, the US Ambassador in London, Joseph Kennedy, sent his son to Glasgow. And the young man who met these people right here was of course their future President, John F. Kennedy.

It was history everywhere. Robert Graves was intrigued and so was the large gathering on this gala night.

The irony of my speaker's award is a topic which can wait another week. For the moment I was just glad to look around and survey the faces, some of them down from Aberdeenshire to support a Buchan man!

The pipers played and that brilliant pianist, Terry Martin, set the scene of the dinner with my kind of music. It was Gershwin, Cole Porter, Jerome Kern, and Richard Rodgers.

This was a banquet as it used to be in the days when Glasgow could boast the old Malmaison and the One-O-One, when stars like Betty Grable could walk along Waterloo Street to the Alhambra Theatre.

I just took my standing ovation and knew that this had to be one of the headiest nights of my life.

THE KINDNESS OF FRIENDS . . .

* 16TH DECEMBER 1996 *

ALONG life's furrow we gather up our experience, distil it into some form of wisdom and seek to pass it on to our inheritors— who may have little thought or caring for our haverings!

But in time perhaps they come back to it and remember. Among the thoughts I tried to impart to my children as they grew up was the one which said: try to get to know as many people as possible as early in your life as possible. Because you may never again come to know folk quite so well.

The truth of that came back to me earlier this year at the centenary of our village school as I gathered round with my classmates of 1936 and resumed a conversation as if we had never been away.

And that same prospect arose the other day as I headed north once more to Aberdeenshire to revisit some of the old haunts.

Next morning I would open the annual bazaar of Turriff Academy, in the town where I started work, and find myself confronted with faces from those early post-war years when the world was gathering itself for the second half of the century.

Young men back from the war and reaching the peak of fitness as members of the local football team came past to shake hands and reveal they were now in their mid-seventies, but luckier than Eddie and Jackie and Johnny and Doodles who were long gone.

From Turriff, on the edge of Buchan, I drove 15 miles eastward to my native Maud for an appointment I could have done without. For I was going from the bazaar to the bizarre.

On this miserable morning they were holding the last-ever auction in the sale-ring from which my father once conducted the biggest weekly cattle market in Britain. He would put through 1,000 store cattle by himself on a Wednesday. But this was a disposal sale and I asked them to reserve me the old stool from his rostrum.

The only consolation on a day like this was the sight of friendly faces from the past.

So I hastened to Fraserburgh (or the Broch as we knew it) where I worked as a young reporter, this time to face the public at Trail's bookshop and once again to meet friends of long ago.

But the highlight would come that evening, back in Aberdeen, where my newspaper colleagues of 45 years ago were laying on a dinner. I thought there would be just a few of us round a table but that generation had survived better than I could have hoped.

So we dined and wined and they recalled my early days of reporting in the North-east, whether it was hauling bodies out of a shipwreck on a stormy night in Gamrie Bay or learning too late the power of champagne at a society wedding on Deeside!

Like that day at Maud School, we resumed our camaraderie where we left off, rich and rewarding, young journalists grown to pensioners and knowing each other as we would know so few.

In the bleary-eyed morning I was out of bed too soon for a live interview with Robbie Shepherd on his BBC radio show, before heading for Glasgow. In Aberdeen they were about to view the television programme *Walking Back to Happiness*, in which I had revisited my calf country earlier this year, much as I was doing last week. But I wouldn't be around to see it since it was for consumption in the area of Grampian Television only.

On the road south I decided on a detour by the land of Lewis Grassic Gibbon, passing his old school and heading down the brae to Arbuthnott Church, which became Kinraddie Kirk in *Sunset Song*.

There wasn't another soul in sight as I stretched my legs in that picturesque howe, with its burn running in spate and a chorus of birds giving a fair imitation of a spring afternoon.

Down Kinraddie way the Lord's door is mercifully unlocked so I carried that symphony inside, mounted the steps of the pulpit, and let my imagination run loose on the life which had existed here in Grassic Gibbon's day. To think that such a figure could still have been with us even now, whereas he has been dead for more than 60 years.

Out in the kirkyard I wandered to that corner where his remains lie buried by the lee of the dyke, alongside his wife and parents.

Suddenly the birds went quiet and I tried to reconstruct Grassic Gibbon's life, year by year, from childhood here before the Great War, to rebellious youth and wanderings in the Middle East, much like Lawrence of Arabia.

Then those precious few years of turning out 17 books in a life which didn't see his 34th birthday.

In that corner where he will lie for ever, I ran my fingers over those words from the eulogy for the men who fell in that first war:

> The kindness of friends
> The warmth of toil
> The peace of rest

Those sentiments had been so vivid on this tour of the Northeast. For I had indeed been reminded of the kindness of friends, with whom I had shared the warmth of early toil. And in this quiet corner of the world, the peace of rest was complete.

THE ENIGMA OF JIM RODGER

* 1 3 T H   J A N U A R Y   1 9 9 7 *

THE legends of a golden age in journalism are toppling at an alarming rate. No sooner had I eulogised over Drew Rennie, who shaped my own career, than we lost the greatest legend of them all, the Jolly Jim Rodger from Shotts.

Jim was the most difficult of all men to describe—an apparently ingenuous soul who went into the darkness of the Lanarkshire pits as a boy, but fought his way to daylight via football journalism, where he occupied a position quite unique in the Fourth Estate.

By no stretch of the imagination was he a writer, nor even a good verbal communicator, because he talked in riddles and kept even his own sports editors guessing until the last gasp of deadline exasperation.

But he would deliver the story, on the certain premise that he was not so much writing it as creating it. Long before the Mister Ten Per Cents came to manipulate the transfer markets, Jim Rodger was playing the mysterious middleman to whom the entire football world would have entrusted its life.

And he did it all for nothing. Well, for not a single penny of the filthy lucre which so distorts the values of our bewildering world. Jim's reward was the exclusive story, enough to nourish the vanity which drives so much of human activity.

Down the pits with men like Jock Stein of Celtic and Andrew Keir, the actor—another Shotts boy—he had made it his business to get to know people and give help beyond all limits of expectation. Whether it was to save an individual in trouble or a charity in despair he would move Heaven and earth, sweeping aside all

295

obstacles to the point of ruthlessness if necessary. Legions were due him a debt they could never repay.

He masterminded the transfers of men like Jim Baxter and Denis Law. During one of his many heart scares I went to visit him at the Bon Secours nursing home at Langside, where the Protestant Jim enjoyed a special rapport with the nuns. At his bedside I found him talking in riddles down a telephone. Jock Stein was lurking in the background and, as was later revealed, I had just eavesdropped on the transfer of Pat Stanton from Hibernian to Celtic.

Football became the vehicle for his extraordinary existence, but his game went far beyond that. It was about people and politics and Christian fellowship, all mixed into a web of intrigue in which he revelled.

Jim Rodger was an enigma wrapped up in mystique, to be unravelled by very few. No other person in the history of journalism had a hot-line to so many high places. He could phone 10 Downing Street and a Prime Minister would speak to him. He could slice bureaucracy to ribbons if his cause was just, embarrassing the minnows of life into action. Within his jolly rotundness lay an awesome power which defied analysis.

He would put it down to the power of his Maker and maybe he was right. For there was a missionary zeal throughout the family. He had a cousin, Bill Armstrong, whose father was a blacksmith at the pits before becoming a Salvation Army leader.

Young Bill had the brain which made him Sir William Armstrong, head of the entire Civil Service, and later Lord Armstrong, chairman of the Midland Bank, one of the most powerful men in the land. What cousin Bill could achieve in high office, Jim could match at street level.

Sir William figured in one of my two most abiding memories of Jim Rodger. It happened on that July night of 1966 when England won the World Cup. Jim and I headed back from Wembley to witness the celebrations at the Kensington Garden Hotel, where we would meet Sir William.

Prime Minister Harold Wilson, going through a sticky patch,

had arrived back that morning from Washington after crucial talks with President Johnson. Cashing in on the euphoria, he joined captain Bobby Moore on the balcony to acknowledge the crowds, then returned to the foyer.

Spotting Jim and Sir William, he came over to chat about the Washington visit. A gents' door burst open and out staggered Foreign Secretary George Brown, who drunkenly insisted that we all come into the banquet. Amid protests that journalists were banned, I found myself propelled, on the coat-tails of Sir William and cousin Jim—who else?—into a historic private occasion. But when we returned to our own hotel, I ran into a major emergency. The pear-shaped, teetotal Jim, who ate too many cream buns and always carried too much weight, collapsed into my arms and said: "Oh Jack, I'm done!" He paled to a look of death as I administered brandy to his lips and thought we had lost him altogether. He was then only 44. But he survived for many another heart scare and had the bonus of 30 more years.

The other abiding memory was at Lourdes, 25 years ago, when I chanced upon a Mass at the shrine of the Virgin Mary and realised that, in the wake of yet another heart attack, thousands were praying for "the survival of Jim Rodger from Shotts"! When I told him later, he just grinned and winked.

The funeral was a roll-call of football's famous, each one touched in some meaningful way by this remarkable figure. If there are any problems within the Pearly Gates, Saint Peter will at least know where to turn. Jim'll Fix It.

THE POWER OF THE SCOTS

* 2 4 T H   F E B R U A R Y   1 9 9 7 *

I HAD just been addressing a gathering at the University Club in New York when a rather distinguished-looking gentleman came up to say he had spent a large part of his life on an assessment of what Scotland had given to the world.

He could have been just another romantic exile with a bursting pride in the land of his fathers and a willingness to drop all native modesty for a breast-beating boast about what a wonderful lot we are. But Duncan Bruce was clearly a man of substance, whose place at the leadership end of the Scots community in America was soon confirmed.

Like many a budding author, he had reached that stage of research when, in the words of the late Sir Iain Moncreiffe, it was time to "write something now rather than everything never".

There were still a few queries (some on the personalities of Scottish football, about which I tried to put him right without bias!) but he was all set for publication. The result of his massive effort, a book called *The Mark of the Scots*, dropped on my desk the other day, quite a remarkable piece of work, an exhaustive research which has been written, not as a mere listing, but as a narrative.

Like everyone who has tried to pinpoint the people of Scots origin, Duncan Bruce faced the problem of dividing lines. How much blood do you need to be a Scot? Anyway, he is at great pains to list his sources and offers us Americans all the way from George Washington and Davy Crocket to Judy Garland—and yes, even Elvis, descended from one Andrew Presley, who emigrated from Scotland.

Although less than 5% of Americans are of Scots descent, more than 75% of their Presidents have had ancestral connections, including the Roosevelts, Harry Truman, and George Bush.

He raises an interesting point about the Scots Plantation people who went to Ireland, Presbyterians who tended on religious grounds to marry among themselves and therefore remained largely Scottish. When their descendants emigrated to America, however, their Scottishness was masked by the fact that they had come from Ireland. As good immigrants, our tendency to blend well in new countries has sometimes militated against us, whereas the Irish have tended to remain more obviously Irish, as in America.

Evidently we can claim explorers from Cook to Scott, and of course Neil Armstrong who, stepping on to the moon in 1969, was congratulated by President Nixon, himself an Armstrong from Dumfries, speaking on the Scots-invented telephone while the whole world watched on the Scots-invented television.

It was in response to a Scottish minister, George Witherspoon, that the Declaration of Independence was signed, after being given to Thomas Jefferson, who was descended from a sister of Robert The Bruce.

And of course Scotland became the centre of the Industrial Revolution, providing a coincidence of genius in Adam Smith, David Hume, Joseph Black, and James Watt. John Napier, who invented logarithms, built the world's first mechanical computing device as far back as 1615—and Lord Byron's daughter, Ada, wrote the first computer programme in 1843 and is regarded by some as the world's first computer scientist.

So you thought the fax machine was something new? The first patent on a facsimile transmission machine was actually issued to Alexander Bain more than 150 years ago, just after the basic technology had been produced by two others of Scottish ancestry, Joseph Henry and Samuel Morse.

Whereas we all knew that Alexander Graham Bell gave us the telephone, did we know that Marconi was encouraged in his invention of radio by his mother, who was Anne Jameson of Scots descent?

Members of our race gave the world its Marriott Hotels and Holiday Inns, its Campbell's soup and Buick cars, and Charles Rolls, of Rolls-Royce, was the son of Georgina MacLean, of the Fitzroy MacLean family. Winston Churchill, himself with Scottish blood, said: "There is only one thing wrong with Scotsmen. There are too few of them."

I didn't know that Barbara Cartland was descended from the noble Hamiltons, nor that the novelist Graham Greene was the grand-nephew of Robert Louis Stevenson. I'm glad to say Duncan Bruce acknowledges this newspaper as the oldest national daily in the world, just as the *New York Herald*, one of the most influential papers in American history, was founded by Gordon Bennett from Keith in Banffshire.

Press barons of course included Lord Beaverbrook, son of a Scottish minister, and Rupert Murdoch, grandson of the minister at Hatton of Cruden, near Peterhead. From my own corner of Aberdeenshire, I should have known more about Thomas Glover from Fraserburgh, who was sent as a young man to Nagasaki by the Jardine Matheson trading company. But he started his own company, became fabulously wealthy, and was the catalyst for bringing Japan into the industrialised world.

He took the first steam locomotive to Japan, opened its first coal mine, ordered its first full-scale dock, which was built in Aberdeen, and founded the Japanese Navy with three ships ordered from Alexander Hall, again in his native North-east of Scotland. Glover is a hero in Japan but hardly known at home. To crown it all with a touch of romance, his affair with a lady called Maki Kaga was apparently the prototype for Puccini's *Madam Butterfly*. What more could we have done for mankind?

THE LAST OF JOHN MAJOR

◆ 1 0 T H   M A R C H   1 9 9 7 ◆

WITH a General Election just weeks away, I went for a close-up of the Prime Minister the other night, curious to see how he was standing the strain, especially in the aftermath of the by-election defeat.

This was to be a glittering gala night for Tories from all over Scotland and, despite the wisecracks that you could hold such an event in our local café at Netherlee, the faithful came flocking from every constituency in such numbers as to raise the question of how 1,250 people could dine together at the Glasgow Moat House. Scotland's largest dining-room, holding 1,100, is to be found at the rival Thistle Hotel but the mystery was solved when the taxi delivered me to a large marquee in the car-park.

Special Branch men were everywhere. But with the Wirral by-election and his own side queuing up to make life impossible for their leader, would this become a wake?

Or perhaps the Last Supper for Honest John and his Disciples as they were piped and applauded to the table and welcomed by Sir Michael Hirst? From a vantage point nearby, I had indeed a clear view of John Major and as I sat there, studying his demean-our, a hasty calculation told me he is the thirteenth Prime Minister of my lifetime. Unlucky?

They began in 1931 with Ramsay MacDonald, a servant's bairn from my native North-east, who broke new ground for the Labour Party. Of more interest to me at the time, he was the spitten image of my grandfather. Then came the Tories' Stanley Baldwin and Neville Chamberlain, who was replaced by Winston Churchill in 1940.

301

Having inspired us through the Second World War, he was promptly dumped even before victory was declared, in favour of Clement Attlee, a clever man who could nevertheless have been doing with a charisma transplant.

Winnie returned to pave the way for Anthony Eden (famous for his hat; infamous for Suez), the rabbit-toothed Harold ("You've never had it so good") Macmillan, and the much underestimated Alec Douglas-Home, before Labour was restored with the wily Harold Wilson, another Harold with a dental problem.

Onward with the baton-waving Ted Heath (frequently confused with the bandleader of the same name) and a taste of Jim Callaghan before the Iron Lady put the Tories on course for a record-breaking 18 years in office. So I looked at John Major and pondered his private thoughts, when few are giving him a survival prospect which rates at more than that of a snowball in hell. The Labour bandwagon is rolling with such confidence as to ease off on the wooing and give warning of how tough they may have to be.

The certainty is that this will be the most extraordinary General Election of our lifetime. From my early covering of these events after the war, the dominant memory is of the surging power of socialism. That landslide of 1945 was taken as such a mandate for social revolution that Attlee and his team embarked on a six-year spree of state ownership which was almost too much to absorb, so hard on the heels of six years of war.

The country took fright and swung back to the Tories for 13 years before Labour re-emerged in diluted form. But they were still socialists. When Hugh Gaitskell, with his upper-crust background, took over from Attlee in 1955, he belonged to the right of the party. In the context of today's New Labour he would be away to the left.

That is the measure of Labour's pragmatic shift, encouraged by the world-wide message that socialism has gone out of fashion. It has gone so far right that many a Tory voter I've spoken to, including businessmen who have been assured they have nothing to fear from Labour, is considering a vote for Tony Blair.

They feel it would be an easy step, if indeed a step at all. They could certainly do so without sacrificing their anti-socialist principles! The real dilemmas rest with the old-style Labour folk. Where on earth can they place their cross?

So John Major got up to speak and conceded that, if the country followed the example of the Wirral, we would indeed have a Labour Government. I was less interested in the political points than in the composure of the man. Whatever else may be said of John Major, he strikes you as a patently honest and decent man.

With the quietly charming Norma by his side, you were left with the impression of a pleasantly modest couple. That may or may not be relevant in the final analysis. But it did remind me of that immodest display by Neil and Glenys Kinnock in the 1992 eve-of-poll rally in Sheffield, where the football-like triumphalism raised last-minute hackles among neutrals who, I'm sure, decided to bring them down a peg. Tony Blair will not make that mistake.

A feature of the Tory bash was the large turnout of young people, interesting in view of the opinion poll which showed the young's distrust of Tony Blair. So the big band struck up and the cabaret brought us the hilarious Allan Stewart (no, not the Member for Eastwood).

It was altogether a poignant night. Euphoria or bravado? John Major gave a broad, courageous smile, took a wistful look around— and was gone.

WHEN I WAS JUST SIXTEEN

* 1 7 T H   M A R C H   1 9 9 7 *

I WENT out for lunch three times last week. No, not to a restaurant, just outside—to the garden. And there's really nothing to beat the alfresco meal, is there? If only we had the weather.

Well, it has been a promising start to 1997 and there I was, lounging with a glass of wine, gazing into the deep blue yonder as the sun beat gently at a temperature of 60 degrees, offering the first hint of a tan.

Despite a heavy schedule of writing I find it hard to resist the sun. Whenever it appears I can be seduced toward the deck-chair, drifting into daydreams and proving once again that I have long since perfected that exquisite art of doing absolutely nothing.

Unbelievably for such weather, we were still in the early days of March and the thoughts which drifted past last week were taking me to this same time of year exactly half a century ago.

Those with memories of 1947 will tell you that we were up to the oxters in snow, in what turned out to be the wildest winter of the century. Winters in rural Scotland had always brought their own particular mixture of hardship and charm, farmers struggling into the village with horse-drawn sledge, like something out of a Christmas card, to collect food supplies for the weeks ahead.

But 1947 was different. Not even the oldest grandmother could remember anything like it. Our Buchan train, which plied the route from Aberdeen to Peterhead and Fraserburgh, splitting into two parts at our village junction of Maud, was hardly known for its speed at the best of times.

But in the blizzard which blew up on January 28, 1947, the

304

confounded thing disappeared altogether, lost in a cutting about Newmachar and not to be seen for many weeks after that.

There is, of course, great drama in a snowstorm, at first much appreciated by the very young. But even they were wearied by the hazards of 1947. For what began in January was still with us in May, snow lying behind the dykes even when a second meteorological phenomenon burst upon us on the first day of June.

I remember that date very well because, just as we had been through the worst winter on record, we were suddenly confronted with what turned out to be the best summer of the century, at least until 1995 (although I still have my doubts about that one).

Out of sheer relief that glorious June day we went out to greet the summer sun. And in my case I overdid it, playing football in the Pleasure Park to the point of exhaustion, then lying down in a burst of sweat till the cooler evening air cast a chill on my slender frame.

Next day it was pneumonia and, when that cleared, Dr Crombie had me off to Aberdeen Royal Infirmary, suspecting that the heart valves had been affected. So there I was, in my 16th summer, with specialists gathered round in a head-shaking exercise to forewarn that I may never work. If I did, it would have to be something quiet, like sitting behind a desk.

Sent home to rest, I was carried out to the front green, to a camp-bed under a canopy, so that I could enjoy the warmth and chat to passing neighbours. Little Miss Hendry stopped to say she had had the same thing when she was my age and here she was, now in her eighties. I knew she was trying to be kind and encouraging.

So there I lay and read the newspapers I had dreamed of working for, even if that was no longer to be. Through that spring into summer my mother was complaining about the meat ration being reduced to a shilling a week (five pence) with further cuts to come for bread. This was the post-war austerity of Sir Stafford Cripps.

The antidote to my mother's misery seemed to be the so-called New Look of fashion, created by Christian Dior—and the fact that we had just had 35 consecutive days of clear blue skies and scorching sunshine.

I read that Henry Ford had just died at the age of 83, Franz Lehar was still active, a Hungarian journalist called Biro had invented a revolutionary pen—and Princess Elizabeth announced her engagement to Prince Philip of Greece.

I would lay down the paper and gaze into space, drifting into daydreams of the life I had envisaged. And that reverie from boyhood came back vividly last week as I sat there in the garden, going through a similarly thoughtful process.

But whereas in 1947 I had been gazing along the tunnel of life's prospects, with all its uncertainties, I was now looking back along that same tunnel, much older, perhaps a little wiser and certainly more grateful.

Because on this Monday morning I enter the 50th year of my career as a writer. The power of youth must have healed the cracks of a faulty heart to turn that dream of a career in journalism into an unexpected reality after all.

At least I had learned to regard every day as a bonus, every breath of fresh air as a stimulant, every ray of sunshine as a soothing balm. I drained the claret and knew how good it felt to be alive.

THE LEGEND OF
BUSBY, STEIN AND SHANKLY

IT may consign me to the ranks of insanity but I will confess that I sat up till half past five the other morning, just to watch the Oscar ceremony coming live from Los Angeles. I'm a sucker for that kind of thing, almost certainly dating back to a thirties childhood when the Playhouse at Peterhead was an escape from the inhospitable climes of Buchan.

One day I would go there perhaps, and one day I did. And if I learned anything at all in that Californian wonderland it is that constant sunshine can bake your brain to a state of nonentity and that the cauld blast of a real Nor'-easter is more surely an anchor to reality.

Yet for all the pouting and posturing of stars and starlets across the full spectrum of silliness, there is something addictive about those Hollywood nights.

The English Patient did us proud, though I have to say the film itself fell well short of my expectations.

As always at the Oscars there was a moment to remember. And for me that moment was the tragic spectacle of Mohammed Ali, trapped in his Parkinson's syndrome, coming up for the documentary award which should have been celebrated with the floating of a butterfly and the stinging of a bee. I could remember only that day in 1965 when I took him to Burns's Cottage at Ayr, sat him in the Bard's own chair, and heard some of the early versifying for which he gained a reputation.

At least the Hollywood show can produce drama, which is more than can be said for another of those showbusiness ceremonies, held in London the other night, when the masterminds of our own *Trainspotting*, trotting on stage to collect their awards, felt obliged to do so in a mixture of shirt-tails, overcoats, and an effing expletive, the bleak uniformity of modern expression.

By far the best theatre, however, was reserved for the weekend when television gave us three consecutive nights of Busby, Stein and Shankly—*The Football Men*, a study of the three greatest managers ever to grace the game in Britain. What struck me first about those legends, all now gone to that distant stadium, is that I am old enough to have seen them as players.

Not that their own strengths lay particularly in performance, rather in the moulding of men who generally had greater skills than themselves.

Each created a team which, in its time, was the greatest in Britain: Shankly with Liverpool, Busby with Manchester United, and Stein with Celtic. Beyond that, their common bond was that they had all worked down the pits.

So this was as much as anything a study of the background which forged men of this character in that period between the wars when they were growing up. Here was Shankly, one of 10 in a cottage where it was a feat for the mother to feed them, never mind instil those qualities of honesty, decency and integrity for which the world cries out today.

Bill Shankly's sayings have become legendary ("No, no, football is not a matter of life or death. It's far more important than that"). The unconscious comedian was honesty personified.

Matt Busby scarcely had time to know the father who was killed in the First World War. Once again a young mother struggled to give him a chance.

In the fifties she watched him create the Busby Babes of Manchester United, a team destroyed in the Munich air crash of 1958. Matt himself drew back from the brink of death and 10 years later had rebuilt a team to win the European Cup. On that memorable Wembley night I found his mother wandering in a daze, wanting to see her boy. I took her to the dressing room, the big friendly bear hugged her and they both cried. And the unspoken name on their lips was that of a man who died in France.

When Joe Loss had struck the last chord at the Russell Hotel that night, Busby made a quiet speech about the importance of people around him. As the man who might as well have been headmaster of a big school, he was idolised by his pupils, not least George Best, who caused him most problems.

Jock Stein, who had his own wayward child in Jimmy Johnstone, made a similar impact at Celtic Park, taking a bunch of local lads and moulding them into world-beaters.

As a one-time ghost writer for all three legends, I could appreciate all the more the skill and perception of Hugh McIlvanney, who fashioned this memorable television in a manner which belongs to himself. Hugh and contributing brother Willie, the distinguished novelist, were themselves the products of a miner's cottage in Kilmarnock and knew so well what they were talking about.

They may yet have a tailpiece. For the feats of Shankly, Busby and Stein could soon be overtaken by the last of the breed, Alex Ferguson, who has uniquely achieved it all in both Scotland and England, and is just a game or two away from the final accolade.

That would wrap up a breed whose style has already taken on the ring of a different age.

LABOUR'S LANDSLIDE

✦5TH MAY 1997✦

AS the polling booths entered their final hours, I was enjoying the music of Broadway and Hollywood, to the dancing of Wayne Sleep and the singing of Lorna Luft, who sounded most like her mother, Judy Garland, as she belted out that great old melody "The Man That Got Away".

By the time I was home and settled down for the late-night session, John Major was facing the music on another scale and contemplating how little time it takes to move the frontiers of history, not only towards a new millennium but to a new era of British politics.

It was no doubt galling to see so many of his policies being hijacked by New Labour but, whatever the opinion of Tony Blair, the overriding impression of election night was that of new beginnings. There is indeed a tide in the affairs of human existence and we mortal creatures need this kind of impetus and excitement every so often.

It reminded me very much of the atmosphere in America at the start of Kennedy's reign. Here was another 43-year-old, identifiable with the youth of the nation and somehow representing the spirit of his time, yet facing the most awesome responsibilities. (Considering how recent the Kennedy years might seem, it is a sobering thought for Mr Blair that the President would now be 80!)

Given the scrutiny of public figures in the 1990s, the new Prime Minister must be glad he kept to his high moral standards in a generation which so readily deserted them. His advantage over Kennedy in this direction is confirmed by the fact that, if the public had known even half the story of the President's philandering, he would not have survived his inauguration ceremony. (Mind you, Bill Clinton is doing not so badly.)

So we entered the full flow of election night, switching channels and catching up with unfolding dramas which threatened to run beyond our grasp. There had never been anything like it. As the word "landslide" began to dominate the screens, I remembered being in Glasgow in 1945 and learning the outcome of that particular election from a billboard in Byres Road. "Labour Landslide", it said. I didn't then know what television was.

Churchill was out, Attlee in. But even that sensational day, before the Second World War was over, was paling to insignificance compared with this. As the pattern became clear, the only purpose now in lingering till dawn was to see how complete the massacre could be. So the platform scenes were repeated in all their familiarity, with one of our Scottish returning officers making a bit of a pompous ass of himself.

So night became morning, as the milkman rattled on the doorstep, the pundits ran out of superlatives, and poor old Peter Snow nearly disappeared up his own swingometer.

And there were the inevitable faces. Richard Branson, all thousand teeth of him, fresh from the multi-million benefits of Tory privatisation, turning up at New Labour's party, refusing to say who he voted for but celebrating just the same. And who is this? Oh God, help us! Richard Attenborough grasping Neil Kinnock's hand and desperate to tell the world how much the victory was due to this man. I just hoped they would get the wee lordie off the set before he began to greet with gratitude.

John Major's result came at 3.30 a.m. and you couldn't help feeling sorry for the man whose time as Prime Minister would run out in a few hours. Whatever the shambles of his party, he was still one of the most decent and honourable politicians of my lifetime.

But his day was gone, patently to be revealed in the cruel light of modern technology. Norma was there, charming as ever. What do you say to your man in moments like these?

311

History was in the making, before our very eyes. The new man of destiny was upon us, his wildest dreams far exceeded as the dawn of reality broke upon his boyish face.

Barracking from the sidelines would no longer do. His team, so far well disciplined if totally without experience, was now on the field to be judged by performance, not rhetoric. What was going through his head? I wondered. Would he be thinking of the hard left and what mischief they could wreak? Having obediently lain low to get themselves elected, would they now take heart from the massive endorsement and push for real, traditional socialism? Only time would tell.

At least Mr Blair had the whip-hand of being able to remind them that broken promises would spell disaster. Sitting in the heart of the Eastwood constituency and watching the Tories swept to oblivion even in this, their Scottish stronghold, one was tempted to think that Allan Stewart could have been their sole man at Westminster, but for his personal misfortunes. Final surrender to sleep was encouraged by the dreary monotones of Martin Bell, whose acceptance speech could put politics out of fashion. I drifted off with one last thought.

Despite the euphoria, Tony Blair, Gordon Brown et al, will soon run into the problems which will in time make them just as unpopular as their predecessors. Has there ever been a Government of lasting popularity? There will come a day when they, too, will face defeat. It is in the cyclical nature of things.

THE JIM CLARK STORY

•19TH MAY 1997•

THE Border lands of Scotland roll out before you in gentle contours which somehow reflect the nature of the Borderers themselves, for long a favourite people of mine.

The signposts tell you of Greenlaw and Hutton Castle (former home of Sir William Burrell) before you draw in for lunch at the welcoming little inn at Allarton. A mile or so further on and you are in Chirnside, which stirs a memory, but the destination for the moment is the neat little town of Duns.

There, in the sweep of a picturesque public park, you put down a couple of jackets for goalposts and try to convince your grandson that you were once a nifty footballer. But children are not easily fooled.

He executes a clever body-swerve, leaves old Grandpa Jack floundering and suggests I might do better in goal.

Living so close to the Border, he looks towards the nearest team of some standing and that of course is Newcastle United. So his heroes are Shearer and Ginola, against whom my offerings of the current Aberdeen team offer pale competition.

But in time we exhaust ourselves and withdraw for a cool drink to the centre of Duns, where my eye catches the name of a hero from a bygone day.

A nearby building announces "The Jim Clark Room".

Jim Clark was a local hero around the Borders, I explain to my grandson, but he was more than that. Clark was the greatest motor-racing driver in the world in his day, some would say of any day.

Yet to Border people he was still the unassuming young farmer who came to market with his cattle and sheep and enjoyed the even tenor of rural life. His hands were long and slender with the grace of an artist. But his artistry was expressed in the fiercest of dare-devil competition on international circuits.

In a short career, he won 25 of his 72 Grand Prix races, was twice world champion (the first-ever Scot) as well as the first Briton to win the famous Indianapolis 500-mile race, setting a record speed.

Curiously, and without knowing it at the time, I had witnessed Jim Clark's very first attempt at motor racing in the 1950s. As the boy who came after four sisters, he was taken to a race by his brother-in-law, Alex Calder, and was bitten by the bug.

Then he accompanied a neighbouring farmer, Ian Scott Watson, who was competing at a Sunday meeting on the wartime aero-drome at Crimond in Aberdeenshire. I happened to be there that day, reporting on this short-lived local excitement which nevertheless drew crowds of 30,000.

After a practise round, Scott Watson said to the teenager: "Go on, have a try. You're far enough from home; your parents won't know." Clark donned the helmet, put up a faster practise time that Scott Watson—and entered the race. Although he came last, the course of his life was set.

He was soon heading for the top, where he enjoyed eight years with the Lotus team. But he was always back home whenever possible, bringing with him such legends of racing as Graham Hill (Damon's father), Jack Brabham and Dan Gurney, who were always happy to attend the annual dinner of Jim's local motor club. (Nowadays, I'm told, top drivers hardly speak to each other, let alone socialise.)

The quiet man from Edington Mains Farm, Chirnside, was popular wherever he went. Though blessed with good looks he was rather shy with girls, but he did have a lasting relationship with Sally Stokes, a top model of the time. Jim Clark's mother was relieved when she gathered that her son was going to give up his dangerous sport in 1968, when he was 32. Alas, that moment didn't quite arrive.

314

A few weeks after his 32nd birthday he took part in a relatively unimportant race at Hockenheim in Germany. Suddenly his Lotus skidded off the track and crashed into a tree.

I remember the news reaching my desk with much the same impact as the assassination of President Kennedy. On that quiet Sunday afternoon, Jim Clark was dead. Having seen his career launched at Crimond, I was now writing his obituary.

In the strange ways of fate, it happened in a part of Germany well known to his farming father, who had been a prisoner in the First World War.

So I told the story to my grandson as we wandered through the Jim Clark Room, viewing his trophies and memorabilia and watching the video of his career. Five years ago, I remembered, there was a poignant moment in this room.

Clark's famous successor, Ayrton Senna of Brazil, turned up one day to pay silent homage to the man who was his inspiration. He stood there thoughtfully, then left without fuss. Little did he know that, at the San Marino Grand Prix, he would soon meet the same fate as his hero.

We drove on to Jim Clark's old home at Edington Mains, on the road to Berwick, surveyed that Border landscape which so enriched his short life and came back to the village of Chirnside to stand respectfully by his plain memorial stone.

Could it really be close to 30 years ago? Or was it only yesterday?

MY FOUNDER'S DAY ORATION

• 2 N D   J U N E   1 9 9 7 •

THE sun was beating on the great quadrangle of Robert Gordon's College in Aberdeen as 1,000 youngsters lined up for the ceremonial which would mark the annual Founder's Day, tribute to the remarkable man whose vision, as well as his money, created one of our finest schools.

I looked again at the Auld Hoose, central building of the college, the opening of which was rather delayed by the arrival of Butcher Cumberland to billet his troops within its classrooms on his way north to Culloden in 1746 and again on his victorious way south, when he raped and plundered the Granite City. A nasty piece of work.

But now it was time to take my place at the head of the parade, complete with pipe band, as we marched out through the famous vaulted gateway and across to the muckle Kirk of St Nicholas for the service of remembrance.

It brought back a rather different memory from more than 50 years ago, when I was shown that same vaulted gateway and asked to leave Gordon's College because I had not reached the minimum of academic requirement.

With tears on my cheeks and the ring of failure in my ears, it was home to Maud and the wrath of a father who would be short of understanding. I was still only a lad of 14, hardly ready for an immediate post-war world of bleak uncertainty.

On Friday, however, those tears were replaced by an inner smile of satisfaction as Robert Gordon's College bestowed its highest honour, letting bygones be bygones and inviting me to deliver the Founder's Day Oration. What a turn up for the book.

316

This used to be the day for British Ambassadors and chairmen of great corporations, but the world is a changing place and I accepted with all the grace at my disposal.

This was no time for idle boasting about academic failure, more a chance to offer a glimmer of hope to those who, for one reason or another, do not shine at school.

Good fortune had eased the way through a career in journalism which took me to the far ends of the earth and into contact with people who would have seemed unreachable from the rural scene of my childhood in Aberdeenshire.

But life is full of surprises and if I had gathered a few shafts of wisdom along the way, now was the time to impart it to a succeeding generation.

Whereas I had thought that, in our Grampian cocoon, we were perhaps a bit behind the wider world, it had been a delight to discover that our basic standards could take us anywhere and dispel all thoughts of inferiority.

Robert Gordon was just one of many enterprising Scots who made that discovery a long time ago, setting out from his home in Aberdeen to be a highly successful merchant on the continent of Europe.

Another lesson I learned was that, no matter the slings and arrows that come your way, there is always a turning point in your fortunes. It has been my experience that, if you stick with it, nothing goes wrong forever.

There was also a timely reminder about the mesmerising magic of the computer, which elevates virtual reality above its station, and a plea for the poor old human brain which remains the finest computer of all.

On a more personal note, there was time to recall my arrival at Gordon's College during the Second World War, a time for bombing raids, underground shelters and food rationing.

It was an Aberdeen of tramcars and dray horses, of Cocky Hunter's junk yard at the Castlegate, Harry Gordon's Beach Pavilion—and a little girl making an early appearance at His Majesty's Theatre under the name of Julie Andrews. On an April

317

day of 1946 Winston Churchill came to receive the freedom of Aberdeen and I did something which would not have been possible in later times of security. I ran alongside the great man's car and reached out to touch him.

It was a strange experience to look down on this vast congregation from the heights of a mighty pulpit and recall events of 50 years ago, already receding far into history and taking us one-fifth of the way back to Cumberland's day.

Time is indeed a fascinating measure and, with the remnants of a memory which was once a major asset of mine, I could pick out faces which were worth whole columns of their own.

There, distinguished as ever, was 87-year-old George Barton, former head of the junior school who remembered my early stammering days.

And here was another familiar face from the more recent past. Yes, it was Ian Black, famous Olympic swimmer and now a successor of Mr Barton as head of the junior school.

The new headmaster of the college, Brian Lockhart, former deputy head of Glasgow High, has inherited a fine tradition. As we crossed the quadrangle, he acknowledged every passing pupil. They in turn responded with a courtesy which heightened the feel-good factor on this, one of the very special days of my life. If there was a tear on the cheek as I bade farewell to that vaulted gateway on Friday, it certainly did not, on this occasion, come from the fount of regret.

HOW CULLODEN GAVE RISE TO NEWSPAPERS

•14TH JULY 1997•

BIRTHDAY celebrations of one kind or another were in the summer air as I headed north towards the land where I was born. Earlier in the week my own milestone had been marked with a splendid barbecue in my son's back garden, reminding me that I was now securely into the age of retirement.

When one of his neighbours arrived to present me with a bottle of champagne—and I realised that she was the wife of a prominent Rangers footballer—I rejoiced in the fact that the prospects for goodwill and reconciliation in this troubled world are far from dead!

So northwards to Aberdeen to join old colleagues in a milestone of another sort—the dinner which would spark off the 250th anniversary of the *Press and Journal*, the local daily newspaper which serves the far reaches of north and west.

At *The Herald* we are magnanimous enough to acknowledge that, while this is the oldest daily newspaper in the English-speaking world, there were others in the weekly field before our own starting date of 1783.

The *Belfast Newsletter*, for example, takes a bit of beating when it comes to longevity. So does the *Press and Journal*, which was gearing up for its first edition in the latter part of 1747 and made its actual appearance on January 5, 1748.

It shatters me to think that I remember clearly the 200th anniversary bash in the Music Hall, Aberdeen, just as I was entering journalism. Now here I was, 50 years later, arriving at the Marcliffe-at-Pitfodels, on the outskirts of the city, for yet another reminder of how time has drifted away.

319

We drank champagne on the lawn and were led to the banqueting room by the skirl of the pipes, representing perhaps the only weekend march which was not re-routed. It was straight to our tables where the main speaker of the night would be Lord Wakeham.

As chairman of the Press Complaints Commission he could have had no complaints about the food, which ranged from Moray coast prawns, Shetland salmon, Stonehaven crabs, Cruden Bay trout, and Peterhead herring to Donside lamb, ice-cream from Rothienorman, and butter biscuits from New Pitsligo.

There was certainly no lack of support for home produce, blessed by Bishop Mario Conti and enjoyed by all. And there, as I surveyed the distinguished gathering, my thoughts were wandering back to those early days of disseminating news, when the fastest means of communication was by horse.

It was really the Battle of Culloden, the last major conflict on British soil, which gave rise to the *Press and Journal*, or the *Aberdeen's Journal*, as it was originally known.

A bright young Aberdonian called James Chalmers, who had been to Oxford University and become fascinated by the art of printing, went on to gain experience in London before returning to Aberdeen in 1736 and setting up his own printing press.

Ten years later the Duke of Cumberland marched his troops into the city on the way to Culloden and Chalmers is said to have been sent by the city fathers to report on that event.

It is perhaps nearer the truth to say that, as a Royalist sympathiser, he actually fought on Cumberland's side, which means he was a lucky man to survive after the defeat of Bonnie Prince Charlie.

In any event, he returned to Aberdeen with a first-hand account of the battle, produced his bulletin in printed form, which received such a reception as to convince James Chalmers there was a market for a regular newspaper. After his death in 1764 he was succeeded by his son, James Chalmers the Second, whose tenure included playing host to some of the most distinguished names of the day.

320

There is a report of the 1773 visit of Dr Johnson, accompanied of course by James Boswell, and a sketch of Robert Burns paying a call on Chalmers at his newspaper office in 1787.

With a fine sense of history, the printing press on which they produced the report of Wellington's victory over Napoleon at Waterloo is beautifully preserved to this day.

At this anniversary dinner, I was thinking even more of the people with whom I had worked on the paper nearly half a century ago, giants of journalism who could give me first-hand accounts of recent legends.

Those old Broad Street offices had been the workplace of men like Eric Linklater and Leslie Mitchell, better known as Lewis Grassic Gibbon. My witnesses were legends in their own right, like that greatest of music and drama critics, George Rowntree Harvey, and splendid writers like George Fraser, who continues to produce his weekly column even now when he is approaching his 102nd birthday.

It was my privilege to pick up the vibrations of a wonderful newspaper heritage, though I wondered, looking around that gathering on Friday night, how much of that heritage has filtered through to the young journalist of today. We need to know our past to make the most of our present and our future. And as I drove away from Aberdeen in the bleary-eyed morning, the Tall Ships were sailing towards the city at the start of a colourful celebration.

As the crowds flocked to the seafront in their tens of thousands, these symbols of a bygone age at least would remind them that, once upon a time, there was a very different way of life.

TRAGEDY OF DIANA

I WENT to a dinner party last weekend and enjoyed a carefree camaraderie until well past midnight. But within hours I was trying to retrace the steps of that evening, moment by moment, seeking to visualise that other candle-lit dinner for two taking place at the Ritz in Paris.

I could pinpoint the moments when Princess Diana and her Dodi would still have been savouring the fullness of life, the tenderness of their new-found love. Roughly, it was possible to gauge when they rose from that table and prepared to drive off to their love-nest.

There would be the inevitable attentions of the paparazzi forever active in Paris and a pest to celebrities seeking privacy on the one hand, if sometimes to be encouraged for the sustaining of an image on the other.

If we could talk to Diana and Dodi right now, there is a suggestion with which, in hindsight at least, they would surely agree. Wouldn't it have been better to leave openly by the front door of the Ritz, giving the photographers a wave before stepping into the limousine and heading off to the Al Fayed home in the care of their proper driver and at a speed within the limits of both the law and good sense.

If the paparazzi had followed on their motorbikes, drawn alongside the car and taken a thousand pictures, would that have been so awful? Those pictures would have shown no more than a couple in the back of a car, happy to declare their love openly and knowing that soon they would be inside the gates of the mansion, safe in their privacy.

322

Instead, fostering the mystique of superstars, they chose to steal away by a side door, committing themselves to a driver who seemed to have been sufficiently fired by drink to negotiate a powerful car with all the responsibility of a madman. Such ploys were a sure guarantee that the photographers would be lured into a high-speed chase.

The fates were lurking in that Paris underpass to remind us that, no matter the height of power or wealth or prestige, there is no privilege of exemption when the hand of death descends. As in the assassination of President Kennedy, we shall forever remember the moment we heard the news. I heard of the accident before I went to sleep at 1.45 a.m., delivered in such calm tones by a World Service announcer that I couldn't quite believe he meant it. At least Diana was still alive, even if her Dodi was dead.

It was a few hours later before the full horror of the night unfolded, before we could exercise our imaginations on the detail of those final seconds—the thud of a high-speed collision, the somersaulting car, the flailing bodies, the fleeting moments of realisation, and then the quiet slide into death.

Diana was 36 when she died. So was Marilyn Monroe, who somehow sprang into my thoughts. Diana was just a year old when that happened. She was just two when Kennedy was shot.

But if we could apply our yardsticks of time, we certainly could not have anticipated public reaction. The shock had to go somewhere and, until matters settled down on Friday, it reached such heights of hysteria as we have never seen before, that swell of emotion almost threatening to run out of control. As always, there was the search for a scapegoat and when the anger directed at the paparazzi diverted to a dead driver, there was a new quest, because living scapegoats are preferred. That was when they turned on the royal family, forgetting that, whatever their differences, without her royal connection we might never have heard of Diana at all.

Personally, I thought the attendance at Crathie Church with William and Harry was courageous and sensible. But that was criticised. Charles should have had his arms around the boys. But

323

what kind of embarrassing gesture would that have been for two teenage lads?

The Queen and her family took the time it needed to comfort the boys at Balmoral and that came clearer when she did return to London with dignity. One failing of human beings is that we have lost all notion of how to deal with grief. Having long abandoned the anchor of God and denied our spirituality, we toss about like a rudderless ship when faced with a storm.

A society in moral decline, we gape into the void of our own souls and realise how weak and vulnerable and helpless we really are.

So if the appalling tragedy of Diana, Princess of Wales, brings us to face our own frailty, if it veers us away from the bleak materialism and aggression which seem to dominate our thinking, if it turns us instead to a more tender and loving and caring way of life, not just for this week but for ever, then she will not have died in vain. And that memorable funeral gave hope that this might be so.

For those who seek the continuity of her spirit, they may find it most obviously in the face and the life of her elder son. As the future King William, this upstanding young man will one day, I believe, be the saviour of the British monarchy.

Other Jack Webster titles from B&W:

THE HERALD YEARS

Voted Newspaper Columnist of the Year in 1996, Jack Webster has won great acclaim over the last decade with his weekly columns in *The Herald*.

This selection of Jack's *Herald* columns reflects the extraordinarily wide range of his interests, experiences, and reflections on life—from reminiscences of childhood to meetings with the famous and infamous; from mysteries like the curious fate of Rudolf Hess to tales of the *Queen Mary* and other great ships of the century. But often it has been the chance encounter or phone call which has provided Jack with his inspiration—for fascinating and moving insights into the lives of ordinary people.

FROM DALI TO BURRELL

In *From Dali to Burrell* Jack Webster tells the story of the fascinating life and times of one of the art world's most influential figures: Tom Honeyman—art collector, friend of Salvador Dali, and the man who brought the Burrell Collection to Glasgow.

Few art gallery directors could rival Honeyman's verve and versatility. His vision and determination led to the acquisition, for Glasgow Art Galleries, of the Dali Crucifixion and a fine collection of work from the Glasgow School—unpopular decisions at the time, but now universally acclaimed. This book charts Honeyman's achievements, from service with the RAMC during the First World War to his distinguished career as director of Glasgow Art Galleries.

THE EXPRESS YEARS

In *The Express Years: A Golden Decade*, Jack Webster focuses on the Swinging Sixties, recreating the unique atmosphere of the period through a cross-section of the articles he was writing at the time for the *Scottish Daily Express*.

Whether interviewing stars like Bing Crosby, or portraying his father back home in Aberdeenshire, Jack brings to his writing the rhythm and warmth which have earned him a deservedly large and loyal following over the years.

GRAINS OF TRUTH

Jack Webster broadened his audience dramatically in the 1980s when he became the award-winning creator of highly personal documentary films for television. These films were based on his two highly-acclaimed volumes of autobiography—*A Grain of Truth* and *Another Grain of Truth*—which looked back on an eventful life stretching from his Aberdeenshire background, including a moving portrayal of the last day on his father's farm at Maud, to a distinguished career in journalism.

A wonderfully evocative and entertaining account of life in the North-east of Scotland and beyond, these two *Grains of Truth* have now been brought together for the first time in one volume.

Available from all good bookshops,
or direct from the publishers:

B&W Publishing,
233 Cowgate, Edinburgh,
EH1 1NQ.

Tel: 0131 220 5551